3. 50

Reading for Writing

Edited by ARTHUR MIZENER

Cornell University

Reading
for Writing

HENRY HOLT AND COMPANY, NEW YORK

To the Teacher

THIS BOOK of selections for freshman study has been made with three main considerations in mind. The first is to provide the teacher with material which is mature in ideas and feelings. The second is to provide a varied selection, so that the teacher may choose among these selections if he wishes. The third is to make the book flexible, so that the teacher will not be limited to the procedure which seems to me—perhaps wrongly—the best one, but may use the book in his own way. In fact, the essays in this book have been selected with as much concern for the teacher who wishes to ignore the editor's plan as for the teacher who does not wish to. These essays may, for instance, be rearranged by subject matter; at the end of this introduction there is an alternate Table of Contents in which they are so rearranged. It is probably needless to describe the other purposes they may be made to serve. But the teacher who wishes to arrange his course by literary types will find examples of satire and irony, of humor and persuasion, of analysis and meditation; and the teacher who wishes to illustrate the various levels of written English will find samples of everything from the brilliant informal English of Mr. Thurber to the parade-ground formality of Macaulay.

I stress this variety because we all know that teachers differ widely in their ideas about the best way to teach Freshman English. To be useful, a book has to lend itself to a variety of courses. At the same time, however, an editor must arrange his selections in some order, and that order will be dictated by his conception of how the selections should be taught and for what purpose. He ought, I think, to make perfectly clear the purpose which has dictated his plan and to provide his fellow teachers with every means for carrying out the plan.

The arrangement of the essays in this book has been made on the conviction that our main purpose in teaching freshmen how to read is to teach them how to write well, or—to speak realistically—to write better than they do. It is commonplace that students' writing does not improve until they acquire concrete knowledge of a subject that interests them and some understanding of the resources of the English language. The first of these needs is the main reason for providing students with essays that range over a variety of subjects and attitudes. The second is the reason for arranging these essays according to the way they are constructed and for providing questions which are directed almost as much to the construction as to the ideas of the essays.

The six sections into which these selections have been divided have no profound theoretical justification; they are meant to be useful. Since there is no general agreement about the best order in which to present the various forms of essays to students, I have kept these six sections relatively independent so that the teacher may, if he wishes, take them up in some other order than the one that seems to me best. For the same reason, I have not tried to give these divisions a spurious logic: *Autobiography* is not the same kind of category as *Comparison and Contrast,* but both are, I believe, pedagogically useful.

A similar policy has governed the arrangement of the selections within each section. Each begins with one or two selections which make an obvious use of the form with which the section is concerned. The rest of the selections in each section are arranged in what I believe is the order of increasing difficulty of form and substance. This arrangement ought to make the students' task easier; it ought also to make it easy for the teacher to adjust the book to his particular purpose, whether that purpose be relatively elementary or relatively advanced college teaching.

To help the student to see what he is expected to do with the questions which follow each selection, I have provided for the first selection in each section a commentary which analyzes the selection in the way a good student will analyze the rest of the selections when he answers the questions about them satisfactorily. The attention of the commentaries is divided between form and substance about as the attention of the questions is. Both also aim to make the reader reach a judgment such as I believe we all hope students will reach after they have thoroughly mastered what they have been reading.

But much the most extensive aid this book provides students is the list of detailed questions after each essay. These questions are arranged to suggest that the student ought to make one unhurried but unanalytical reading of the essay to grasp its main ideas and general form, and then a second, careful and analytical reading, through which he may guide himself by following the remainder of the questions. If he does so, he ought to emerge with a fairly detailed knowledge of the essay's ideas and attitudes and with a fairly clear idea of its structure.

I have made these questions numerous and detailed. How the teacher uses them will depend on whether he plans to use this book for a full year's work, as he can, or only for a term. Though the questions are arranged in order and lead from one point to another by what I hope is a series of logical steps, each one raises a specific problem within the essay and—with rare exceptions—is independent of other questions, so that the teacher may select among the questions without confusion or loss. In other words, I believe the student will gain something by studying a given set of questions in order, without skipping any of them; but I believe, too, that if the teacher asks the student to answer only selected questions, he will be able to do so without getting into difficulties.

However the teacher uses these questions, he will see that they have been written on the assumption that the only good reading is a close and careful reading. This is the reason these selections are short. If we ask the student to read closely and to discover all the meaning, we must not ask too much of his span of attention. Brevity is probably even more desirable if we are going to ask him to visualize the design of the selection: unpracticed readers find this task difficult and usually succeed with it only when the selection is a short one; yet, if the student is going to learn something from his reading which will help him in his own writing, this is probably the most important task he can perform. For these reasons, too, we probably ought not to ask our students to write very long passages, both because their precise knowledge of most subjects is limited and because they find it difficult to maintain the design of their essay over any very extended number of ideas and words. Unfortunate as these limitations are in many ways, they have this compensation: they allow us to assign a great many more pieces of writing, to read these assignments with much more care, and to discuss them in much greater detail at conferences.

The "Suggested Topics" which follow the questions for each selection are supplementary to the questions and sometimes overlap them. The teacher will find among the questions for each selection a number that provide satisfactory topics for writing assignments, and the topics specifically suggested for writing assignments are for the teachers who need a large number of such topics.

Let me conclude by saying once more that, though the method of teaching which has determined the arrangement of this book has always seemed to me the best one, I am far from being quite certain that it is; and that, though the machinery of this book has always worked well for me, I am not sure it will suit everyone. I have therefore tried to make a selection of essays that lend themselves to a variety of other purposes than the one represented by this book's arrangement, and to plan the machinery of this book in such a way that it can be used as a whole, or in part, or not at all.

A. M.

Cornell University
November 1, 1957

Contents

IV. Autobiography

V. Feeling and Attitude

VI. Definition

Table of Contents for a Course
Arranged by Subjects

xi

V. Education

VI. Politics

VII. Science

VIII. Economics

IX. Language and Literature

X. Religious and Spiritual Problems

THOMAS BABINGTON MACAULAY

SUSANNE K. LANGER

HAROLD TAYLOR

GILBERT SELDES

PETER F. DRUCKER

KATHERINE ANNE PORTER

ERWIN PANOFSKY

i. Comparison and Contrast

1 / The Baconian Philosophy*

THOMAS BABINGTON MACAULAY

ON THE GREATEST and most useful of all human inventions, the invention of alphabetical writing, Plato did not look with much complacency. He seems to have thought that the use of letters had operated on the human mind as the use of the go-cart in learning to walk, or of corks in learning to swim, is said to operate on the human body. It was a support which, in his opinion, soon became indispensable to those who used it, which made vigorous exertion first unnecessary and then impossible. The powers of the intellect would, he conceived, have been fully developed without this delusive aid. Men would have been compelled to exercise the understanding and the memory, and, by deep and assiduous meditation, to make truth thoroughly their own. Now, on the contrary, much knowledge is traced on paper, but little is engraved in the soul. A man is certain that he can find information at a moment's notice when he wants it. He therefore suffers it to fade from his mind. Such a man cannot in strictness be said to know anything. He has the show without the reality of wisdom. These opinions Plato has put into the mouth of an ancient king of Egypt. But it is evident from the context that they were his own; and so they were understood to be by Quinctilian. Indeed, they are in perfect accordance with the whole Platonic system.

Bacon's views, as may easily be supposed, were widely different. The powers of the memory, he observed, without the help of writ-

* From *Essay on Lord Bacon* by Thomas Babington Macaulay.

25 ing, can do little toward the advancement of any useful science.
He acknowledges that the memory may be disciplined to such a
point as to be able to perform very extraordinary feats. But on
such feats he sets little value. The habits of his mind, he tells
us, are such that he is not disposed to rate highly any accomplish-
30 ment, however rare, which is of no practical use to mankind. As
to these prodigious achievements of the memory, he ranks them
with the exhibitions of rope-dancers and tumblers. "These two
performances," he says, "are much of the same sort. The one is an
abuse of the powers of the body; the other is an abuse of the
35 powers of the mind. Both may perhaps excite our wonder; but
neither is entitled to our respect."

To Plato, the science of medicine appeared to be of very disputable advantages. He did not indeed object to quick cures for
acute disorders, or for injuries produced by accidents. But the
40 art which resists the slow sap of a chronic disease, which repairs
frames enervated by lust, swollen by gluttony, or inflamed by wine,
which encourages sensuality by mitigating the natural punishment
of the sensualist, and prolongs existence when the intellect has
ceased to retain its entire energy, had no share of his esteem. A life
45 protracted by medical skill he pronounced to be a long death. The
exercise of the art of medicine ought, he said, to be tolerated, so
far as that art may serve to cure the occasional distempers of men
whose constitutions are good. As to those who have bad constitutions, let them die; and the sooner the better. Such men are unfit
50 for war, for magistracy, for the management of their domestic
affairs, for severe study and speculation. If they engage in any
vigorous mental exercise, they are troubled with giddiness and
fulness of the head, all which they lay to the account of philosophy. The best thing that can happen to such wretches is to have
55 done with life at once. He quotes mythical authorities in support
of this doctrine; and reminds his disciples that the practice of the
sons of Aesculapius, as described by Homer, extended only to the
cure of external injuries.

Far different was the philosophy of Bacon. Of all the sciences,
60 that which he seems to have regarded with the greatest interest

was the science which, in Plato's opinion, would not be tolerated in a well-regulated community. To make men perfect was no part of Bacon's plan. His humble aim was to make imperfect men comfortable. The beneficence of his philosophy resembled the beneficence of the common Father, whose sun rises on the evil and the good, whose rain descends for the just and the unjust. In Plato's opinion man was made for philosophy; in Bacon's opinion philosophy was made for man; it was a means to an end; and that end was to increase the pleasures and mitigate the pains of millions who are not and cannot be philosophers. That a valetudinarian who took great pleasure in being wheeled along his terrace, who relished his boiled chicken and his weak wine and water, and who enjoyed a hearty laugh over the Queen of Navarre's tales, should be treated as a *caput lupinum* because he could not read the *Timaeus* without a headache, was a notion which the humane spirit of the English schools of wisdom altogether rejected. Bacon would not have thought it beneath the dignity of a philosopher to contrive an improved garden chair for such a valetudinarian, to devise some way of rendering his medicines more palatable, to invent repasts which he might enjoy, and pillows on which he might sleep soundly; and this though there might not be the smallest hope that the mind of the poor invalid would ever rise to the contemplation of the ideal beautiful and the ideal good. As Plato had cited the religious legends of Greece to justify his contempt for the more recondite parts of the art of healing, Bacon vindicated the dignity of that art by appealing to the example of Christ, and reminded men that the great Physician of the soul did not disdain to be also the physician of the body.

To sum up the whole, we should say that the aim of the Platonic philosophy was to exalt man into a god. The aim of the Baconian philosophy was to provide man with what he requires while he continues to be a man. The aim of the Platonic philosophy was to raise us far above vulgar wants. The aim of the Baconian philosophy was to supply our vulgar wants. The former aim was noble; but the latter was attainable. Plato drew a good bow; but, like Acestes in Virgil, he aimed at the stars; and therefore, though

there was no want of strength or skill, the shot was thrown away.
His arrow was indeed followed by a track of dazzling radiance, but
it struck nothing. Bacon fixed his eye on a mark which was placed
100 on the earth, and within bow-shot, and hit it in the white. The
philosophy of Plato began in words and ended in words, noble
words indeed, words such as were to be expected from the finest
of human intellects exercising boundless dominion over the finest
of human languages. The philosophy of Bacon began in observa-
105 tions and ended in arts.

COMMENTARY

THIS SELECTION from Macaulay's essay on Bacon has, at least
as its most obvious intention, the desire to make clear to us the essential purpose for which Bacon thought and wrote. This main intention
is, therefore, uncomplicated, but the plan of the selection is not quite
so simple as this intention might lead us to expect. Macaulay has
chosen to explain the essential character of Bacon's philosophy by
comparing it to the essential character of Plato's philosophy. At first
glance this may strike us as an unnecessarily roundabout way of defining Bacon's purpose. But if we stop to think of the ways in which
we explain things to others, we will see that this is one of the commonest. We very frequently explain things by showing the ways in
which they are like other things and the ways in which they differ
from other things. Frequently, in fact, we do both, and much of the
time we take the likeness for granted and concentrate on the resem-
blances, as Macaulay takes it for granted that two philosophers will
be alike in the largest sense and spends his time pointing out the
ways in which they differ. This procedure has a special advantage
for Macaulay as we shall see.

Once Macaulay is committed to the method of comparison and
contrast, his success depends on his ability to think of aspects of the
main subject, philosophy, about which Bacon and Plato had clearly
defined opinions, but about which they differed in the same way that
they differed in basic principles. His task is then to set forth in order,
first Plato's view and then Bacon's, on each of these aspects of philosophy and to indicate that the two philosophers differed about each

aspect in a way which reveals the differences in their basic principles. Having shown the way these basic principles governed their thinking in particular instances, Macaulay must then conclude by contrasting the principles themselves.

Thus the method of explanation Macaulay has chosen logically determines the structure of this selection. He begins with the subject of writing and reading and devotes one paragraph to Plato's view of it (lines 1–22 of the foregoing selection), followed by a contrasting paragraph which describes Bacon's view of it (lines 23–36). He then moves to his second subject, medicine, and does the same thing (lines 37–88). Finally, he sums up with a paragraph in which he contrasts the general principles of Plato and Bacon which governed their views of these particular subjects and were clearly implied in the preceding paragraphs, where these subjects were described (lines 89–105).

There are two things which are of the greatest importance if Macaulay is to keep this plan and its purpose clearly before the reader. The first is available to a writer whatever form of essay he is using; that is, to keep the reader aware, at each stage of the explanation, of exactly what he is doing. This means that at the very beginning of the first paragraph he must tell us that the subject we are concerned with in this paragraph is "writing," and that in this paragraph we are going to think about Plato's view of it. Because writing will also be the subject of the second paragraph and Plato of interest to us only in the first, Macaulay even goes so far as to invert the syntax of the first sentence, so that the subject, "alphabetic writing," may come to our attention before Plato does. Since the second paragraph continues with the subject of writing but shifts our attention to Bacon's view of that subject, Macaulay is careful to begin the second paragraph with a reference to Bacon's "widely different" views of the subject.

The contrast between Plato's views and Bacon's on the subject of medicine, Macaulay's second example, is not so simple as the contrast between their views on the subject of writing. Plato, he tells us, saw some merit in the art of medicine, but he thought it was useless or harmful in one respect (lines 37–58), and this was precisely the respect in which Bacon thought it most useful (lines 59–88). Therefore, though Macaulay is careful to begin this pair of paragraphs with a reference to the subject, medicine, and to the man, Plato, just as he did the first pair of paragraphs, he has to keep the predication of his sentence—"of very disputable advantages" (lines 37–38)—less simple and decisive than the predication of the sentence with which he began his discussion of the first subject (lines 1–3). Nevertheless both the subject and the man are clearly referred to in this sentence; and just as the second paragraph opens with a direct reference to "Bacon's views" (line 23), so the fourth paragraph opens with a direct reference to "the philosophy of Bacon" (line 59). For these same reasons, the final paragraph opens with a phrase—"to sum up the whole" (line 89)—that warns us Macaulay is now going to draw a conclusion from these illustrations, to generalize the principles which underlie the contrasting views illustrated by his two examples.

The second thing Macaulay does to keep his plan clear for the reader is to keep in mind in the development of each paragraph about Bacon the order in which he has stated the views of Plato in the preceding paragraph. If he does so, the reader will find that the contrasting paragraphs are parallel with each other, almost sentence by sentence, in subject matter, but that they contrast with each other, point by point. Of course Macaulay must not make the structure of parallel and contrast too mechanical, for then the paragraphs would become diagrams, and we would cease to believe that what they described was the thought of two independent philosophers. But within this limit, he works carefully to make his contrasts striking by keeping the subjects alike. Thus, for example, the first paragraph begins with Plato's disapproval of writing as a substitute for the "exercise of the understanding and memory," (lines 9–13) and gives us a comparison of writing to the go-cart or corks (lines 4–6), a comparison which emphasizes the harmfulness, in Plato's view, of using writing as a support. In the second paragraph, in precise contrast, Macaulay describes Bacon's disapproval of excessive dependence on memory (lines 26–28), and gives us a comparison—this time one of Bacon's own—which emphasizes Bacon's feeling that "prodigious achievements of the memory" are stunts, not much more useful than the stunts of "ropedancers and tumblers" (lines 30–36). The parallels and contrasts of the two paragraphs on medicine are less simple, because the situation here is less simple than in the first two paragraphs, but the method Macaulay uses for developing paragraphs three and four is essentially the same as the method he uses for developing the first two paragraphs.

When he comes to the last, summing-up paragraph, Macaulay has to do something slightly different from what he has done in the previous paragraphs. Up to this point he has been contrasting one paragraph with another; now he must make his contrast within the paragraph. He does so in two ways. First, he opens the paragraph with two pairs of contrasting sentences in which the first sentence describes Plato's aim and the second Bacon's (lines 89–94). He then gives us a sentence in which he evaluates these two aims (lines 94–95). Second, this evaluation is followed by a pair of sentences that expand the evaluation of Plato by comparing Plato's philosophy to the shooting of an arrow at the stars (lines 95–99), and by a single sentence that expands the evaluation of Bacon by describing his philosophy as like shooting an arrow at an actual target and hitting it in the bull's-eye (line 99–100). Macaulay ends the paragraph with a pair of sentences which repeat in other words the judgment of the two philosophies he gave at the beginning of the paragraph and thus restate the conclusion toward which he has been working from the start of this selection (lines 100–105).

At the end of the first paragraph of this Commentary, it was remarked that this method of parallel and contrast had a special advantage for Macaulay, and we must now consider what that is. It will be obvious to every reader that, though Macaulay has a deep respect for Plato, his sympathies are with Bacon. However much our main purpose may be explanation, we are all likely to sympathize more with one view of our subject than another. There is nothing wrong with our doing so; in fact our doing so is a positive good, so long as we do not misrepresent the point of view with which our sympathies do not lie. It is not always easy to be fair to the point of view with which we do not sympathize: it is much too easy to score off a man who cannot answer us. Perhaps it is only fair to say that Macaulay is not wholly without fault in this respect, and his partial failure limits the effectiveness of what he has to say. For, quite apart from the question of fairness, a writer defeats his own purpose (unless, of course, his purpose is simply to be belligerent) by misrepresenting an opponent or by loading his description in favor of the view with which he sympathizes. There is nothing a reader detects more quickly than such concealed bias, and nothing that leads him more quickly to lose faith in everything that the writer is telling hm.

Macaulay is very far from being grossly unfair to Plato's view. The careful reader will have noticed that, in order to balance the satiric description of "prodigious achievements of memory" which he has found in Bacon and plans to use in the second paragraph (lines 30–36), Macaulay has invented an equally satiric comparison for Plato (lines 3–6). In the third paragraph, he is at pains to repeat from Plato the bad kinds of chronic diseases which made Plato impatient of the medicine that was concerned to cure them (lines 39–44). In the last paragraph he pays Plato a high compliment as "the finest of human intellects" (lines 102–103). Nonetheless, we are made to feel, from the first, the futility, almost the absurdity, of Plato's aim "to exalt man into a god" (line 90). However grand this purpose may be, Macaulay seems to be implying, it has very little value because it "is of no practical use to mankind" (line 30). How does he create this impression?

He has two main ways of doing so, one of which is open to the writer whatever form he uses, the other of which is the special advantage Macaulay gains for this purpose by using the form of parallel and contrast. The first way is easy to see. When Macaulay is talking about Plato's views, he is very careful to show their impracticality and their drastic consequences. Thus he describes Plato's distrust of the effects of writing by saying that to Plato the man who depends on writing "cannot *in strictness* be said to know anything" (lines 16–17). This makes Plato's opinion sound almost like a quibble. And when Macaulay is describing Plato's view of medicine, he insists on the least attractive consequences of adopting that view: "As to those who have bad constitutions, let them die; and the sooner the better" (lines 48–49). This makes Plato appear cruel. But when Macaulay is talking about Bacon or the things Bacon approved of, he emphasizes advantages, not limitations or dangerous consequences. Thus the very first sentence describes writing, which Bacon is going to approve of, as "the greatest and most useful of all human inventions" (lines 1–2). Even if we accept this statement as true, we ought to remember what Macaulay does not help us to remember, though it was crucial to Plato's attitude, that there are things man possesses which he did not invent but were granted by the gods, things which, in Plato's view, were more valuable than anything man ever has or ever will invent. In this way, Macaulay regularly emphasizes for us the value of the kind of usefulness Bacon emphasized and encourages us to overlook what was to Plato the most important consideration, that man lives neither by bread alone nor by his own grace.

This bias is even more heavily enforced by the means which are made available to Macaulay by the method of parallel and contrast. Perhaps the least skillfully managed passage in this selection is at the end of paragraph three, where Macaulay tells us that Plato quoted mythical authorities to support his view of medicine (lines 55–58). Most readers will feel a little uncomfortable at this: the point seems irrelevant; it certainly does not strengthen Plato's argument for us. The reason Macaulay introduced this passage at the end of paragraph three becomes clear when we look at the parallel passage with which he ends the next paragraph, where he describes Bacon's view of medicine: "As Plato had cited the religious legends of Greece . . . , Bacon vindicated the dignity of that art by appealing to the example of Christ" (lines 83–86). Macaulay knows very well that his readers will greatly prefer to find themselves on the side of Christ here, and therefore he allows himself to refer to "the religious *legends* of Greece" (line 84) when he is speaking of Plato, but to "the *example* of Christ" (line 86) when he is speaking of Bacon. This is a particularly skillful—perhaps cunning is not too strong a word—use of the advantage given Macaulay by the method he has chosen; it is cunning because, when we stop to think, we remember that, however much Christ was concerned with the relief of human suffering, he was even more concerned with the salvation of men's souls and that in some ways his example supports Plato's attitude better than it does Bacon's. Yet to hear Macaulay tell it, one might almost suppose that even when Christ was concerned with men's souls, his interest was rather psychiatric than redemptory: he was "the great Physician of the soul" (line 87). This view of Christ is carefully planted earlier in the paragraph when Macaulay suggests that Bacon's concern with making men "comfortable" was comparable to the beneficence of "the common Father," namely, God himself (lines 64–65). It is, but only in a very narrow and secondary respect which Macaulay is careful not to make clear to us.

Quite apart, then, from the skill with which Macaulay uses parallel and contrast to explain and clarify Bacon's philosophy, he also takes advantage of this method to reinforce other means, open to any writer, to make readers share our attitude toward the subject we are discussing. There is both skill and cunning in the way Macaulay does so. We ought to be alert to detect a writer's cunning in this use of language and to guard ourselves against falling into it in our own writing; we ought to be equally alert to admire responsible skill in it and to train ourselves to take advantage of it.

QUESTIONS

1. Macaulay's essay on Bacon was written over a hundred years ago, in 1837. It therefore uses certain words that were more familiar in his day than in ours, and others that are reasonably familiar to us in senses that are not. It is important for us to be sure we know the meanings of these words exactly; if we do not, we shall have at best an inexact understanding of what Macaulay is saying. Make sure you know the exact meaning of the following words and phrases: complacency (line 3); delusive aid (line 10); assiduous (line 12); suffers (line 16); supposed (line 23); science (line 25); sap (line 40); enervated (line 41); mitigating (line 42); distempers (line 47); magistracy (line 50); valetudinarian (line 70); *caput lupinum* (line 74); recondite (line 85); vulgar (line 93); arts (line 105).

2. Just as Macaulay is careful about maintaining a parallel between paragraphs, so he is careful about maintaining a parallel within the paragraphs and even within the sentences of his essay. A good illustration of parallelism between sentences is provided by lines 89–95; a good example of parallelism within the sentence is provided by the sentence beginning in line 76. This kind of parallelism is not easy to produce because it requires the writer to use exactly the same syntactical pattern twice, to say different, but parallel, things. Explain the parallelism of the sentence beginning at line 83. Point out other places where Macaulay makes skillful use of such parallelism.

3. Perhaps the most complicated paragraph in this essay is the fourth. The opening of the paragraph, for example, is not parallel to the opening of the third paragraph. Why do you think he used this opening? Would the essay be better or worse if it were omitted?

4. The section of paragraph four which begins at line 70 is parallel to the third paragraph. Show how what is said here contrasts with what is said in paragraph three.

5. In lines 64–66 Macaulay says that Bacon's philosophy resembled the common Father's in that it refused to distinguish, so far as illness was concerned at least, between the just and the unjust. He then goes on to say that its purpose was "to mitigate the pains of millions who

are not and cannot be philosophers." Are these *ideas* parallel? How do we know that the valetudinarian of the next sentence is not a philosopher? If he is not, are we to assume that he is one of the unjust, perhaps one of the evil, who are referred to in lines 65–66?

SUGGESTED TOPICS

1. With the material provided in paragraphs three and four, write a paragraph in which you make the reader sympathize with Plato rather than Bacon by using the same method of parallel and contrast that Macaulay uses.

2. Write a paragraph in which you describe, without making any comparison to Plato, the main principles of Bacon's philosophy so far as you can deduce them from Macaulay.

3. Write a paragraph in which you outline the main principles of Macaulay's philosophy so far as you can determine them from this essay.

2 / The Lord of Creation*

SUSANNE K. LANGER

A SYMBOL is not the same thing as a sign; that is a fact that psychologists and philosophers often overlook. All intelligent animals use signs; so do we. To them as well as to us sounds and smells and motions are signs of food, danger, the pres-
5 ence of other beings, or of rain or storm. Furthermore, some animals not only attend to signs but produce them for the benefit of others. Dogs bark at the door to be let in; rabbits thump to call each other; the cooing of doves and the growl of a wolf defending his kill are unequivocal signs of feelings and intentions to be reck-
10 oned with by other creatures.

We use signs just as animals do, though with considerably more elaboration. We stop at red lights and go on green; we answer calls and bells, watch the sky for coming storms, read trouble or promise or anger in each other's eyes. That is animal intelligence raised to
15 the human level. Those of us who are dog lovers can probably all tell wonderful stories of how high our dogs have sometimes risen in the scale of clever sign interpretation and sign using.

A sign is anything that announces the existence or the imminence of some event, the presence of a thing or a person, or a
20 change in a state of affairs. There are signs of the weather, signs of danger, signs of future good or evil, signs of what the past has been. In every case a sign is closely bound up with something to be noted

* Reprinted by Special Permission from the January 1944 issue of *Fortune Magazine*; Copyright 1944 by Time, Inc.

or expected in experience. It is always a part of the situation to which it refers, though the reference may be remote in space and time. In so far as we are led to note or expect the signified event we are making correct use of a sign. This is the essence of rational behavior, which animals show in varying degrees. It is entirely realistic, being closely bound up with the actual objective course of history—learned by experience, and cashed in or voided by further experience.

If man had kept to the straight and narrow path of sign using, he would be like the other animals, though perhaps a little brighter. He would not talk, but grunt and gesticulate and point. He would make his wishes known, give warnings, perhaps develop a social system like that of bees and ants, with such a wonderful efficiency of communal enterprise that all men would have plenty to eat, warm apartments—all exactly alike and perfectly convenient— to live in, and everybody could and would sit in the sun or by the fire, as the climate demanded, not talking, but just basking, with every want satisfied, most of his life. The young would romp and make love, the old would sleep, the middle-aged would do the routine work almost unconsciously and eat a great deal. But that would be the life of a social, superintelligent, purely sign-using animal.

To us who are human, it does not sound very glorious. We want to go places and do things, own all sorts of gadgets that we do not absolutely need, and when we sit down to take it easy we want to talk. Rights and property, social position, special talents and vir- tues, and above all our ideas, are what we live for. We have gone off on a tangent that takes us far away from the mere biological cycle that animal generations accomplish; and that is because we can use not only signs but symbols.

A symbol differs from a sign in that it does not announce the presence of the object, the being, condition, or whatnot, which is its meaning, but merely *brings this thing to mind*. It is not a mere "substitute sign" to which we react as though it were the object itself. The fact is that our reaction to hearing a person's name is quite different from our reaction to the person himself. There are

certain rare cases where a symbol stands directly for its meaning:
60 in religious experience, for instance, the Host is not only a symbol
but a Presence. But symbols in the ordinary sense are not mystic.
They are the same sort of thing that ordinary signs are; only they
do not call our attention to something necessarily present or to be
physically dealt with—they call up merely a conception of the
65 thing they "mean."

The difference between a sign and a symbol is, in brief, that a
sign causes us to think or act *in face of* the thing signified, whereas
a symbol causes us to think *about* the thing symbolized. Therein
lies the great importance of symbolism for human life, its power to
70 make this life so different from any other animal biography that
generations of men have found it incredible to suppose that they
were of purely zoological origin. A sign is always embedded in
reality, in a present that emerges from the actual past and stretches
to the future; but a symbol may be divorced from reality altogether.
75 It may refer to what is *not* the case, to a mere idea, a figment, a
dream. It serves, therefore, to liberate thought from the immediate
stimuli of a physically present world; and that liberation marks the
essential difference between human and nonhuman mentality. Animals think, but they think *of* and *at* things; men think primarily
80 *about* things. Words, pictures, and memory images are symbols
that may be combined and varied in a thousand ways. The result
is a symbolic structure whose meaning is a complex of all their re-
spective meanings, and this kaleidoscope of *ideas* is the typical
product of the human brain that we call the "stream of thought."
85   The process of transforming all direct experience into imagery
or into that supreme mode of symbolic expression, language, has
so completely taken possession of the human mind that it is not
only a special talent but a dominant, organic need. All our sense
impressions leave their traces in our memory not only as signs dis-
90 posing our practical reactions in the future but also as symbols,
images representing our *ideas* of things; and the tendency to ma-
nipulate ideas, to combine and abstract, mix and extend them by
playing with symbols, is man's outstanding characteristic. It seems
to be what his brain most naturally and spontaneously does. There-

fore his primitive mental function is not judging reality, but *dream-* 95
ing his desires.

Dreaming is apparently a basic function of human brains, for
it is free and unexhausting like our metabolism, heartbeat, and
breath. It is easier to dream than not to dream, as it is easier to
breathe than to refrain from breathing. The symbolic character of 100
dreams is fairly well established. Symbol mongering, on this in-
effectual, uncritical level, seems to be instinctive, the fulfillment of
an elementary need rather than the purposeful exercise of a high
and difficult talent.

The special power of man's mind rests on the evolution of this 105
special activity, not on any transcendently high development of
animal intelligence. We are not immeasurably higher than other
animals; we are different. We have a biological need and with it a
biological gift that they do not share.

Because man has not only the ability but the constant need of 110
conceiving what has happened to him, what surrounds him, what
is demanded of him—in short, of symbolizing nature, himself, and
his hopes and fears—he has a constant and crying need of *expression.* What he cannot express, he cannot conceive; what he cannot
conceive is chaos, and fills him with terror. 115

If we bear in mind this all-important craving for expression we
get a new picture of man's behavior; for from this trait spring his
powers and his weaknesses. The process of symbolic transformation
that all our experiences undergo is nothing more nor less than the
process of *conception,* which underlies the human faculties of ab- 120
straction and imagination.

When we are faced with a strange or difficult situation, we cannot react directly, as other creatures do, with flight, aggression, or
any such simple instinctive pattern. Our whole reaction depends on
how we manage to conceive the situation—whether we cast it in 125
a definite dramatic form, whether we see it as a disaster, a challenge, a fulfillment of doom, or a fiat of the Divine Will. In words
or dreamlike images, in artistic or religious or even in cynical form,
we must *construe* the events of life. There is great virtue in the
figure of speech, "I can *make* nothing of it," to express a failure to 130

understand something. Thought and memory are processes of *mak-ing* the thought content and the memory image; the pattern of our ideas is given by the symbols through which we express them. And in the course of manipulating those symbols we inevitably distort
135 the original experience, as we abstract certain features of it, em-broider and reinforce those features with other ideas, until the con-ception we project on the screen of memory is quite different from anything in our real history.

Conception is a necessary and elementary process; what we do
140 with our conceptions is another story. That is the entire history of human culture—of intelligence and morality, folly and superstition, ritual, language, and the arts—all the phenomena that set man apart from, and above, the rest of the animal kingdom. As the re-ligious mind has to make all human history a drama of sin and
145 salvation in order to define its own moral attitudes, so a scientist wrestles with the mere presentation of "the facts" before he can reason about them. The process of *envisaging* facts, values, hopes, and fears underlies our whole behavior pattern; and this process is reflected in the evolution of an extraordinary phenomenon found
150 always, and only, in human societies—the phenomenon of lan-guage.

Language is the highest and most amazing achievement of the symbolistic human mind. The power it bestows is almost inesti-mable, for without it anything properly called "thought" is im-
155 possible. The birth of language is the dawn of humanity. The line between man and beast—between the highest ape and the lowest savage—is the language line. Whether the primitive Neanderthal man was anthropoid or human depends less on his cranial capacity, his upright posture, or even his use of tools and fire, than on one
160 issue we shall probably never be able to settle—whether or not he spoke.

QUESTIONS

1. Why does the author begin this selection with the sentence: "A symbol is not the same thing as a sign"?

2. The first two paragraphs of this selection are largely concerned with offering examples of signs. What kind of signs are used for illustrations in the first paragraph? What kind in the second?

3. The last sentence of the second paragraph (lines 15–17) refers to the interpretation of signs by animals. Is it therefore illogical in this paragraph, or is there some reason for introducing this idea here?

4. The Macaulay selection which precedes this one falls into three units, the unit about writing, the unit about medicine, and the final paragraph of generalization. Does the third paragraph of this selection relate to the preceding paragraphs in a similar way?

5. The fourth and fifth paragraphs of this selection (lines 31–52) offer us another illustration of what signs are by imagining for us what human society would be like had man "kept to the straight and narrow path of sign using." It therefore makes the plan of this part of the selection somewhat more complicated than the plan of the Macaulay selection. Explain why the writer used this more complicated plan.

6. The sixth paragraph (lines 53–65) is a transition between the main subject of the first half of the selection and the main subject of the second half, though we may not perhaps become absolutely sure that it is until we get to the last clause of this paragraph (lines 64–65). Why?

7. The first half of this selection began with two paragraphs of examples of signs. The second half contains no examples to illustrate its subject. Can you give a reason why the author offers no examples of this subject?

8. The seventh paragraph of this selection (lines 66–84) begins with the phrase, "A symbol differs from a sign in that. . . ." It does so partly because of something the author had written in the previous paragraph. What is that and why does it make this a particularly good way to open paragraph seven?

9. Is the seventh paragraph devoted to the ways in which "a symbol differs from a sign"? If it is, show how each sentence in it supports this assertion, being particularly careful to show how the fourth sentence (lines 75–76) does.

10. The seventh paragraph ends by asserting that symbols call up in our minds a "conception," that this is the sense in which they may be said to "mean" something. In what way does the eighth paragraph elaborate this assertion? Be sure you know what the full meaning of "conception" is.

11. The second sentence in paragraph eight (lines 88–93) makes an assertion about one of the conclusions men have drawn from their habit of thinking symbolically instead of merely in signs, the conclusion that it is "incredible to suppose that [men] were of purely zoological origin." To what kind of ideas about the origin of men is the author referring here?

12. The ninth paragraph (lines 97–104) advances the argument of this selection beyond the definition of a symbol to an assertion about the priority of symbolic thinking in the consciousness of men. It asserts that this kind of thinking "is man's outstanding characteristic." What else in the paragraph asserts the same thing? What is there in the paragraph to suggest that symbolic thinking is not only the most fundamental habit of man's mind but the first one he developed in time?

13. The tenth paragraph (lines 105–109) seeks to reinforce these assertions; how does it do so?

14. The eleventh paragraph (lines 110–115) brings us back to the point of the author's original comparison between signs and symbols. How? Is there some special reason for introducing a brief summing-up of what has gone before just at this point?

15. The next three paragraphs (lines 116–151) discuss some of the consequences which logically follow from our accepting the author's argument that man thinks symbolically. In these three paragraphs, three words are italicized. Why?

16. The fifteenth paragraph begins: "Conception is a necessary and elementary process. . . ." What earlier statement does this one refer to? Why is it referred to at this precise point?

17. In the fourth paragraph, at line 33, the author said: "[Man] would not talk, but grunt and gesticulate and point." Did she include this statement at that early point in the essay because she wanted to anticipate something she was going to say in these last two paragraphs of the selection? What is that? Does she anticipate this subject anywhere else in the selection?

18. The most obvious way to visualize the structure of this selection is probably to think of it as containing four parts; in this scheme, the first part would be the discussion of "a sign"; the second would be the discussion of "a symbol." What would the third and fourth parts be?

SUGGESTED TOPICS

1. Write a paragraph in which you make clear, in your own words, the distinction between signs and symbols. This paragraph ought not to contain more than five sentences.

2. Write a paragraph in which you explain what language is according to this selection.

3. Write a paragraph in which you illustrate, with specific examples not given in the selection, the way human beings use signs.

3 / Conservatism and American Culture*

HAROLD TAYLOR

I BEGIN with the Greek citizen Pericles, who had so much to do with the public life of Athens.

"Unlike other cities," said Pericles, "Athens expects every citizen to take an interest in public affairs; and, as a matter of fact, most
5 Athenians have some understanding of public affairs. We do believe in knowledge as a guide to action: we have a power of thinking before we act, and of acting too, whereas many peoples can be full of energy if they do not think but when they reflect they begin to hesitate. We like to make friends abroad by doing
10 good and giving help to our neighbors; and we do this not from some calculation of self-interest but in the confidence of freedom in a frank and fearless spirit. I would have you fix your eyes upon Athens day by day, contemplate her potentiality—not merely what she is but what she had the power to be, until you
15 become her lovers. Reflect that her glory has been built up by men who knew their duty and had the courage to do it. Make them your examples and learn from them that the secret of happiness is freedom, and the secret of freedom, courage."

This is also the secret of Athens' greatness in the greatest days
20 of Greek civilization, and I believe it to be profoundly true. I be-

* Excerpt from a speech, reprinted by permission of Harold Taylor.

22

lieve what Pericles has said about knowledge as a guide to action, and I know what he means when he says that people can be full of energy when they do not think, but when they reflect, they begin to hesitate. I also believe what he says about giving help to our neighbors, at home and abroad, not from some calculation of self- 25 interest but in the confidence of freedom and in a frank and fearless spirit.

This is what we should teach in our schools and our colleges, this is the spirit which should animate our communities.

How do we teach it? 30

By the examples of courage told by the poets, the philosophers, and the writers who have captured the image of nobility in action, who show man behaving with grace under stress. By the examples of courage in action, by the commitment of teachers, citizens, community leaders and public figures to principle and ideal. By giving 35 our children and our citizens the knowledge on which to act, since without knowledge it is impossible to act intelligently, and without intelligence, courage may degenerate into foolishness. But most of all, we teach the young and their elders to be courageous when we give them the self-confidence and faith that when they think and 40 act for themselves, when they speak out and refuse to conform to the society which presses upon them, they are fulfilling their duty as citizens.

In view of the prevailing characteristics of our age, this is the most important single thing we can teach. 45

At present we are in the grip of a conservative trend which has taken our eyes away from the necessity of making personal choices, of making commitments, away from the necessity of thinking for ourselves. The characteristics of the period in which we live are those of caution, conservatism, security and the negative emotions 50 which make people less willing and able to speak for themselves and to be themselves, and make people long for the security of the group so that their own opinions won't show. I have noticed more and more blocks put before people, young and old, who want to think and act on their own. If a suggestion is made to do some- 55 thing—anything—a thousand little men run out from everywhere with reasons why it shouldn't or can't be done. Or everyone waits for someone else to move so that he can be proved wrong if he does, or lacking in initiative if he doesn't. If an action is proposed, 60 instead of everyone saying, Let's try it, everyone says, Let's refer it to a committee. Or even worse, everyone says, Let's send out a questionnaire. Such an amount of time is spent peeking and peering before and behind and around and inside for possible errors and things for which you might be blamed that very little fresh and 65 new gets started.

Under another heading, this is called the search for security. There certainly do seem to be a lot of people seeking it, all the way from Mr. Dulles who does it by brinkmanship and travelling a lot, to the Government offices where they have tucked away the 70 scientist who has so many brilliant top secret ideas that security regulations won't clear him to work with them. Then there are the general run-of-the-mill security seekers who are looking for peace of mind, emotional serenity and positive thinking and no trouble about anything, while the whole of business and industry 75 has devoted itself to making life completely smooth and empty of any possible difficulty. Out in New York, nobody breathes ordinary air any more, it's all air-conditioned, no books, plays, television shows or movies are just plain good ones, they are either sensational, selling to millions, with colossal success, or they are noth- 80 ing. I came across my favorite breakfast food the other day—it doesn't snap, it doesn't crackle, it doesn't pop, it guarantees just to lie there at the bottom of its bowl and absorb its milk.

I bring you the news of a conference two weeks ago at Sarah Lawrence College which included a cross-section of 300 college students 85 from forty colleges, and eight discussion leaders, among whom were W. H. Whyte, Jr., who has just written *The Organization Man*, a book dedicated to the proposition that we have all become conformists, and Robert Hutchins, a man who has always refused to conform. The conference undertook to consider the character 90 of the present college generation. It was agreed among the students that this is an age of the security-minded and the conformist, an age of public relations in which the problem, Mr. Hutchins said, is not to *be* good, but to *look* good. Mr. Hutchins commented further on the fact that the magazines were full of articles on dieting, a sign that we all have too much. He found the spirit of the age in an article in the current issue of *Coronet*, whose title is, How To *Look* Ten Pounds Lighter.

The students said that this was the age of the safe man, the man who, right from his kindergarten to his college days, wants to be adjusted, well-liked, popular, noticed and successful. One student said that the ideal was to be well-rounded, well-rounded that is, in the sense that all the rough edges had been smoothed off until a man was perfectly round like a tennis ball with a little friendly fuzz on top.

But is this what it means to be a student?

To be a student is an honorable and highly respected position to occupy. In Burma, in Indonesia, in Ceylon, in Africa, to be a student is to accept the responsibility for becoming a leader of one's country, of being educated to bring one's gifts to the country's service at a time when education has not been able to catch up with the enormous demands for educated men and women who can build new countries.

But is the student in America in a very different situation? Is there not a shortage of educated and informed leadership in our country? Is the American student not responsible, quite as much as the Burmese student, for putting his education at the service of his country and not merely putting it at the service of a commercial career? We can not promise our American youth that after a college education he will go directly into a Cabinet post or a place in a United Nations delegation. But we can promise him that his presence as an informed and interested citizen, aware of political and social issues, is wanted in the government, in politics, in public administration, in education, in the law, in business and everywhere else in our society.

In most other countries, the student does not go to the university merely to increase his chances of a higher income in later years. He goes to develop those talents which in the view of the university are needed to carry on a civilization. In this country, at this point

in our prosperity and material success, we hear constantly of the
130 values of an education in raising one's income. It works out, I believe, to around $100,000 more over a lifetime for a B.A. degree
than without one. But our youth should be reminded not to go on
to the PH.D. or any higher degree. The income seems to fall off
sharply after the B.A.

135 Emphasis upon the personal advantage of an education has dis-
tracted many people from thinking of the true values of higher
learning and the true mission of the student and the citizen. I
would like to suggest that the task of the colleges and the universities is to enable the young to find a personal identity and to
140 help the young to find ways of serving humanity. I would like to
suggest that this is what students are in college to do, and that if
they are not doing that, they are failing to achieve a true education.

QUESTIONS

1. Like the preceding selections, this one uses the device of comparison and contrast; in fact, it uses two comparisons which, though
they are closely connected, are still distinguishable. It begins by describing what the speaker thinks is "the secret of Athens' greatness."
With what does it contrast this account of Athens?

2. In the process of describing what the speaker wishes to contrast
with Periclean Athens, he makes some remarks about American students. What train of thought led him to this subject?

3. The subject of American students brings the speaker to his
second comparison. What is it?

4. What part of the first section of the speech, the section which
runs from lines 1–82, prepares us for the second comparison?

5. This selection is a speech. It therefore does a good many things
that a carefully composed essay might not; for instance, it paragraphs
very frequently and it uses dramatic rhetorical questions (for example,
"How do we teach it?" line 30). What purpose did these devices serve
in the text for a speech? Why would they probably not be used in an
essay composed wholly for reading?

6. At line 46, the author writes, "At present we are in the grip of a

conservative trend which has taken our eyes away from. . . ." Give some specific reasons why, had he been writing an essay, he might not have written quite this sentence. Do you find other examples of this kind of casual statement in the selection?

7. The author makes himself and quotes from others a certain number of informal ironic remarks. Explain what you think is the point of the remarks in lines: 53; 56; 60–61; 80–82; 92–93; 101–104.

8. In spite of the informality and the loose organization of this selection, it has a serious purpose which dictates the two related comparisons it makes. Try to sum up the conception of a society and of the individual members of that society which the author admires.

9. Explain how this conception leads him to make the two comparisons he does.

10. If you turn this last problem around, you will ask yourself what conception of the function of an education and therefore of colleges Mr. Taylor holds. See if you can state this conception. You will have to deduce this conception, in part at least, from the author's description of the society he admires.

11. How closely does he relate what he has to say about Pericles and Athens to his conception of the good society?

SUGGESTED TOPICS

1. In paragraphs eight, nine, and ten (lines 66–104) the author offers a series of examples to illustrate what seems to him the characteristic attitude of our time. These examples are strung together in the loose style of an informal speech. See if you can arrange them in the more closely ordered structure of the kind of paragraph or paragraphs that would be suitable for a carefully composed essay.

2. Write two or three paragraphs in which, depending on your own preferences, you (a) defend the impulse to conform which the author is criticizing; (b) point out some of the defects of the nonconformist kind of man whom the author admires; (c) give further illustrations of inadequacies of the kind of conformism the author is attacking.

4/ The Maturity of American Movies*

GILBERT SELDES

T HE ACCOLADE of maturity is usually given to European
pictures. Some of these are so alien to our modes of thinking that comparisons are useless; but the British product is close
to our own in general method and purpose. I take, for example, a
straight cops-and-robbers picture, *Odd Man Out,* directed in 1947
by Carol Reed for Filippo del Guidice, and *Naked City,* produced
by the late Mark Hellinger for Universal (1948).

In each an act of violence is committed at the beginning; in each
the police track down the criminal; in *Odd Man Out* a number of
people take an interest in the man; some of them hide him, some
expose him to his enemies; while in *Naked City* the police are
hindered chiefly by accomplices; in each picture the criminal is
brought to bay and killed by the police. Having said this much, I
have told nothing of the essence of *Odd Man Out* and, at the same
time, have said everything worth saying about *Naked City* except
that the final chase, along the superstructure of a New York bridge,
was excellently photographed and thrilling.

The technical wizards in Hollywood cannot duck the question:
By what means did a British variation of our specialty, the escape-
and-chase picture, manage to be something like a serious work of

* From *The Great Audience* by Gilbert Seldes. Copyright 1950 by Gilbert
Seldes. Reprinted by permission of The Viking Press, Inc., New York.

art? Why was it profoundly exciting when it stopped being a thriller? Why did its theme seem important, its passions intense, its tragic end so satisfying? The last question is, in a way, the answer to the others. That a cops-and-robbers picture should have a guiding line of thought, that its people should be moved and shaken and reconciled by profound human passions, that the death of the hunted hero-criminal should be tragic—these are the elements our gangster pictures deliberately avoid.

The robbery which launches the story of *Odd Man Out* is undertaken to get funds for a secret political movement vaguely defined as "the Organization." Alien as this is to American experience, it was convincing; the somber fanaticism of the men as they planned the raid gave the Organization actuality and significance, so that a groundwork of sympathy for the robbers was laid, and out of this sympathy rose all of the later emotions of the audience. Before we had lived with them five minutes we saw evil deeds flowing out of a noble motive and were committed from that moment to pity for good men who could never be good again because they were involved in murder; we felt hope and anxiety and fear, the dreadful sense of time running out while the force of law, admirable in its action and not without pity itself, closed in; it was not a simple matter of choosing sides, because we had the feeling that both the hunter and the hunted would give their lives to undo the murder, the feeling that life sometimes traps the good into evil ways and we are helpless.

In that mood we see Johnny shot by a mill-guard and returning the fire in a desperate attempt to get away; he cannot hold on to the car and falls; the driver is afraid to go back for him, and his other companions see him staggering into a side street; returning later, they fail to find him. From that point the picture divides into two lines which run parallel, then cross, and finally converge. One is the story of the wounded man trying to get away, dragging himself through mean streets, interrupting children at play, fainting in a shelter and waking to overhear the whispers of lovers, stumbling unseen into a cab in the rainy night and so passing the cordon of police. The other line brings in all the people who want

Johnny: the police to arrest him; the jeweled Teresa, smuggler's
fence and falsely warm hostess to the Organization's boys, who
wants to square herself with the police by betraying Johnny; mem-
60 bers of his gang who sacrifice themselves to draw off the pursuers;
a nondescript little bird fancier who finds him and tries to sell him
to a priest; the priest who wants to save his soul; the Samaritans
who give him first aid but no more; the failed medical student who
patches him up so that he can go to his fate; the artist who wants
65 to paint the look of death in his eyes; the girl who loves him and
wants to save him or die with him.

It has something of the effect of a diagram: faith, science, art,
society, love—all competing for the body and soul of man. But
with one exception, the artist, all the characters are saved from be-
70 coming abstractions, each has a life of his own; they are equipped
not with superficial little characteristics but with complete and
rounded characters; each has lived before the picture started, and
the survivors of the tragedy will live on after it is ended. The
streets through which they move are alive with junkyards and book-
75 stalls and charwomen eating fish and chips from greasy papers and
trams slewing round corners and factory whistles and men talking
politics as they drink beer in saloons and women doing a bit of late
marketing; they generate a sense of actuality so that the Belfast I
have never seen is more real and palpable to me than the familiar
80 ways of New York in the glossy brightness of *Naked City*.

The instant creation of a powerful emotion and the persisting
sense of actuality are two of the three major elements in *Odd Man
Out*; the third, the most subtle, is the satisfaction of a profound
subconscious need: the picture makes you feel that it exists in time.
85   This is an extraordinarily difficult thing to do in the movies,
which are seen in one unbroken sequence, but it is indispensable.
Unless we feel that time is passing, we can have no sense of reality.
Whenever we go to the movies we must live in two durations at
once; first, our own in the theater, knowing while we sit there that
90 at the end of two hours we must catch a train or stop at the deli-
catessen; and second, the duration of events on the screen, which
may be shorter than our own in a Marx Brothers sequence or many

times as long in a biography of Pasteur. (In a remarkable tour de force Alfred Hitchcock identified the two durations; all the events in *Rope* take place in a span of eighty minutes, and eighty minutes is precisely the time it takes the spectator to watch them unroll; the sense that time is passing is not, however, missing.) In *Odd Man Out*, skillful cutting between the two parallel actions, picking up the fugitive not where we last saw him but at a further stage on his doomed way, changes in light and in the pitch of the sound that the streets give off, all contribute; but, most of all, the admirable players themselves make us feel that they are living through events, their voices convey to us the passage of the hours, and we have in the end the final sense of reality, because we have, without knowing it, forgotten our own time, our trains and our errands, and have endured as long as the characters on the screen.

Could Hollywood make such a picture? The answer is that fifteen years ago Hollywood did; in a sense, Hollywood made this same picture, for *Odd Man Out* is a lineal descendant of *The Informer*, and in many ways *The Informer* is the more daring and the more successful. The central character is not a handsome hero played by a popular actor; in place of James Mason's Johnny there is the doltish confused Gyppo played by Victor McLaglen, an actor of known inadequacy upon whom a miracle was worked by the brilliant director, John Ford. Here, too, the minor people are rounded, the streets and barrooms are sound and solid, the alien air (of an Irish city again) is still the air we breathe. Liam Flaherty's book is a finer work than F. L. Green's *Odd Man Out*, and the screen play derived from it by Dudley Nichols is one of the movies' rare instances of creative adaptation. John Ford and Carol Reed have both been influenced by D. W. Griffith, the first man who tried to transmit a dominant emotion through atmosphere on the screen, so the two pictures are technically parallel. *The Informer* also creates the illusion of time passing, and in pace, in pitch of voices, and in lighting, both directors deliberately "underplayed": the murmur of human conversation gives its tone to the pictures, not the projection of dialogue, and dramatic scenes are played for their full value without staccato interruptions of

fresh angle-shots. A defect of *The Informer* is that almost all of
130 it is played in semidarkness; the fearful atmosphere of Dublin in
the days of The Trouble is impressive, but the picture is hard
to see.

The history of *The Informer* is enlightening. Like other distinguished works, it was not a studio enterprise, and an executive of
135 RKO whom I congratulated on the production said, with a rare
mixture of grace and candor, "We aren't entitled to credit. John
Ford wanted to do it and we let him." As things go, letting a successful director do a picture out of which the studio expects no
profit is infrequent, and sometimes the studio is startled by the
140 result. Favorable notices and Academy Awards went to Nichols,
Ford, and McLaglen for the best screen play, the best direction,
and the best performance by an actor, yet *The Informer* was not,
by Academy standards, the best movie of the year, an honor which
went to *Mutiny on the Bounty*. (The "Oscars" represent the per-
145 sonal judgment of people in the industry, choosing among pictures
proposed by other people in the industry.) *The Informer* continued to be shown profitably for several years and is still revived
occasionally.

I have compared one of the best melodramas ever made with
150 a picture considerably above the Hollywood average and have introduced *The Informer*, one of a handful of great pictures, to indicate that the making of movies satisfactory to the adult intelligence is not a national prerogative of the British. The pictures I
have mentioned here are on the serious side, but any picture in
155 which an intelligent adult can take pleasure should be considered
mature, and of these Hollywood has made many. *The Great Mc-
Ginty* and *Hail the Conquering Hero, Hold Back the Dawn*,
which had a rare and authentic feeling of romance, *My Man God-
frey, Mr. Deeds Goes to Town, The Farmer's Daughter, The Jol-
160 son Story, Hell's Angels*—these are titles picked among the average
A pictures. They were made by writers and directors and players steeped in the Hollywood tradition. They are not cited as examples of great art, but they are far from infantile, and they prove
that Hollywood not only can make intelligent pictures but can
make a huge profit out of them.

QUESTIONS

1. Like the preceding selections, this one depends on comparison and contrast but it differs in several ways from the standard essay which uses comparison and contrast. It uses only one example of British pictures and two of American, and it arranges these examples in an unusual order. Explain what this order is and why the author uses it.

2. The author begins this selection by asserting, not that European pictures are different from American pictures, but that "the accolade of maturity is usually given to European pictures." This is presumably, then, his main subject. Logically, it involves him in showing two things: (1) what maturity consists in; and (2) whether, in his opinion, giving the accolade of maturity to European pictures is just. How does he make clear to us what he thinks constitutes maturity in a picture?

3. Does he, at any point, sum up for us the characteristics which seem to him to constitute maturity in a picture? If he does, does he do so before or after he has analyzed these characteristics?

4. If this essay had had only the first of the two purposes mentioned under Question 2, it would have ended sooner than it does. Point to what seems to you the logical place for it to have stopped if its author had been writing only about what constitutes maturity in a picture.

5. The second purpose mentioned under Question 2 caused the author to write what comes after the stopping place you have selected in answering the previous question. This section of his essay cannot say that the Europeans do not make mature pictures for the simple reason that the previous part of the essay implies that they do; how does it do that?

6. If the conclusion of this essay cannot logically say the Europeans do not make mature pictures, can it, nonetheless, say that it is not entirely just to give the accolade of maturity to European pictures? What is an "accolade"? To what extent *does* this essay qualify its opening assertion about the usual award of the accolade of maturity?

7. Go back now to the problem of how the author defines, in the body of his essay, the quality he calls maturity; how many characteristics which constitute maturity does he list? Which precise sections of his essay are devoted to making these qualities clear to us?

8. Now consider the way he proceeds at the end of the essay. For instance, what is his purpose in telling us about his conversation with "an executive of RKO" (lines 133–137)? Why does he tell us that *The Informer* did not receive the Academy Award for the best movie of the year?

9. Taking into account the points you have been noticing in Questions 7 and 8, and considering the exact phrasing of the last four sentences in the essay (lines 153–165), try to state as exactly as you can the extent to which the author believes the accolade of maturity can be given to Hollywood pictures.

SUGGESTED TOPICS

1. Write two or three paragraphs about a picture you have seen recently in which you analyze what happens and what it means in the way Mr. Seldes analyzes *Odd Man Out* or *Naked City*.

2. Explain in your own words what Mr. Seldes means in line 78 by "a sense of actuality" and give an illustration of this effect from a picture you have seen.

3. Mr. Seldes says (lines 85–87) that it is difficult for a picture to make you feel that it exists in time because a picture is seen "in one unbroken sequence." Explain why that makes the task difficult and explain then why it is important for a picture not to fail at it.

5 / The Myth of American Uniformity*

PETER F. DRUCKER

"HOW CAN YOU AMERICANS stand all this uniformity?" Every one of the dozens of visitors from all over Europe who, during these past few years, have discussed their American impressions with me, has asked this question in one form or another. Yet what makes every single one—businessman, clergyman, or scientist; teacher, lawyer, or journalist; labor leader or civil servant—come to me for information is bewilderment, if not shock, at the incomprehensible and boundless diversity of this country.

"But *somebody* must lay out the standard curriculum for the liberal arts colleges. If the federal or the state governments do not do it, who does?"

"In what grade does the American high school student start Latin? How many hours a week are given to it? And what works of Shakespeare are normally read in the American high schools?"

"It can't really be true that there is no one labor union policy on industrial engineering. I am told that some unions actually insist on a time and motion study of each job, some unions acquiesce in it, and others refuse to allow any industrial engineers. But surely no union movement could possibly operate pulling in opposite directions on a matter as important as this?"

* From "The Myth of American Uniformity," *Harper's Magazine* (May 1952). Reprinted by permission of Peter F. Drucker.

"Please explain to us what American managements mean when they talk of 'decentralization.' Wouldn't this mean that different units of a company would do things differently, adopt different policies, follow different ideas? And how could any management allow that and still keep its authority and control?"

The going gets really rough when the talk turns to political institutions or to the churches. That it makes all the difference in the world what congressional committee a pending bill is assigned to, will upset even the urbane visitor—if indeed he believes it. And among the most frustrating hours of my life was an evening spent with a Belgian Jesuit who insisted that there must be one simple principle that decides when and where agencies of the Catholic Church in this country work together with other faiths, and when not. The only comfort was that he obviously had got no more satisfaction from his American brethren in the order than from me.

Yet it is quite clearly not in diversity that the visitors see the essence of America. They are baffled by it, shocked by it, sometimes frightened by it. But they don't really believe in it. Their real convictions about this country come out in the inevitable question: "But don't you find it trying to live in so uniform a country?"

It is not only the casual visitor, spending a few weeks here, who believes in "American uniformity" despite all he sees and hears. The belief survives extended exposure to the realities of American life.

A few months ago a well-known English anthropologist, reviewing an exhibition of American paintings for a most respectable London Sunday paper, explained the "mediocrity of American painting" by a reference to "the uniformity of the American landscape—all prairie and desert." One might remind the reviewer that nothing is more startling to the immigrant who comes to America to live than the tremendous variety of the landscape and the violence of the contrasts in the American climate, soils, geology, fauna, and flora. Or one might reduce the argument to its full absurdity by asking which of these sons of Kansas, for example, is the typically uniform prairie product—William Allen White, Earl Browder, or General Eisenhower? But the essential fact is not that the argument is nonsense. It is that Geoffrey Gorer, the anthropologist, knows this country well, and that the newspaper that printed his nonsense is unusually knowledgeable about things American on the whole. Yet though they know all about New England or Virginia or Minnesota or Oregon, though they probably also know about the artists who paint in the desert of Cape Cod—or is it a prairie? —they immediately think of "uniformity" when something Ameri- can needs explanation.

I am not discussing here the *quality* of American culture, whether it be crude, shallow, vulgar, commercialized, materialist, or, as Marxists maintain, full of "bourgeois idealism." My concern here is solely with the prevailing European conviction of American uniformity. And that conviction is an obvious absurdity. Nor could it be anything else considering the pragmatic bent of the American people and their deeply engrained habit of voluntary and local community action and community organization.

Indeed any serious student of America has to raise the question whether there is not *too much* diversity in this country. There is the danger that diversity will degenerate into aimless multiplicity —difference for difference's sake. Jefferson, de Tocqueville, and Henry Adams, as well as recent critics of American education such as Robert Hutchins, have seen in this the major danger facing American society and culture.

There is actually more uniformity in European countries, both materially and culturally, than in the United States. It may no longer be true that the French Minister of Education knows at every hour exactly what line of what page of what book is being read in every French school. But still, in education, in religious life, in political life, in business as well as in its cultural ideals, European countries tend to have at most a few "types," a few molds in which everything is formed. What then can the European possibly mean when he talks of the "uniformity of America"?

He himself, as a visitor, unconsciously furnishes the answer in the way he sorts out his American experiences, in the questions he asks, in the answers he understands and those he doesn't. When

he thinks of "diversity" he tends to think of the contrast between
95 the ways in which social and economic classes live. He is used
to seeing a definite and clear-cut upper-class civilization and culture
dominating. And that indeed he does not find in this country.
Therefore the bewildering differences in American life appear to
him meaningless—mere oddities.
100   I still remember how the sage of our neighborhood in suburban
Vienna, the wife of the market gardener across the street, explained
the "Great War," the war of 1914–18, when I was a small boy of
ten or eleven: "The war had to come because you couldn't tell
maids from their ladies by their dress any more." Frau Kiner's ex-
105 planation of history differed from that offered during the nineteen
twenties by Europe's learned sociologists, whether of the Right or
of the Marxist persuasion, mainly by being brief and simple. They
all assumed that there must be a distinct upper-class way of life,
an upper-class architecture, upper-class dress, upper-class goods in
110 an upper-class market—and contrasted with it the "folk culture" of
the peasantry or the equally distinct ways of life of the middle
class and working class. Indeed that eminently sane, that notori-
ously Americophile magazine, the London *Economist*, echoed
Frau Kiner only a few months ago when it reported with apparent
115 amazement that "to the best of their ability—and their ability is
great—the [American] manufacturers make clothes for the lower
income groups that look just as smart as those they make for the
more fortunate"—and explained this perverse attempt to make the
maids look like their ladies as the result of the "egalitarian obses-
120 sion" of this country.
    The class-given differentiation in Europe is even more pro-
nounced in the nonmaterial, the cultural spheres. One example is
the tremendous importance of the "right speech" in practically
every European country; for the "right speech" is upper-class
125 speech. Another example is the extent to which European educational systems are based on the education of a ruling class. The
Renaissance Courtier, the Educated Man of the Humanists, the
Christian Gentleman of nineteenth-century England—the ideal
types which embody the three basic educational concepts of mod-

ern Europe—were all in origin and intent ruling-class types. The [130] rising middle class not only did not overthrow the class concept of education, it emphasized it as a symbol of its own emergence into the ruling group. Similarly, in Occupied Germany the working-class leaders—to the chagrin as well as the complete bewilderment of American educational advisers—have shown no enthusiasm for [135] the plan to convert the traditional *"Gymnasium"* into an American high school. To deprive these schools of their ruling-class character would actually deprive them of social meaning for the working-class children.

Europe has even succeeded in turning diversities and differences [140] that were not social in their origin into class distinctions. One of the best examples of this is the way in which the "gentry" and its retainers became identified with the Church of England while the "tradesman" went to "Chapel"—a distinction that held till very recent times and is not quite gone yet.   [145]

Thus the European myth of American uniformity tells us less about America than about Europe. For it is based, in the last analysis, on Frau Kiner's belief that a class structure of society is the only genuine moral order.

That today the theme of "American uniformity" is played on [150] above all by Communist propaganda is thus no accident. For the "proletariat" of communist ideology is indeed a "master class." It is a reaffirmation of the European ruling-class concept and of its ruling-class way of life in an extreme form—only turned upside down. On this rests to a considerable extent the attraction of Com- [155] munism for European intellectuals. There is an old Slav proverb: "There will always be barons for there must always be peasants." All Vishinsky would have to do to change it into an orthodox Soviet proverb would be to change "barons" to "proletarian commissars." And Frau Kiner's philosophy of history he would not [160] have to change at all.

But Frau Kiner's statement could never have been made in this country, not even by a sociology professor in a three-volume tome. Whether the United States really has no ruling class at all—or whether, as the Marxists assert, the classes are only camouflaged in [165] this country, one thing is certain: this country knows no distinct upper-class or lower-class "way of life." It knows only different ways of making a living.

Indeed there has been only one genuine ruling-class way of life 170 in this country since its beginning: that of the plantation aristocracy in the Old South between 1760 and 1860. When the *nouveaux riches* in that period between the Civil War and the first world war made the attempt to set themselves up as "Society" they failed miserably. They could not even develop an upper-class 175 American architecture—and of all the arts architecture is the mirror of the way of life. The tycoons had to be content with imitation French châteaux, Italian Renaissance palaces, and Tudor manors—the white elephants which their servantless grandchildren are now frantically turning over to monasteries, hospitals, or 180 schools. (It is not entirely an accident, perhaps, that the people most eager to live today in the baronial halls of yesterday's capitalists seem to be the Soviet delegates.) To find an upper-class way of life the tycoons had to gate-crash the Scottish grouse moors, the Cowes Regatta, or the Kaiser's maneuvers in Kiel. In this 185 country it was difficult indeed to lead a ruling-class life.

The closest we come today in this country to anything that might be called an "upper-class way of life" is to be found in the top hierarchy of the big business corporations. The way people in some of these companies talk about the "twelfth floor" or the 190 "front office" faintly echoes Frau Kiner's concept of the "ladies." At work the big business executive has indeed some of the trappings of a distinct style of living in the ceremonial of receptionist, secretary, and big office, in his expense account, in the autographed picture of the "big boss" on the wall, the unlisted telephone, and 195 so forth. But only at work. As soon as he leaves the office the "big shot" becomes simply another business man, anonymous and indistinguishable from millions of others. And he is quite likely to live, like the president of our largest corporation, in an eight-room house in a pleasant and comfortable but not particularly swank 200 suburb.

In fact, it does not even make too much sense to talk of this

country as a "middle class" society. A middle class has to have a
class on either side to be in the middle. There is more than a grain
of truth in the remark made jokingly by one of my European
visitors, an Italian student of American literature: "If there were ₂₀₅
such a thing as a working-class literature, *Babbitt* and *Arrowsmith*
would be its models."

QUESTIONS

1. This selection and the one that follows it illustrate some of the
complicated ways in which comparison and contrast may be used.
The central scheme of Mr. Drucker's essay is to explain to us that the
notion that America is hopelessly uniform is a myth by showing us
the contrasts between America and Europe in this matter of uniformity
and variety. But he does not start by simply saying, "America is uniform in these respects and diverse in those whereas Europe is diverse
in these respects and uniform in those." The opening section of his
essay, which runs from lines 1–66, describes the comments of a number of Europeans who have visited America. How does this section
serve his purpose?

2. What do you think his essay gains by starting in this less obvious
and more difficult way?

3. This opening section of the selection divides into two parts at
line 36. How do these two parts differ in making the point Mr. Drucker
wishes to make clear to us in this first part?

4. Mr. Drucker begins this section of his essay with the question
asked him by all his European visitors, "How can you Americans
stand all this uniformity?" When does he come back to this question
for the first time? For the second time? Why does he come back to it
at these points?

5. Lines 10–36 consist of a number of short paragraphs. What is
the logical point of this frequent paragraphing? See if you can state
in one word the subject of each paragraph in lines 10–26, and in two
words the subject of the paragraph in lines 27–36.

6. Mr. Drucker offers two arguments to suggest that Mr. Geoffrey
Gorer's explanation of the "mediocrity of American painting" is nonsense (lines 49–51); explain these arguments.

7. Mr. Drucker has now posed a problem for us: "Intelligent people from Europe, who know America and have seen and felt America's diversity [can you point out the place in the essay where he says this?], nonetheless continue to assert that America is depressingly uniform; why?" Where in his essay does he start to solve this problem?

8. What is he doing in the passage—we might almost call it a parenthesis—which comes between the posing of this problem, which concludes at line 46, and the beginning of his solution of this problem?

9. What is the basic idea by which Mr. Drucker solves this problem?

10. What is the point of Mr. Drucker's little anecdote about Frau Kiner (lines 103–104)?

11. What attitude toward society is applied by the London *Economist* when it explains the practice of American clothing manufacturers by referring to America's "egalitarian *obsession*" (lines 119–120)?

12. In lines 121–145, Mr. Drucker offers us a series of illustrations of "differentiation" in European society. They are all calculated to show that European society is differentiated in only one main way, which is of extreme importance to Europeans. What is that way?

13. Explain how what Mr. Drucker has to say about speech, about education, about church-going supports his idea that there is one major way in which European society is differentiated.

14. Show how this discussion of European ways of life in lines 121–145 contrasts with the aspects of American society Mr. Drucker's European visitors questioned him about (lines 10–36) and thus explains why they asked these questions.

15. In the last section of his essay, beginning at line 150, Mr. Drucker examines American society in the light of the idea which governs the differentiation of European society. What is the argument by which he explains the importance of the myth of American uniformity in Communist propaganda in Europe (lines 150–161)?

16. The key to Mr. Drucker's discussion of American society in this last section of his essay is his distinction between "ways of life" and "ways of making a living." What is this distinction?

17. Can you, from your own knowledge of American history, provide some evidence to show how "the plantation aristocracy in the Old South between 1760 and 1860" was a "genuine ruling class" (lines 169–171)? Mr. Drucker's remark about architecture (in lines 174–176) may help you here.

18. Can you identify some of the "tycoons" referred to in line 176? Can you identify some of the houses they built (lines 176–178)?

19. Why is the parenthesis in lines 180–182 relevant to Mr. Drucker's argument?

20. To what extent does Mr. Drucker admit in the next paragraph (lines 186–200) that there is an "upper-class way of life" in America?

21. What is the point of the European visitor's joke about *Babbitt* and *Arrowsmith* (lines 205–207)?

SUGGESTED TOPICS

1. Write a paragraph in which you present some other aspects of American society that might disturb a European as do those given by Mr. Drucker in lines 10–36.

2. Write a paragraph in which you explain why the three sons of Kansas listed by Mr. Drucker in lines 57–58 reduce Mr. Gorer's argument to its full absurdity.

3. Write a paragraph in which you explain, a) industrial engineering (lines 17–19); b) de Tocqueville; c) Henry Adams; d) the idea of "the Renaissance Courtier" (line 127); e) a *Gymnasium;* f) a French château (line 177); g) the front office (line 190). Some of these you may know about already; some you will have to look up in the library.

6 / The Future Is Now*

KATHERINE ANNE PORTER

NOT SO LONG AGO I was reading in a magazine with an enormous circulation some instructions as to how to behave if and when we see that flash brighter than the sun which means that the atom bomb has arrived. I read of course with the
5 intense interest of one who has everything to learn on this subject; but at the end, the advice dwindled to this: the only real safety seems to lie in simply being somewhere else at the time, the farther away the better; the next best, failing access to deep shelters, bomb-proof cellars and all, is to get under a stout table—that is, just what
10 you might do if someone were throwing bricks through your window and you were too nervous to throw them back.

This comic anticlimax to what I had been taking as a serious educational piece surprised me into real laughter, hearty and care-free. It is such a relief to be told the truth, or even just the facts,
15 so pleasant not to be coddled with unreasonable hopes. That very evening I was drawn away from my work table to my fifth story window by one of those shrill terror-screaming sirens which our excitement-loving city government used then to affect for so many occasions: A fire? Police chasing a gangster? Somebody being got
20 to the hospital in a hurry? Some distinguished public guest being transferred from one point to another? Strange aircraft coming over, maybe? Under the lights of the corner crossing of the great

avenue, a huge closed vehicle whizzed past, screaming. I never knew what it was, had not in fact expected to know; no one I could possibly ask would know. Now that we have bells clamoring away instead for such events, we all have one doubt less, if perhaps one expectancy more. The single siren's voice means to tell us only one thing.

But at that doubtful moment, framed in a lighted window level with mine in the apartment house across the street, I saw a young man in a white T-shirt and white shorts at work polishing a long, beautiful dark table top. It was obviously his own table in his own flat, and he was enjoying his occupation. He was bent over in perfect concentration, rubbing, sandpapering, running the flat of his palm over the surface, standing back now and then to get the sheen of light on the fine wood. I am sure he had not even raised his head at the noise of the siren, much less had he come to the window. I stood there admiring his workmanlike devotion to a good job worth doing, and there flashed through me one of those pure fallacies of feeling which suddenly overleap reason: surely all that effort and energy so irreproachably employed were not going to be wasted on a table that was to be used merely for crawling under at some unspecified date. Then why take all those pains to make it beautiful? Any sort of old board would do.

I was so shocked at this treachery of the lurking Foul Fiend (despair *is* a foul fiend, and this was despair) I stood for a moment longer, looking out and around, trying to collect my feelings, trying to think a little. Two windows away and a floor down in the house across the street, a young woman was lolling in a deep chair, reading and eating fruit from a little basket. On the sidewalk, a boy and girl dressed alike in checkerboard cotton shirts and skintight blue denims, a costume which displayed acutely the structural differences of their shapes, strolled along with their arms around each other. I believe this custom of lovers walking enwreathed in public was imported by our soldiers of the First World War from France, from Paris indeed. "You didn't see that sort of thing here before," certain members of the older generation remarked quite often, in a tone of voice. Well, one sees quite a

lot of it now, and it is a very pretty, reassuring sight. Other citizens
60 of all sizes and kinds and ages were crossing back and forth; lights
flashed red and green, punctually. Motors zoomed by and over the
great city—but where am I going?—I never read other peoples'
descriptions of great cities, more particularly if it is a great city I
know. It doesn't belong here anyway, except that I had again that
65 quieting sense of the continuity of human experience on this earth,
its perpetual aspirations, set-backs, failures and re-beginnings in
eternal hope; and that, with some appreciable differences of dress,
customs and means of conveyance, so people have lived and moved
in the cities they have built for more millennia than we are yet able
70 to account for, and will no doubt build and live for as many more.

Why did this console me? I cannot say; my mind is of the sort
that can often be soothed with large generalities of that nature.
The silence of the spaces between the stars does not affright me,
as it did Pascal, because I am unable to imagine it except poetically;
75 and my awe is not for the silence and space of the endless universe
but for the inspired imagination of man, who can think and feel
so, and turn a phrase like that to communicate it to us. Then too,
I like the kind of honesty and directness of the young soldier who
lately answered someone who asked him if he knew what he was
80 fighting for. "I sure do," he said, "I am fighting to live." And as for
the future, I was once reading the first writings of a young girl, an
apprentice author, who was quite impatient to get on with the
business and find her way into print. There is very little one can
say of use in such matters, but I advised her against haste—she
85 could so easily regret it. "Give yourself time," I said, "the future
will take care of itself." This opinionated young person looked
down her little nose at me and said, "The future is now." She may
have heard the phrase somewhere and liked it, or she may just
naturally have belonged to that school of metaphysics; I am sure
90 she was too young to have investigated the thought deeply. But
maybe she was right and the future does arrive every day and it is
all we have, from one second to the next.

So I glanced again at the young man at work, a proper-looking
candidate for the armed services, and realized the plain, homely

fact: he was not preparing a possible shelter, something to cower under trembling; he was restoring a beautiful surface to put his books and papers on, to serve his plates from, to hold his cocktail tray and his lamp. He was full of the deep, right, instinctive, human belief that he and the table were going to be around together for a long time. Even if he is off to the army next week, it will be there when he gets back. At the very least, he is doing something he feels is worth doing now, and that is no small thing.

This lunatic atom bomb has succeeded in rousing the people of all nations to the highest point of unanimous moral dudgeon; great numbers of persons are frightened who never really had much cause to be frightened before. This world has always been a desperately dangerous place to live for the greater part of the earth's inhabitants; it was, however reluctantly, endured as the natural state of affairs. Yet the invention of every new weapon of war has always been greeted with horror and righteous indignation, especially by those who failed to invent it, or who were threatened with it first . . . bows and arrows, stone cannon balls, gunpowder, flintlock pistols, the dumdum bullet, the Maxim silencer, the machine gun, poison gas, armored tanks, and on and on to the grand climax—if it should prove to be—of the experiment on Hiroshima. Nagasaki was bombed too, remember? Or were we already growing accustomed to the idea? And as for Hiroshima, surely it could not have been the notion of sudden death to others that shocked us? How could it be, when in two great wars within one generation we have become familiar with millions of shocking deaths, by sudden violence of most cruel devices, and by agonies prolonged for years in prisons and hospitals and concentration camps. We take with apparent calmness the news of the deaths of millions by flood, famine, plague—no, all the frontiers of danger are down now, no one is safe, no one, and that, alas, really means all of us. It is our own deaths we fear, and so let's out with it and give up our fine debauch of moralistic frenzy over Hiroshima. I fail entirely to see why it is more criminal to kill a few thousand persons in one instant than it is to kill the same number slowly over a given stretch of time. If I have a choice, I'd as lief be killed by an atom bomb as by

a hand grenade or a flame thrower. If dropping the atom bomb is an immoral act, then the making of it was too; and writing of the formula was a crime, since those who wrote it must have known what such a contrivance was good for. So, morally speaking, the
135 bomb is only a magnified hand grenade, and the crime, if crime it is, is still murder. It was never anything else. Our protocriminal then was the man who first struck fire from flint, for from that moment we have been coming steadily to this day and this weapon and this use of it. What would you have advised instead? That the
140 human race should have gone on sitting in caves gnawing raw meat and beating each other over the head with bones?

And yet it may be that what we have is a world not on the verge of flying apart, but an uncreated one—still in shapeless fragments waiting to be put together properly. I imagine that when we want
145 something better, we may have it: at perhaps no greater price than we have already paid for the worse.

QUESTIONS

Mr. Drucker's essay, which precedes this one, might be said to complicate the simple form of comparison and contrast because it wants to work in the maximum number of examples for each side of its comparison and because it wants to provide room for some related but not essential ideas about its subject. This selection complicates the simple form for another reason. It was written by one of the finest contemporary short-story writers and it shows very clearly the different way a short-story writer's thoughts move. If we were to list, as in a topic outline, the subjects of the paragraphs in this essay, the list might look something like this: 1) Reading an essay on Civil Defense; 2) Watching the life of the city from my apartment window; 3) Watching a young man in the apartment across the way finishing a table; 4) Watching the life of the city from my apartment window; 5) Various observations about space and time; 6) Watching the young man in the apartment across the way finishing a table; 7) The effect of the atom bomb on our feelings, particularly our moral feelings; 8) A hopeful view of the future. Such a list certainly makes this essay look both jumbled and repetitive. In order to read it successfully, we have to look for the things in it which make this order of paragraphs not only sensible but brilliantly right. This means we have to see that the author is not so much concerned with moving logically—in the very narrow sense of the word—from one point in her comparison to another, but with moving from one feeling about her experience to another comparable or contrasting feeling. The questions which follow are aimed at drawing your attention to these movements.

1. What was it about the magazine article on what to do when the atom bomb falls that surprised the author into real laughter (line 13)?

2. Why does she describe this laughter as "carefree" (lines 13–14)?

3. If you know that when this essay was written, during the last war, a rule had just been set up that sirens should be reserved for air-raid warnings and that all other users of sirens had to substitute bells, can you explain the connection between the account in lines 1–11 of the author's reading the magazine article and the account in lines 15–28 of her going to look out her apartment window?

4. Logically speaking, the author makes clear to us, the shift of her attention from the street scene to the young man in the apartment house across the street is accidental. Is there some connection in the way she feels about him in lines 29–44 and the way she had felt about the siren in lines 15–28?

5. What is there in her feelings about the young man which leads her to begin the next paragraph (lines 45–48) with a statement about despair? At the beginning of the following paragraph (line 71) she says, "Why did this console me?" referring to what she has said in lines 48–70. What is consoling about this passage?

6. What, in particular, is consoling about the young woman lolling in a deep chair (lines 49–50), about the boy and the girl with their arms around one another (lines 50–54)? Why, in discussing the boy and girl, does the author stop to remember what certain members of the older generation have said about the kind of thing they are doing (lines 54–58)?

7. What is the connection between Pascal's remark about the silence of the spaces (lines 73–77), the young soldier's remark about what he was fighting for (line 80), and the young girl's observation that "the future is now" (lines 80–87).

8. The paragraph which begins at line 93 (paragraph 6, which looks, in our topic outline, like a repetitious paragraph) begins, *"So I glanced again at the young man at work. . . ."* Why?

9. This sixth paragraph is the most important in the essay; in it the author indicates what are to her the two most important things in life and even what the relation between these things is. Can you say what they are?

10. "At the very least," this paragraph concludes, "he is doing something he feels is worth doing now. . . ." Has this observation about the young man any connection with what the young girl in the previous paragraph said to the author?

11. The seventh paragraph, which begins at line 103, starts on the subject of the atom bomb. How has the author prepared us for this discussion of the bomb?

12. Why does the author insist on reminding us that Nagasaki was bombed as well as Hiroshima (line 116)?

13. At the conclusion of her paragraph on the atom bomb, the author asks us whether we should have advised the human race, at its beginning, to stick to "sitting in caves gnawing raw meat and beating each other over the head with bones" (lines 139–141). Explain why she specifies these three activities of primitive men.

14. What is the connection between the point she makes in this last sentence of paragraph seven (lines 139–141) and the atom bomb?

15. How does the qualified hope expressed in the last paragraph (lines 142–146) follow from the conclusion of the previous paragraph?

SUGGESTED TOPICS

1. Write a paragraph in which you state as clearly and logically as you can what seems to you the essential line of reasoning the author is following in the paragraph on the atom bomb (lines 103–141).

2. Write a paragraph in which you describe what the author thinks are the important and good things in life, basing your discussion on what you can deduce from lines 25–32, 40–52, and 79–87.

3. Write a paragraph in which you describe the attitude Miss Porter thinks we ought to take toward the existence of the atom bomb.

7 / Humanism*

ERWIN PANOFSKY

NINE DAYS before his death Immanuel Kant was visited by his physician. Old, ill and nearly blind, he rose from his chair and stood trembling with weakness and muttering unintelligible words. Finally his faithful companion realized that he would not sit down again until the visitor had taken a seat. This 5 he did, and Kant then permitted himself to be helped to his chair and, after having regained some of his strength, said, "Das Gefühl für Humanität hat mich noch nicht verlassen"—"The sense of humanity has not left me." The two men were moved almost to tears. For, though the word *Humanität* had come, in the eighteenth 10 century, to mean little more than politeness or civility, it had, for Kant, a much deeper significance, which the circumstances of the moment served to emphasize: man's proud and tragic consciousness of self-approved and self-imposed principles, contrasting with his utter subjection to illness, decay and all that is implied in the 15 word "mortality."

Historically the word *humanitas* has had two clearly distinguishable meanings, the first arising from a contrast between man and what is less than man; the second, between man and what is more. In the first case *humanitas* means a value, in the second a limita- 20 tion.

* From *Meaning in the Visual Arts* by Erwin Panofsky. Copyright © 1955 by Erwin Panofsky, reprinted by permission of Doubleday & Co., Inc.

The concept of *humanitas* as a value was formulated in the circle around young Scipio, with Cicero as its belated, yet most explicit spokesman. It meant the quality which distinguishes man,
25 not only from animals, but also, and even more so, from him who belongs to the species *homo* without deserving the name of *homo humanus*; from the barbarian or vulgarian who lacks *pietas* and παιδεία—that is, respect for moral values and that gracious blend of learning and urbanity which we can only circumscribe by
30 the discredited word "culture."

In the Middle Ages this concept was displaced by the consideration of humanity as being opposed to divinity rather than to animality or barbarism. The qualities commonly associated with it were therefore those of frailty and transience: *humanitas fragilis,*
35 *humanitas caduca.*

Thus the Renaissance conception of *humanitas* had a two-fold aspect from the outset. The new interest in the human being was based both on a revival of the classical antithesis between *humanitas* and *barbaritas*, or *feritas*, and on a survival of the medieval
40 antithesis between *humanitas* and *divinitas*. When Marsilio Ficino defines man as a "rational soul participating in the intellect of God, but operating in a body," he defines him as the one being that is both autonomous and finite. And Pico's famous "speech," "On the Dignity of Man," is anything but a document of paganism. Pico
45 says that God placed man in the center of the universe so that he might be conscious of where he stands, and therefore free to decide "where to turn." He does not say that man *is* the center of the universe, not even in the sense commonly attributed to the classical phrase, "man the measure of all things."
50 It is from this ambivalent conception of *humanitas* that humanism was born. It is not so much a movement as an attitude which can be defined as the conviction of the dignity of man, based on both the insistence on human values (rationality and freedom) and the acceptance of human limitations (fallibility and frailty);
55 from this two postulates result—responsibility and tolerance.

Small wonder that this attitude has been attacked from two opposite camps whose common aversion to the ideas of responsibility and tolerance has recently aligned them in a united front. Entrenched in one of these camps are those who deny human values: the determinists, whether they believe in divine, physical or social 60 predestination, the authoritarians, and those "insectolatrists" who profess the all-importance of the hive, whether the hive be called group, class, nation or race. In the other camp are those who deny human limitations in favor of some sort of intellectual or political libertinism, such as aestheticists, vitalists, intuitionists and hero- 65 worshipers. From the point of view of determinism, the humanist is either a lost soul or an ideologist. From the point of view of authoritarianism, he is either a heretic or a revolutionary (or a counterrevolutionary). From the point of view of "insectolatry," he is a useless individualist. And from the point of view of libertinism he 70 is a timid bourgeois.

Erasmus of Rotterdam, the humanist *par excellence*, is a typical case in point. The church suspected and ultimately rejected the writings of this man who had said: "Perhaps the spirit of Christ is more largely diffused than we think, and there are many in the 75 community of saints who are not in our calendar." The adventurer Ulrich von Hutten despised his ironical skepticism and his unheroic love of tranquillity. And Luther, who insisted that "no man has power to think anything good or evil, but everything occurs in him by absolute necessity," was incensed by a belief 80 which manifested itself in the famous phrase: "What is the use of man as a totality [that is, of man endowed with a body and a soul], if God would work in him as a sculptor works in clay, and might just as well work in stone?"

QUESTIONS

1. In this selection we have, as we had in "Conservatism and American Culture," a double contrast and comparison. This double comparison is constructed more simply and clearly, perhaps, even than President Taylor's; nonetheless this selection is the most difficult in this section because the ideas dealt with in it are themselves difficult.

Let us begin with the structure. The essay obviously reaches a turning point in lines 50–55, where the author asserts that two similar but contrasting conceptions of *humanitas* contributed to the renaissance conception of humanism. These conceptions of *humanitas* are briefly summarized in lines 51–54, but in order to understand this summary, we must look back at what has been said in three preceding paragraphs (lines 17–35). Explain which part of these three paragraphs makes clear the meaning of the phrase "insistence on human values" and which part makes clear the phrase "acceptance of human limitations," and show how each does so.

2. Explain how Professor Panofsky's explanation of these two conceptions leads him to describe the first as "a value" and the second as "a limitation" (lines 20–21).

3. In the three paragraphs of explanation which we are considering (lines 17–35) Professor Panofsky uses some foreign words and expressions which may discourage us by making us feel we can never understand them unless we know Latin and Greek (for instance, *homo humanus, pietas, παιδεία, humanitas fragilis, humanitas caduca*). Actually he defines each of these foreign words or expressions in the course of his explanation. Show that you have found these definitions and that you can therefore define each of these strange-looking words.

4. If you look in any good dictionary (Webster's New Collegiate, Webster's New World, The American College, for example), you will find a noun, *caducity,* and an adjective derived from it, *caducous.* One of the meanings the dictionary gives for *caducity* is "transitoriness" and one of the meanings it gives for *caducous* is "transitory." If you look at the etymologies (a word you may also have to look up) for these two words, you will be able to tell whether this information helps you to understand the meaning of *"humanitas caduca"* or not. The English words certainly look as if they were connected with the Latin word, but you must never assume such a connection without checking the etymology and the definitions of the English word, since it is very easy to be fooled about this kind of connection. For example, look up *piety* in the dictionary, note its etymology, and then see if you can find a definition in the dictionary which corresponds to the one Professor Panofsky gives for *pietas.* You will find an even more complicated and therefore potentially misleading situation if you look in the dictionary for English words that look like the Greek

word παιδεία, which may be transliterated into our alphabet as "*paideia.*" If you look up "paid-" in the dictionary, you will get on the trail of this complicated situation. This exercise should teach you that, on the one hand, you can learn a great deal about foreign words from an English dictionary if you use it cleverly, and, on the other, that you have to be on your guard against all sorts of pitfalls in doing so.

5. If we now turn our attention back to the plan of Professor Panofsky's essay, we will notice that before he begins the explanation (lines 17–35) which leads up to his summary (lines 51–54), he has a paragraph in which he relates an anecdote about Kant and then comments on it. Explain how this anecdote shows what Professor Panofsky's comment on it in lines 13–16 says it shows.

6. How does this anecdote fit as an introduction to the explanation which follows it in the next three paragraphs (lines 17–35)?

7. The fifth paragraph, beginning at line 36, offers two illustrations of how *humanitas* "had a two-fold aspect" in the renaissance. Show how the remarks about Ficino (lines 40–43) and about Pico (lines 43–49) illustrate this point.

8. After the turning-point paragraph (lines 50–55) in which Professor Panofsky summarizes his explanation of the two-fold nature of humanism, he has two further paragraphs in which he comments on the situation of humanism from the renaissance to our own time. He says it has been attacked from two opposite camps and then describes these two camps in two ways, by telling us what they stand for, and by telling us what their members characteristically think of humanists. But if we are to follow him in this paragraph, we must be sure we realize when he has ceased telling us the first of these things and started telling us the second. Indicate the place where he changes from the first to the second.

9. How many different groups or parties who "deny human values" does Professor Panofsky list? How many who "deny human limitations"?

10. Show that you recognize which of the attitudes toward humanists listed in the second half of the paragraph goes with which of the parties listed in the first half.

11. In the last paragraph (lines 72–84) Professor Panofsky illustrates the attacks on humanism by the attacks which were made on Erasmus. He tells us about three attacks on Erasmus and each of these attacks is made by a party or group he has described in the preceding

paragraph; however, he does not mention them in this paragraph in the same order in which they are mentioned in the preceding paragraph. Show that you understand which party described in the previous paragraph is represented by (a) the church (lines 73–76); (b) the adventurer Ulrich von Hutten (lines 76–78); (c) Luther (lines 78–80).

12. What is there about the sentence quoted from Erasmus in lines 81–84 which would have incensed a man who believed what Luther is quoted as saying in lines 78–80?

13. Explain why it was perfectly logical for the Catholic Church to be suspicious of the man who said what Erasmus is quoted as saying in lines 81–84.

SUGGESTED TOPICS

1. Explain in your own words and without reference to Professor Panofsky's historical explanation the two conceptions which were joined in the idea of humanism.

2. Write a paragraph in which you show how the contrast between the two conceptions which contributed to humanism, the contrast which is explained in the first half of the essay (lines 17–49), is reinforced by the contrast in the second half of the essay (lines 56–84), the contrast between the two camps which attack humanism from opposite sides.

3. Write an essay on the anecdote about Kant which shows that— at least as Professor Panofsky has given it to us—it forms a small fable of the humanist account of man.

CARL BECKER

PETER F. DRUCKER

OLIVER WENDELL HOLMES, JR.

ALLEN TATE

ARTHUR M. SCHLESINGER, JR.

LIONEL TRILLING

EDMUND BURKE

JAMES THURBER

ALISTAIR COOKE

JOHN MAYNARD KEYNES

ii. Separation and Discrimination

8 / Individual Freedom in a Democratic Society*

CARL BECKER

THE PRINCIPLE of individual freedom in the economic realm, although not much stressed in the propaganda of the great crusading days, was always an integral part of the liberal-democratic ideology. For the needed emancipation of industry from the hampering restraints of monopolistic privilege and petty governmental regulation, it was a sound working principle; but applied without qualifications it could only benefit the industrial bourgeoisie at the expense of the underlying population of peasants and workers. As set forth in the *Wealth of Nations,* and in the more rigorous and apparently more scientific works of the English classical economists, the principle was indeed scarcely more than pure rationalization of the business interests of capitalist employers; but this ominous fact was long concealed because the principle was formulated in terms of the word liberty, the magic of which was sufficient at that time to give a general sanction even to the brutalities of cut-throat competition and the systematic degradation of women and children. The present misery of the workers could be more easily contemplated and dismissed because it could be regarded as a necessary but temporary phase in the operation of a divinely ordained law of progress. The average humane

* From *Modern Democracy* by Carl Becker. Reprinted by permission of the Yale University Press.

59

middle-class man, whether employer or not, could therefore accept the principle of individual freedom in the economic realm, along with the other great freedoms, since it so happily enabled him to reconcile his selfish with his altruistic impulses by assuring him
25 that he could best serve God and his neighbor by doing as he pleased. "Private advantage a public benefit"—such was the succinct formula by which the prosperous middle classes justified their amiable expectation that when everyone was free all would presently be equal, when all were equal everyone would presently have
30 enough, when all had enough no one would any longer be unjust or inhumane.

The expectation was surely naïve, in no sort of harmony with the relevant facts of social experience. Even under the most favorable circumstances, a society of uprooted and freely competing in-
35 dividuals must have functioned to the advantage of the few who by good fortune, intelligence, or lack of scruple were able to acquire wealth and to employ it to advance their interests through the mechanism of politics: the times would always be ripe for a sufficient number of not-too-good men to come to the aid of the
40 party. But this result was greatly accelerated and intensified by those changes in the economic and material conditions of life which, effected without blare of trumpets and scarcely perceived at the time, are now known as the industrial or technological revolution of modern times.

45 In terms of the ideal there should have emerged from the liberal-democratic revolution a relatively simple society of free, equal, and prosperous citizens, fraternally cooperating to effect, by rational discussion and mutual concession, the common good. In fact there emerged an extremely complex society in which highly in-
50 tricate and impersonal economic forces, stronger than good will or deliberate intention or rational direction, brought about an increasing concentration of wealth and power in the hands of the fortunate few, and thereby nullified, for the majority of the people, many of those essential liberties which provide both the
55 theoretical justification and the necessary conditions for the practical success of democratic institutions.

If then the democratic way of life is to survive we must distinguish the kinds of individual freedom that are essential to it from those that are unessential or disastrous. Broadly speaking, the kinds that are essential are those which the individual enjoys in his intellectual and political activities; the kind that are unessential are the relatively unrestrained liberties he has hitherto enjoyed in his economic activities. The distinction is comparatively easy to make in theory, but will be extremely difficult to effect in practice. Not the least of the difficulties arises from the fact that in the traditional ideology the freedoms of the individual in the political, the intellectual, and the economic realms are so intimately associated that they seem to stand or fall together. The result is that any proposal to regulate by governmental authority the system of free economic enterprise is sure to be opposed on the ground that if the system of free economic enterprise cannot be maintained the other freedoms of democracy, freedom of thought and political freedom, must in the end be abandoned also. Whether this is true can only be determined by the event. Whatever the event may be, the difficult but essential task which confronts all democratic societies today may be formulated as follows: how in practice to curtail the freedom of the individual in economic enterprise sufficiently to effect that equality of opportunity and of possessions without which democracy is an empty form, and at the same time to preserve that measure of individual freedom in intellectual and political life without which it cannot exist.

COMMENTARY

IN THIS SELECTION from his book, *Modern Democracy*, Carl Becker seeks to reach a conclusion in a matter which he finds confused and difficult, by separating what he thinks is not strictly relevant and therefore confusing from what he thinks is essential. This selection therefore suggests that the form of exposition Becker is using is particularly well fitted to puzzling or controversial matters. The form encourages us to separate the subject into its constituent elements, which we must do before we can hope to establish agreement about which element produces a particular result, or leads to a particular conclusion, or calls for the application of a particular law. Very often the writer who uses this method will prefer one result to another or will favor one side of a controversy rather than another. But if he is an honest writer, he will analyze the subject fairly, so that those who disagree with him can still accept his analysis, and he will probably either admit that they may be right and he wrong (as Becker does at the end of this selection), or show that his opponents are right that certain elements produce certain effects and only wrong in believing that these elements are present in the problem under consideration (as Holmes does in a later selection).

But whatever attitude the user of this form of composition may take towards the elements of his subject, the main part of his essay will consist of an effort to discriminate among the elements which constitute his subject. When you have read this selection from Carl Becker, you will see that he distinguishes three forms of individual freedom in a democratic society, namely, intellectual freedom, political freedom, and economic freedom (lines 59–63). Moreover, when you have read the whole selection, you will see that Becker's conclusion depends on his separating the third of these freedoms from the other two and showing that the third is not essential to democracy but that the first and second are. This is the reason he begins his discussion with the subject of economic freedom, or, as the first phrase of this selection puts it, "the principle of individual freedom in the economic realm" (line 1). He is careful to make clear to us why this principle was originally made a part of "the liberal-democratic ideology" and to agree that it should have been (lines 3–6), but he follows this statement immediately with a counter-statement that, useful and necessary as this principle was when believers in democracy were trying to overthrow an undemocratic society, it was harmful to most people once a society that embodied "the liberal-democratic ideology" actually existed (lines 6–9). This statement is the key to the whole selection, because it indicates the reason for the establishment of the debatable principle (the reason which will continue to be offered for it by those who continue to benefit from it), and then joins directly to this assertion a succinct statement of the reason why Becker thinks this principle is not a true part of the democratic creed and cannot be proved so by the arguments of its supporters. In this way the first seven lines of the selection outline for us the whole plan of what follows.

Since Becker's outline has contrasted the use of the principle of economic freedom in the fight for democracy with its use in an established democratic society, and since his purpose is to show that in the second situation its use is a mistake, the next logical step for him to take is to discuss the arguments that have been offered for continuing to use the principle in an established democratic society. This is what he does. Notice how carefully the sentence in lines 9–17 follows the plan laid out in the previous clause (lines 6–9): the first part of the sentence in lines 9–17 tells us how the arguments for the principle show that it existed for the benefit of "the industrial bourgeoisie," and the second part (lines 15–17) how its application hurt "the underlying population."

But as a historian Becker understood well that the people who argued for this principle did not do so cynically but believed in it sincerely and thought that it operated for the good—at least the ultimate good—of the whole society. He thinks these people were wrong, and he makes it quite clear that he does so ("this ominous fact," line 13; "brutalities," line 16; "degradation," line 16), but he wants to make sure we understand how these people came to believe sincerely in the principle of economic freedom. Therefore he spends the rest of the paragraph outlining the argument they used and suggesting the reasons why it was so very convincing to them. He points out that, in the first place, they found it easy to think of this principle as beneficial to the whole society, and not just to their own class alone, because it appeared to them to be an instance of "liberty," and "liberty" was for them a powerfully emotional idea. He also points out how important to their argument their belief in the idea of progress was, because it allowed them to think, even if they admitted the "present miseries" of other classes, that these miseries were only temporary and that they were necessary to the eventual achievement of progress. In this way Becker makes clear to us how the attitude which seems to him selfish came to seem patriotic and generous to those who believed in it. In the last six lines of the paragraph (lines 26–31) he sums up the argument of those who came in this way to believe in unqualified economic freedom, but once more, he makes it clear that he finds this argument unconvincing. Consider "their amiable expectation," in line 28. Can you explain how this phrase reveals Becker's lack of belief in their argument for unqualified economic freedom?

Having set forth the argument used by those who think the principle of unqualified economic freedom is essential to a democracy, and having implied throughout his discussion of this argument his disagreement with it, Becker then devotes two paragraphs to pointing out why he thinks this argument unconvincing. Notice how careful he is to tell us in the very first sentence of this paragraph exactly what he is going to do in it and how he connects this sentence with the one that immediately precedes it at the end of the previous paragraph. This is what you may have heard described as "transition." Theoretically, if a discussion is arranged perfectly logically, the reader ought to see without help why he is being asked to move from one point to the next, but the best writers seem to feel that it is not entirely safe to count on the reader in this matter and are consequently always careful to offer the reader any assistance they can. On the other hand, transition in itself, if the relation between the paragraphs is not a logical one, can do more harm than good; it only makes matters worse if you carefully point out to the reader that you are now about to move from point A to point B if there is no reasonable connection between these two points.

The first reason Becker offers for thinking the argument for the principle of unqualified economic freedom is unconvincing occupies lines 33–40. It points out that men differ—in luck, in ability, in unscrupulousness—so greatly that the principle of economic freedom allows certain ones excessive wealth and therefore excessive political power, even when historical conditions are favorable to political equality. He sums this argument up with a piece of wit that depends on your recognizing the familiar saying, "Now is the time for all good men to come to the aid of the party." The second reason he offers occupies the rest of the paragraph and the whole of the next paragraph (lines 40–56). It follows very closely from the first reason, because it asserts that, contrary to the assumption behind the first reason, the actual historical conditions in which democratic society developed, namely the conditions produced by the industrial revolution, were not favorable to democracy but, on the contrary, were such as to maximize the damage done by the operation of the principle of unqualified economic freedom. The result, Becker says (lines 53–56), was that liberties which are *essential* to democracy were nullified by the effects of a liberty which was *inessential* to democracy.

This last assertion in the paragraph prepares us for the conclusion

Becker reaches in the next and final paragraph. In this paragraph he clearly distinguishes for us the essential principles of democracy. But first, just as he did at line 32, he provides a clear transition (lines 57–59). He then goes on to tell us that, if we agree unqualified economic freedom is not only inessential to democracy but also destroys the two freedoms which are essential to it, we must still recognize how difficult it is going to be to limit economic freedom. He is even prepared to discover that it may be impossible to do so. If it turns out that it is impossible to do so, he says, that will be because the argument of believers in unqualified economic freedom—the argument that all three kinds of liberty are bound up together—is right (lines 65–73). One thing, however, he feels sure of (lines 73–81): democracy will survive under modern conditions only if this argument is not true, only if we can succeed in separating the principle of economic freedom from the other two and in limiting it without damage to the other two principles. Notice how the effectiveness of this final point is increased by the clear and carefully balanced sentence at the end of the paragraph in which Becker states it (lines 76–81). Every essential of his argument is present in this sentence without confusing or overcrowding it: the necessity for the curtailment of economic freedom, the reason for that necessity, the risk it involves, and the reason that risk must be avoided.

We are now in a position to see clearly the plan Becker has followed in this selection and to understand why he has used it. His purpose was to separate one kind of freedom which many people in democratic society have believed essential to democracy from two other kinds of freedom, and to show that the first kind of freedom is not essential and that, unless we can separate it from the other two, in practice as well as theory, democracy will not survive. This summary can be reduced even more by saying that Becker has three objects: to separate the three kinds of freedom; to show that one is inessential: to show that that one must be limited. Since he has three main objects, Becker divides his discussion into three parts. The first gives us a brief history of the principle of unqualified economic freedom and of the arguments some people have used to try to prove that it is essential to democracy. The second section gives us Becker's reasons for thinking that the actual history of democratic society does not bear out the arguments for this principle and, indeed, shows that the operation of the principle has nullified the two other principles, which are essential to democracy. The third section gives us the conclusion which we must logically draw from the first two. We can sum up Becker's essay even more briefly: 1) supporters of unqualified economic freedom say it operates in a certain way in a democratic society; 2) the facts of history show that it operates in another way; 3) therefore, we must, if possible, limit the operation of economic freedom, or democracy will not survive.

9/ Is There Really a Lack of Opportunity?*

PETER F. DRUCKER

OPPORTUNITIES for advancement in the industrial enterprise [in Western society] are greater than they have ever been in any society. Statistically, opportunities are increasing apace; the industrial enterprise depends on a steady increase in the executive and middle class positions. Every major company in this country has had to start a systematic recruitment and training program for supervisory and executive personnel, as the supply is not equal to an ever-increasing demand.

And yet it is becoming increasingly difficult to rise in industrial society; the promise of equal opportunities is being fulfilled less and less. Outside of the United States this is perhaps not so important. The rise from the rank and file into the management was the exception in Europe rather than the rule. In this country, however, the promise of equal opportunities for every one in industry has been regarded as a basic promise, one of the foundations of "democracy."

The key to the riddle lies in the character of the "skill" required of the new middle and upper groups, the industrial middle class and the executive group. These are not "skills" in the traditional sense, based on experience and long practice. Theoretical knowl-

* From *The New Society* by Peter F. Drucker. Copyright, 1950, by Peter F. Drucker. Reprinted by permission of Harper & Brothers.

edge and administrative ability are required. A rank-and-file job,
however skilled, will not give the worker the knowledge needed
for a supervisory job; nor will it give him an opportunity to demonstrate his ability for supervisory work. A supervisory or middle-
25 management job, by the same token, will not give the knowledge
needed for an executive position nor an opportunity to show executive ability. As a result, the chances of a working man to be promoted to supervisor, or of a supervisor to be promoted into the
managerial group are actually becoming smaller, even though the
30 number and proportion of supervisory and managerial positions
are increasing. The increased demand tends to be filled by direct
appointment of men from the outside rather than by promotion
up the ladder. At the same time, the irrelevance of the worker's
performance as a criterion for performance as a supervisor, and
35 of the supervisor's performance as a criterion for managerial performance, means that promotions are not rational and under-
standable to the group out of which the promoted man comes.

One important result is the almost general complaint that promotions are not made on merit but by favoritism, whim or preju-
40 dice. Of course, there is always justification for such a charge; only
the decision of the Recording Angel is based on complete knowledge of a man. But the belief is as strong in plants where management has tried to develop a rational, objective and impersonal
promotion policy as it is in plants which depend on the "hunch"
45 of the superior. The qualities that make a worker outstanding are
not too relevant to his qualifications as a foreman; the qualities
that make a foreman an outstanding foreman are not too relevant
to his promotion into middle management. Thus even the most
rational decision is likely to appear incomprehensible, irrational
50 and arbitrary to the group out of which the man is promoted.
Hence the strong pressure for seniority as the sole criterion for
advancement; at least it is a simple, clear and indisputable criterion,
however little it may have to do with merit or with the qualifications for the job.

55   That the development is not something peculiarly American—
let alone something peculiarly "capitalist"—is indicated by the

experience of the only other country where the worker once had
an opportunity to become an executive: Soviet Russia.

Twenty years ago, when the Russian industrialization drive
started, opportunities for the worker were practically unlimited. 60
The positions of the managerial group of prerevolutionary days
had become vacant; there were in addition, all the positions in the
new industries to be filled. The Russians promoted every worker
who showed any ability at all as fast as he could learn the new
job. From 1926 until 1936 Russia knew indeed unequalled op- 65
portunities; a boy fresh from the farm could be almost certain of
attaining quickly a major position if he showed ability and industry. But while Russia got good gang bosses out of the ranks,
she did not get good technicians and executives out of the gang
bosses. Very soon she found out that it was on these that the 70
performance of industry depends. Hence in 1936, practically overnight, the whole policy was changed. Able workers now can make
a good deal of money; indeed, under the Russian incentive system
their wage is three or four times the average. But they cannot become executives or even supervisors. Supervisory positions above 75
that of "gang boss" are reserved for the graduates of the technical
schools and universities who are to be the future executives, and
who in turn are usually the children of technicians, executives and
government officials. The extremism of the change in policy is
indeed typical of a regime based on ideological absolutes such as 80
Communism. The change itself, though, was not ideologically motivated but was a reaction to the realities of the industrial situation.

In this country the tremendous pressure for a college education
is a sign that our younger generation does not believe any longer
that opportunities for advancement from the bottom really exist. 85
They believe that the only chance to rise to the top is by starting
well above the ground.

QUESTIONS

1. It is clear from the opening of the third paragraph of this selection (line 17) that the basic form of this essay is going to be the same

as that of the others in this group. But here the form is being used to solve a problem, not to suggest an attitude in a controversy. The problem is set forth in the first two paragraphs. Why does the author use two paragraphs?

2. In the third paragraph the author says that "the key to the riddle lies in the character of the 'skill' required. . . ." (line 17). What is this character?

3. Why does the author emphasize (by naming them twice in lines 18–19) the two groups that are involved in the riddle? Does he continue to distinguish between these two groups?

4. By the end of paragraph three (lines 17–37) Mr. Drucker has solved his riddle. Indicate the lines in which he sums up this solution.

5. Lines 33–37 serve as a transition to another effect of the circumstances which create the riddle; how do they do so?

6. Why is this second effect closely related to the riddle?

7. In lines 55–83 Mr. Drucker gives us an account of the promotion system in Russian industry; why?

8. Point out evidence in lines 59–83 that Mr. Drucker is conscious of the reason he is including this paragraph in the selection.

9. Does Mr. Drucker believe that the attitude of the younger generation, which he describes in lines 84–88, is right?

10. Why does Mr. Drucker think it is important for us to understand the solution to the riddle he is discussing in this selection?

SUGGESTED TOPICS

1. Write a paragraph in which you make clear why Mr. Drucker thinks it necessary to discuss the situation in both the United States and the Soviet Union.

2. There is a connection between the situation described in this selection and the conservatism discussed by President Taylor; what is that connection?

3. Write a paragraph in which you discuss what Becker (Selection 8) would say to Mr. Drucker's assertion that "the promise of equal opportunities for everyone in industry has been regarded as . . . one of the foundations of democracy" (lines 14–16).

10 / Abrams *v.* United States

OLIVER WENDELL HOLMES, JR.

THIS INDICTMENT is founded wholly upon the publication of two leaflets which I shall describe in a moment. The first count charges a conspiracy pending the war with Germany to publish abusive language about the form of government of the United States, laying the preparation and publishing of the first leaflet as overt acts. The second count charges a conspiracy pending the war to publish language intended to bring the form of government into contempt, laying the preparation and publishing of the two leaflets as overt acts. The third count alleges a conspiracy to encourage resistance to the United States in the same war and to attempt to effectuate the purpose by publishing the same leaflets. The fourth count lays a conspiracy to incite curtailment of production of things necessary to the prosecution of the war and to attempt to accomplish it by publishing the second leaflet to which I have referred.

The first of these leaflets says that the President's cowardly silence about the intervention in Russia reveals the hypocrisy of the plutocratic gang in Washington. It intimates that "German militarism combined with Allied capitalism to crush the Russian revolution," goes on that the tyrants of the world fight each other until they see a common enemy—working-class enlightenment—when they combine to crush it; and that now militarism and capitalism combined, though not openly, to crush the Russian revolu-

71

tion. It says that there is only one enemy of the workers of the
25 world and that is capitalism; that it is a crime for workers of America, &c., to fight the workers' republic of Russia, and ends "Awake!
Awake, You Workers of the World!" Signed "Revolutionists." A
note adds, "It is absurd to call us pro-German. We hate and despise German militarism more than do you hypocritical tyrants.
30 We have more reasons for denouncing German militarism than
has the coward of the White House."

The other leaflet, headed "Workers—Wake Up," with abusive
language says that America together with the Allies will march for
Russia to help Czecho-Slovaks in their struggle against the Bol-
35 sheviki, and that this time the hypocrites shall not fool the Russian emigrants and friends of Russia in America. It tells the
Russian emigrants that they now must spit in the face of the false
military propaganda by which their sympathy and help to the
prosecution of the war have been called forth and says that with
40 the money they have lent or are going to lend "they will make
bullets not only for the Germans but also for the Workers' Soviets
of Russia," and further, "Workers in the ammunition factories,
you are producing bullets, bayonets, cannon, to murder not only
the Germans but also your dearest, best, who are in Russia fighting
45 for freedom." It then appeals to the same Russian emigrants at
some length not to consent to the "inquisitionary expedition to
Russia," and says that the destruction of the Russian revolution
is "the politics of the march on Russia." The leaflet winds up by
saying "Workers, our reply to this barbaric intervention has to be
50 a general strike!" and after a few words on the spirit of revolution,
exhortations not to be afraid, and some usual tall talk, ends "Woe
unto those who will be in the way of progress. Let solidarity live!
The Rebels."

No argument seems to me necessary to show that these pro-
55 nunciamentos in no way attack the form of government of the
United States, or that they do not support either of the first two
counts. What little I have to say about the third count may be
postponed until I have considered the fourth. With regard to that
it seems too plain to be denied that the suggestion to workers in

the ammunition factories that they are producing bullets to mur- 60
der their dearest, and the further advocacy of a general strike, both
in the second leaflet, do urge curtailment of production of things
necessary to the prosecution of the war within the meaning of the
Act of May 16, 1918 . . . amending §3 of the earlier Act of 1917.
But to make the conduct criminal that statute requires that it 65
should be "with intent by such curtailment to cripple or hinder
the United States in the prosecution of the war." It seems to me
that no such intent is proved.

I am aware of course that the word intent as vaguely used in
ordinary legal discussion means no more than knowledge at the 70
time of the act that the consequences said to be intended will
ensue. Even less than that will satisfy the general principle of
civil and criminal liability. A man may have to pay damages, may
be sent to prison, at common law might be hanged, if at the time
of his act he knew facts from which common experience showed 75
that the consequences would follow, whether he individually could
foresee them or not. But, when words are used exactly, a deed is
not done with intent to produce a consequence unless that consequence is the aim of the deed. It may be obvious, and obvious to
the actor, that the consequences will follow, and he may be liable 80
for it even if he regrets it, but he does not do the act with intent
to produce it unless the aim to produce it is the proximate motive
of the specific act, although there may be some deeper motive
behind.

It seems to me that this statute must be taken to use its words 85
in a strict and accurate sense. They would be absurd in any other.
A patriot might think that we were wasting money on aeroplanes,
or making more cannon of a certain kind than we needed, and
might advocate curtailment with success, yet even if it turned
out that the curtailment hindered and was thought by other minds 90
to have been obviously likely to hinder the United States in the
prosecution of the war, no one would hold such conduct a crime.
I admit that my illustration does not answer all that might be
said but it is enough to show what I think and to let me pass to
a more important aspect of the case. I refer to the First Amend- 95

ment to the Constitution that Congress shall make no law abridging the freedom of speech.

I never have seen any reason to doubt that the questions of law
that alone were before this Court in the cases of *Schenck, Froh-*
100 *werk* and *Debs,* were rightly decided. I do not doubt for a moment
that by the same reasoning that would justify punishing persuasion to murder, the United States constitutionally may punish
speech that produces or is intended to produce a clear and imminent danger that it will bring about forthwith certain substan-
105 tive evils that the United States constitutionally may seek to prevent. The power undoubtedly is greater in time of war than in time
of peace because war opens dangers that do not exist at other
times.

But as against dangers peculiar to war, as against others, the
110 principle of the right to free speech is always the same. It is only
the present danger of immediate evil or an intent to bring it about
that warrants Congress in setting a limit to the expression of
opinion where private rights are not concerned. Congress certainly
cannot forbid all effort to change the mind of the country. Now
115 nobody can suppose that the surreptitious publishing of a silly
leaflet by an unknown man, without more, would present any
immediate danger that its opinions would hinder the success of
the government arms or have any appreciable tendency to do so.
Publishing these opinions for the very purpose of obstructing, how-
120 ever, might indicate a greater danger and at any rate would have
the quality of an attempt. So I assume that the second leaflet, if
published for the purpose alleged in the fourth count, might be
punishable. But it seems pretty clear to me that nothing less than
that would bring these papers within the scope of this law.

125   An actual intent in the sense that I have explained is necessary
to constitute an attempt, where a further act of the same individual
is required to complete the substantive crime, for reasons given
in *Swift & Co. v. United States,* 196 U. S. 375, 396. It is necessary
where the success of the attempt depends upon others, because if
130 that intent is not present the actor's aim may be accomplished
without bringing about the evils sought to be checked. An intent

to prevent interference with the revolution in Russia might have been satisfied without any hindrance to carry on the war in which we were engaged.

I do not see how anyone can find the intent required by the 135 statute in any of the defendant's words. The second leaflet is the only one that affords even a foundation for the charge, and there, without invoking the hatred of German militarism expressed in the former one, it is evident from the beginning to the end that the only object of the paper is to help Russia and stop American 140 intervention there against the popular government—not to impede the United States in the war that it was carrying on. To say that two phrases taken literally might import a suggestion of conduct that would have interference with the war as an indirect and probably undesired effect seems to me by no means enough to 145 show an attempt to produce that effect.

I return for a moment to the third count. That charges an intent to provoke resistance to the United States in its war with Germany. Taking the clause in the statute that deals with that in connection with the other elaborate provisions of the act, I think that 150 resistance to the United States means some forcible act of opposition to some proceeding of the United States in pursuance of the war. I think the intent must be the specific intent that I have described and for the reasons that I have given I think that no such intent was proved or existed in fact. I also think that there is no 155 hint at resistance to the United States as I construe the phrase.

In this case sentences of twenty years' imprisonment have been imposed for the publishing of two leaflets that I believe the defendants had as much right to publish as the Government has to publish the Constitution of the United States now vainly invoked 160 by them. Even if I am technically wrong and enough can be squeezed from these poor and puny anonymities to turn the color of legal litmus paper—I will add, even if what I think the necessary intent were shown—the most nominal punishment seems to me all that possibly could be inflicted, unless the defendants are to be 165 made to suffer not for what the indictment alleges but for the creed that they avow—a creed that I believe to be the creed of

ignorance and immaturity when honestly held, as I see no reason
to doubt that it was held here, but which, although made the sub-
170 ject of examination at the trial, no one has a right even to consider
in dealing with the charges before the Court.

Persecution for the expression of opinions seems to be perfectly
logical. If you have no doubt of your premises or your power and
want a certain result with all your heart you naturally express your
175 wishes in law and sweep away all opposition. To allow opposition
by speech seems to indicate that you think speech impotent, as
when a man says that he has squared the circle, or that you do not
care wholeheartedly for the result, or that you doubt either your
power or your premises.

180   But when men have realized that time has upset many fighting
faiths, they may come to believe even more than they believe the
very foundations of their own conduct that the ultimate good desired is better reached by free trade in ideas—that the best test of
truth is the power of the thought to get itself accepted in the com-
185 petition of the market, and that truth is the only ground upon
which their wishes safely can be carried out. That, at any rate, is
the theory of our Constitution. It is an experiment, as all life is an
experiment. Every year if not every day we have to wager our salvation upon some prophecy based upon imperfect knowledge. While
190 that experiment is part of our system I think that we should be
eternally vigilant against attempts to check the expression of opinions that we loathe and believe to be fraught with death, unless
they so imminently threaten immediate interference with the law-
ful and pressing purposes of the law that an immediate check is re-
195 quired to save the country.

I wholly disagree with the argument of the Government that the
First Amendment left the common law as to seditious libel in
force. History seems to me against the notion. I had conceived that
the United States through many years had shown its repentance for
200 the Sedition Act of 1798 by repaying fines that it imposed. Only
the emergency that makes it immediately dangerous to leave the
correction of evil counsels to time warrants making any exception
to the sweeping command, "Congress shall make no law . . .

abridging the freedom of speech." Of course I am speaking only of
expressions of opinion and exhortations, which were all that were   205
uttered here, but I regret that I cannot put into more impressive
words my belief that in their conviction upon this indictment the
defendants were deprived of their rights under the Constitution
of the United States.

QUESTIONS

1. In this famous dissenting opinion in a civil liberties case, Justice
Holmes is seeking to distinguish his conception of the relevant parts
of the law from the conception held by the majority of the Supreme
Court and thus to show that "the defendants were deprived of their
rights under the Constitution of the United States" by the majority
opinion. Before he gives his reasons for dissenting from the majority
opinion, he does two other things (lines 1–53). Describe these two
things and explain why Justice Holmes does them. Why does he divide
his account of these two things into three paragraphs?

2. Why do you think Justice Holmes called the two pamphlets
"pronunciamentos" (lines 54–55)? Do you find other remarks which
suggest a similar attitude toward the pamphlets?

3. Justice Holmes begins his discussion by saying that he deems it
unnecessary even to argue that these pamphlets "attack the form of
government of the United States" (lines 54–56). Explain why he
deems it unnecessary.

4. Why does Justice Holmes say the pamphlets "do not support
either of the first two counts" (line 56)?

5. In the rest of the fourth paragraph Justice Holmes agrees that
the second pamphlet does urge "curtailment of production" and therefore might support the fourth count of the indictment (lines 12–15),
but he goes on to quote a passage from the applicable Act about "intent" (lines 66–67) and says that the meaning of this passage pre-
vents the application of the Act to the defendants. This logically requires him to make a distinction between the meaning of "intent" in
"ordinary legal discussion" and the meaning he understands it to have
in this Act. Explain in your own words the first of these two meanings
of "intent."

6. Explain in your own words the second of these two meanings of "intent."

7. In the paragraph which begins at line 69, Justice Holmes shows why the second of these two meanings of "intent" must be the one used in the Act. Explain how he does so.

8. In line 95, Justice Holmes indicates that he will now pass on to "a more important aspect of the case," namely, its relation to the First Amendment. What is the use, for this purpose, of the matter discussed in the next paragraph (lines 98–108)?

9. In lines 114–124, Justice Holmes is arguing that, if the defendant is guilty under count four, it is only because what he did had "the quality of an attempt." By what line of reasoning does he reduce the possible guilt of the defendant to this one item?

10. Justice Holmes has now logically returned to the problem of "intent" which he dealt with earlier (lines 65–84). The paragraph which follows (lines 125–134) is a difficult one, partly because we may at first be unsure of the reference of "It" in the sentence which starts at line 128. What is the reference?

11. This paragraph is also difficult because the difference between two kinds of intent is crucial to Justice Holmes's argument. Either or both of these kinds of intent might theoretically have been in the defendant's mind. What are they?

12. The next paragraph (lines 135–146), by referring to the contents of the second pamphlet, shows why Justice Holmes thinks one and not another of these kinds of intent was in the defendant's mind. Look back at paragraph three (lines 32–53); do the contents of that pamphlet, in your opinion, prove what Justice Holmes says they do?

13. After a brief paragraph devoted to showing that what he has already argued settles the question of the third count (lines 147–156), Justice Holmes moves on to another topic. Like Becker in an earlier selection, he says in effect, "Suppose I am wrong in this argument and that the defendant is in fact guilty" (lines 161–164); even so the penalty imposed is so heavy that it must have been imposed, not just for the crime proved, but also for the political opinion held by the defendant. He says this, not only because he is indignant that such a heavy penalty was imposed, but because it provides the justification for the final point he wants to make in this opinion, namely, the reasoning which lies behind the First Amendment. Why, then, does he

begin this final point, at line 172, by asserting that persecution for the expression of opinions seems to be perfectly logical?

14. What argument does he offer in support of the First Amendment? What is the logical connection between this argument and the argument made in lines 172–179?

SUGGESTED TOPICS

1. Justice Holmes asserts that "An intent to prevent interference with the revolution in Russia might have been satisfied without any hindrance to carrying on the war in which we were engaged" (lines 131–134). Write a paragraph in which you show how this might be true and why Justice Holmes thinks that in this case it was.

2. Write a paragraph in which you explain in your own words the argument by which, according to Justice Holmes, we justify the First Amendment.

3. Write a paragraph in which you explain the conception of "clear and imminent danger" (lines 103–104) which Justice Holmes uses in his argument.

11 / Ezra Pound and the Bollingen Prize[*]

ALLEN TATE

FROM THE TIME I first read Pound's verse more than thirty years ago I have considered him a mixed poet. In an essay written in 1931, on the first thirty Cantos, I expressed views which the later accretions to the work have not changed: the work
5 to which I helped to give the Bollingen Prize [1] is formless, eccentric, and personal. The Cantos are now, as I said then, "about nothing at all." They have a voice but no subject. As one of the commentators on Mr. Barrett's article put it, they have no beginning, middle, or end. I used similar language in 1931. It is a strik-
10 ing fact that in talking about this work one must say "Canto XX of the *Cantos*"; there is always a canto of Cantos, not a Canto of a substantive work with a title like Canto XX of the *Purgatorio* of the *Divina Commedia*.

Mr. Pound is incapable of sustained thought in either prose or
15 verse. His acute verbal sensibility is thus at the mercy of random flights of "angelic insight," Icarian self-indulgences of prejudice which are not checked by a total view to which they could be sub-

[1] In 1949, the Fellows of the Library of Congress awarded the Bollingen Prize for the best volume of poems published by an American in 1948 to Ezra Pound for *The Pisan Cantos*. Mr. Tate was one of the Fellows and voted with the majority.

[*] From Allen Tate, *The Forlorn Demon*. Reprinted by permission of Allen Tate and the Henry Regnery Company.

ordinated. Thus his anti-semitism—which, as Mr. Auden has said, all Gentiles have felt (I have felt it, and felt humiliated by it)— his anti-semitism is not disciplined by an awareness of its sinister implications in the real world of men. Neither Mr. Pound nor any other man is to be censured for his private feelings; but every man must answer for what he does with his feelings. It has been often observed that Pound fails to get into his verse any sort of full concrete reality. In so far as the *Cantos* have a subject it is made up of historical materials. But if there is any poetry of our age which may be said to be totally lacking in the historical sense, the sense of how ideas move in history, it is Pound's *Cantos*. His verse is an anomaly in an age of acute historical awareness.

I do not know what reasons, motives, or prejudices prompted the other affirmative votes. There has been some public conjecture upon this subject, but I consider it a gross impropriety. I shall do well if I am able to speak honestly for myself. I have little sympathy for the view that holds that Pound's irresponsible opinions merely lie alongside the poetry, which thus remains uncontaminated. The disagreeable opinions are right in the middle of the poetry. And they have got to be seen for what they are: they are personal, wilful, and unrelated; and they are not brought together under a mature conception of life as it is now or ever was. I infer the absence of such a mature view in the main from the incoherence of the form; but it is only the latter that concerns me. Apart from specific objections to his anti-semitism and fascism, there is a formal principle which, if severely applied, would have been a good enough reason for voting against *The Pisan Cantos*. Not only the anti-semitism but all the other "insights" remain unassimilated to a coherent form. The assumption of many persons, that a vote for *The Pisan Cantos* was a vote for "formalism" and a vote against "vitality" in poetry, makes no sense at all to me.

There is nothing mysterious about coherent form. It is the presence of an order in a literary work which permits us to understand one part in relation to all the other parts. What should concern us in looking *at* the *Cantos* is the formal irresponsibility; in looking *beyond* the work, the possible effects of this irresponsibility upon

society. (If Pound's *Cantos* expressed *anti*-fascist opinions, my for-
55 mal objections would be the same; but I should think that the
formlessness would make him a good Communist party-line poet.)
But just as Pound's broadcasts over Radio Rome never influenced
anybody in this country, and were chiefly an indignity perpetrated
upon himself, I cannot suppose that the anti-semitism of the
60 *Cantos* will be taken seriously by anybody but liberal intellectuals.
Anti-semites will not "use" it. It is too innocent. I take it seriously
in the sense of disliking it, and I cannot "honor the man" for it, as
the Fellows of the Library were charged with doing; but I cannot
think that it will strengthen anti-semitism.

65   I respect differences of opinion on this question, about which I
am not well-informed. What I have already said is enough to indicate that my vote for *The Pisan Cantos* was not an easy step to
take: I could have voted against it. But this is not all. I had, as
many men of my generation might have had, personal reasons
70 for not voting for Mr. Pound. In so far as he has noticed my writings at all, in conversation and correspondence—which the international literary grapevine always reports—he has noticed them
with contempt.

Nevertheless I voted for him, for the following reasons: the
75 health of literature depends upon the health of society, and con-
versely; there must be constant vigilance for both ends of the process. The specific task of the man of letters is to attend to the
health of society *not at large* but through literature—that is, he
must be constantly aware of the condition of language in his age.
80 As a result of observing Pound's use of language in the past thirty
years I had become convinced that he had done more than any
other man to regenerate the language, if not the imaginative
forms, of English verse. I had to face the disagreeable fact that
he had done this even in passages of verse in which the opinions
85 expressed ranged from the childish to the detestable.

In literature as in life nothing reaches us pure. The task of the
civilized intelligence is one of perpetual salvage. We cannot decide
that our daily experience must be either aesthetic or practical—
art or life; it is never, as it comes to us, either/or; it is always

both/and. But as persons of a particular *ethos*, of a certain habit 90
and character, we discharge our responsibilities to society from the
point of view of the labors in which we are placed. We are placed
in the profession of letters. We cannot expect the business man
and the politician, the men who run the state, to know that our
particular responsibility exists; we cannot ask them to understand 95
the more difficult fact that our responsibility to them is for the
language which they themselves use for the general welfare. They
are scarcely aware of language at all; what one is not aware of one
almost inevitably abuses. But the medium cannot be extricated
from the material, the how from the what: part of our responsi- 100
bility is to correct the monism of the statesman who imagines that
what he says is scarcely said in language at all, that it exists apart
from the medium in a "purity" of action which he thinks of as
"practicality." If men of letters do not look after the medium, nobody else will. We need never fear that the practical man will fail 105
to ignore our concern for the health of language: this he has already done by indicting Pound as if Pound, like himself, were a
monist of action. Pound's language remains our particular concern. If he were a convicted traitor, I should still think that, in another direction which complicates the problem ultimately beyond 110
our comprehension, he had performed an indispensable duty to
society.

QUESTIONS

1. After the first paragraph, this selection divides itself into two
sections. Where does the division between the two sections come?

2. The first paragraph shows that the author thinks Ezra Pound
a "mixed poet." Where, later, does he return to this point and why is it
important to his argument?

3. The first paragraph asserts (line 7) that the *Cantos* "have a
voice but no subject." Has this statement any connection with the two
sections into which the rest of the selection is divided?

4. The second paragraph (lines 14–29) is devoted to evidence
that Mr. Pound "is incapable of sustained thought." How many pieces

of evidence for this assertion does it offer? Explain how each supports the assertion.

5. Explain the phrase "Icarian self-indulgence."

6. Explain the difference between censuring a man for his private feelings and making him answer for what he does with his feelings (lines 21–23).

7. Do you think the assertion in lines 22–23 has any connection with the assertion in lines 31–32?

8. There is a serious, ironic rebuke to people who conjecture on other people's motives in "I shall do well if I am able to speak honestly for myself" (lines 32–33). Why?

9. The opening sentences of paragraph three (lines 30–33) say the author will now discuss his motives for voting in the affirmative. But paragraph three seems to consist entirely of motives for not voting in the affirmative. How do you explain this?

10. At the end of paragraph three (lines 41–46) Mr. Tate suggests that an objection to the formal principle of the *Cantos* is as important for him as an objection to its political opinions and in the next paragraph (lines 49–56) he explains why. Can you make clear in your own words the line of reasoning here?

11. At the end of paragraph four (lines 57–64) Mr. Tate gives his reasons for thinking that Pound's anti-semitism and his "treason," much as Mr. Tate personally dislikes them, have little practical importance. What are these reasons?

12. What explanation would you offer for the fact that Mr. Tate has saved up until lines 68–73 the personal reason which might have made him vote against Mr. Pound?

13. In paragraph six (lines 74–85) Mr. Tate finally comes to his central reason for voting for Mr. Pound. Why, in stating this reason, does he make an exception—"if not the imaginative forms" (lines 82–83)?

14. Why does Mr. Tate think that what Mr. Pound has done "to regenerate the language" is so important for him that he must let it outweigh all the considerations he has mentioned previously?

15. In the final paragraph of the selection, beginning at line 86, Mr. Tate tells us why he thinks the thing that made him vote for Mr. Pound is important, not just to him, but to society. Why does he think it is important for businessmen and politicians?

16. You may feel that lines 105–106 are more complicated than

they need to be, that Mr. Tate might have written something simpler, like, "Practical men will never worry about language." Explain why he wrote what he did instead.

SUGGESTED TOPICS

1. Coleridge once observed that a poem "is discriminated by proposing to itself such delight from the *whole,* as is compatible with a distinct gratification from each component *part."* Write a paragraph in which you discuss the relation between this idea about a poem and Mr. Tate's distinction about Pound's poetry, that it has done much "to regenerate the language, if not the imaginative forms, of English verse."

2. Write a paragraph in which you explain why Mr. Tate makes such a point of the fact that with Pound we must talk about "Canto XX of the *Cantos"* (lines 9–13).

3. Write a paragraph in which you explain why it is a mistake for anyone to think that "what he says is scarcely said in language at all, that it exists apart from the medium in a 'purity' of action which he thinks of as 'practicality' " (lines 102–104).

12/ The Legacy of Andrew Jackson*

ARTHUR M. SCHLESINGER, JR.

I

ANDREW JACKSON has long been the symbol of fighting democracy in American political life. On the lips of Democratic spellbinders his name is a call-to-arms: Jefferson, the sage of Monticello, is the serene philosopher of democracy, but
5 Jackson is its militant champion, rude, brawling and irresistible. Schoolbook history adds the photo-montage: backwoods Andy Jackson, rough, tough and lusty, hard as nails and irascible as a bumblebee, defying successively the British, the Indians, the Eastern aristocrats, the United States Bank, the Supreme Court—all in
10 the name of the common people, the unpolished, uncouth, good-hearted rabble, clad in buckskin and flourishing bowie knives, who stormed the White House on the day of his inaugural.

It is a good story; and it ought to be, for enough talents of diverse kinds went into inventing and perpetuating it. As a young
15 man, Jackson was no doubt a roisterer; but he was sixty-one years old on his inauguration as seventh President in 1829. A quarter century on a spacious Tennessee plantation had given him the bearing and instincts of an aristocrat. His manners had long since grown urbane and confident; and his temper had succumbed to
20 the control of ambition, calculation and experience. As one Wash-

* From *The American Mercury*. Reprinted by permission of Arthur M. Schlesinger, Jr.

ington hostess put it, Jackson possessed "quite as much *suaviter in modo* as *fortiter in re*." Daniel Webster, later to become one of his determined enemies, observed in 1824, "General Jackson's manners are more Presidential than those of any of the candidates. . . . My wife is for him decidedly." (The other candidates that year 25 included John Quincy Adams of the famous Massachusetts family and Henry Clay, the polished and cosmopolitan Kentuckian.) Like Thomas Jefferson and Franklin Roosevelt, Andrew Jackson was a country squire in the White House.

But the opponents of Jackson found it smart politics to spread 30 a legend of his crudeness and ignorance. He was portrayed as a senile, semi-literate and impassioned old fool, dominated by a clique of cunning radicals. From this propaganda campaign came such tales as the one that "O.K." originated in Jackson's belief that he was abbreviating the words "all correct." Webster and Clay 35 in their speeches on the Hill developed the same basic picture in more sonorous tones. For many years the leading historians of the period, men in the Whig-Republican tradition, copied their judgments from Webster and Clay, whose oratorical flights they mistook for sober historical analysis. The Jackson myth was thus 40 solidly imbedded in the written history.

In recent years the legend has received support from a new source, supposedly pro-Jackson in character. The cult of the proletariat created a movement to proletarianize all American democratic heroes by a process of retroactive historical interpretation. 45 The stereotype of Jackson fabricated by Whig propaganda in the 1830's thus became a natural for the sentimental leftism of the 1930's. One of the more ludicrous results was the attempt to press Jackson into the service of the Communist Party line—as in *The Merry Andrew*, a novel written by a fellow-traveling Hollywood 50 writer named Dalton Trumbo. In this curious book the ghost of Jackson appears to warn the hero against sinister British attempts to inveigle him into the imperialist war against Hitler and the Nazis. (Needless to say, this book was written before the attack on the USSR disclosed to Trumbo that Hitler was a menace to world 55 democracy.)

The tip-off is the use of the nickname. No one ever called Jackson "Andy Jackson" during his Presidency—at least, in some years of research on the 1830's I never came upon it—but the literary
60 phonies today unfailingly dub Jackson with the folksy "Andy," as their successors in another century will doubtless speak of that great proletarian Frankie Roosevelt.

Jackson was perhaps not quite the symbol of fighting democracy that he has appeared in the schoolbooks. But in a more funda-
65 mental sense he remains the classic symbol in American life of the political and economic struggle for the common man. Franklin Roosevelt, who knew his American history, perceived fully both Jackson's essential significance and his own remarkable kinship to Jackson. "We look back on his amazing personality," Roosevelt
70 once said, "we review his battles because the struggles he went through, the victories he won are part and parcel of the struggles, the enmities, the defeats and the victories of those who have lived in all the generations that have followed."

II

The great paradox of democracy is that its moral ideas preceded
75 its political and economic problems. Democracy drew its values and goals from the eighteenth century, its basic practical issues from the nineteenth century. Jefferson set forth the democratic dream in terms so compelling and universal that they have held broadly good for all subsequent generations. But his specific demo-
80 cratic presuppositions were derived from an agricultural society of small freeholds. His identification of democracy and rural life was so complete that he looked upon cities and upon a property-less working class with a horror he did not conceal. "The mobs of great cities," he said, "add just so much to the support of pure
85 government, as sores do to the strength of the human body."

Jefferson wrote, of course, before industrialism had begun to transform the basis of American life. As President he tried to grapple with some of the first repercussions of this transformation. But he died before any one could effectively measure the conse-
90 quences of industrialism for democracy or restate the problems of

democracy in terms of an industrial society. Jefferson's Virginia successors in the White House—Madison and Monroe—simply folded before the demands of the vigorous new business community; and John Quincy Adams, the sixth President, sympathized, on the whole, with these demands. 95

Jackson was thus the first President to take up the challenge to American democracy presented by a business community whose resources were greatly expanded by the Industrial Revolution. The business community had reached out for political power: involuntarily, perhaps, its objective became, not just to produce goods and 100 make profits, but to control the state. Once in power it had crudely identified the broad interests of American society with the narrow cash interests of the businessmen. ("What is good for business," as the National Association of Manufacturers put it a century later, "is good for you.") The consequence was a series of measures 105 which alarmed and threatened to impoverish the farmers, the workers, the professional people, the intellectuals and even the small businessmen.

The incompetence of business rule created a massive but inchoate movement of social protest. Jackson forged this protest into 110 an effective political party, as he had forged the rag, tag and bobtail of the South into a fighting force at the battle of New Orleans. Businessmen inevitably denounced him for setting class against class. But in fact he was simply representing the groups in America outside the business community (and a good many enlightened 115 businessmen as well) in a battle to preserve the foundations of American democracy.

His following included the farmers, mechanics and workers. It included the heads of the young and struggling trade union movement—in 1834 the Democrats sent Ely Moore, first president of 120 the National Trades Union, to the House of Representatives where his fiery pro-labor speeches frightened the Southern Democrats and appalled John Quincy Adams. It included the efficient machines in the large Northern cities; it had its conservative Southern wing and its agricultural bloc. It included most of the leading 125 writers of the day—Nathaniel Hawthorne, William Cullen Bryant,

Walt Whitman, James Fenimore Cooper, Washington Irving, George Bancroft and many others. Anticipating the election to Congress of actress Helen Gahagan Douglas by a century, the
130 Democrats of New York City even ran Edwin Forrest, the popular actor, for Congress in 1838.

Business aspirations came to focus under the leadership of Nicholas Biddle, president of the United States Bank. In 1832 Biddle determined on a campaign to secure the recharter of the
135 Bank, both with its special access to the government and its special immunities from public control. A frenzy of lobbying, press hysteria and pressure group activity, stimulated along lines all too familiar to us today, pushed the Bank bill through both houses of Congress. Jackson sent it back with a resounding veto. "When the
140 laws," wrote Jackson, "undertake . . . to make the rich richer and the potent more powerful, the humble members of society—the farmers, mechanics, and laborers—who have neither the times nor the means of securing like favors to themselves, have a right to complain of the injustice of their Government."
145 The issue then went to the country, which triumphantly sustained Jackson in the 1832 election. With this mandate behind him Jackson removed the government deposits from the Bank. Against the nearly unanimous opposition of the business community, his successor, Martin Van Buren, established the independent treasury
150 system, and thereby gave the deathblow to the theory that private banks had a proprietary right to the use of government funds.

III

This pattern has recurred periodically in our history. "Free enterprise," left alone, contains strong inherent tendencies toward monopoly—tendencies which no one has recognized with more
155 acuteness than Adam Smith. Government has then to intervene in order to prevent competition from being extinguished. But the very act of intervention—particularly against the desire of the largest and most powerful elements of the business community—strengthens the authority of the government and increases the dis-

position of the people to look to the state for the solution of its 160 problems.

Jackson's war against Biddle and the Bank transformed the central government from a mild and innocuous agency into an instrument with powers of coercion. He bared the teeth of the Constitution, and his victory established as a basic tenet of American 165 democracy that in the last analysis the people's government has to be kept more powerful than any private group controlled by men not responsible to the people.

This meant, of course, that Jackson had to expand the executive powers in proportion to the vigor of Biddle's challenge. His Presi- 170 dency almost transformed the character of the office, unfolding new Constitutional resources both for public and for party leadership. He used the veto, for example, more often than all his predecessors put together; and he first employed Federal patronage on a large scale as a means of maintaining his party organization. 175

Business denounced these acts as the prelude to dictatorship. At one point in his second term, after the removal of the government deposits from the Bank, the Senate actually passed a resolution charging the President with having violated the Constitution; and, when Jackson responded with a long protest, the Senate re- 180 fused to enter it into its records. But Jackson was always confident in his appeal over the heads of Congress to the people. Before his second term ended, the Senate rescinded its resolution of censure.

Jackson's energy inevitably entangled him with the Supreme Court. Eventually he was able to fill the Court with his own ap- 185 pointees who promptly handed down a series of decisions which threw the business community into panic. Daniel Webster wrote gloomily that the Court was "gone . . . and almost everything is gone, or seems rapidly going." But the nation managed even to survive the change in the personnel of the Court. 190

IV

Jackson thus laid out in firm lines the pattern for all the Presidents who have had to pick up the pieces after a period of business rule. The problem has always been with us. In one hundred and

fifty years business has produced only one leader with a genuinely
195 national viewpoint—Alexander Hamilton. Since the time of the
Federalists, businessmen and their political servants have displayed
no governing capacity in the realm of national politics. In the crises
of American life the people have always turned to a coalition of
non-business groups behind some militant democratic leader; the
200 leader must tap all the resources of the Presidential power to fight
for the democratic program against the Congress and the Supreme
Court, which are both more likely to be under conservative control; and the record shows that the business community has always
provided savage resistance to the policies which in the end have
205 saved them.

Big government is thus not the result of a wild-eyed radical
conspiracy. It is the direct creation of big business; for only
through big government can the people impose their veto on the
action of big business—the veto so indispensable to the workings
210 of democratic society. As business itself has grown more complex,
bureaucratic and centralized, so too has government machinery for
controlling it.

Thus a difference of degree, rather than a difference in purpose,
divides the age of Franklin Roosevelt from the age of Jackson. The
215 New Deal did not invent government intervention in business,
government appeals to a broad popular coalition against the business community, or the expansion of Presidential power. It simply
stepped up these methods to meet the challenge of an ever more
powerful and more centrally controlled business community.

220 Government intervention certainly presents thorny problems of
its own. Roosevelt once said, "We have built up new instruments
of public power. In the hands of a people's Government this
power is wholesome and proper. But in the hands of political pup-
pets of an economic autocracy such power would provide shackles
225 for the liberties of the people." The example of totalitarianism in
Germany and Russia is chastening. But let us not delude ourselves
that all Federal regulation is Communist-inspired, that any proposal for government controls was born in Moscow. This is the
type of myth which since the days of Jefferson and Jackson the

business community has been fostering in order to protect itself 230
from scrutiny and control.

Andrew Jackson may never have been quite the raw and roman-
tic figure that some of his leftist admirers imagine. No one called
him Andy. His table manners were good, and he could read and
write. But his contributions to the development of American de- 235
mocracy have been fundamental just the same. He adapted Jeffer-
sonianism to the harder, tougher necessities of industrial society.
He showed future democratic Presidents how to restrain the business community when it tries to assert its political will to the det-
riment of the humble members of society. At a time when politi- 240
cal power has swung back to the Right, liberals will find new inspiration in his fighting spirit.

QUESTIONS

1. This selection complicates the form of essay we have been considering by making two distinctions which, though they are related
and can be worked out together, have to do with two separate things.
The first distinction it wishes to make is between the popular and the
accurate conceptions of President Andrew Jackson; the second is between the view of big government taken by businessmen and the view
of big government suggested by history. How does Professor Schlesinger connect his discussion of Andrew Jackson's character with his
discussion of big government?

2. The first paragraph of this selection (lines 1–12) summarizes
the popular view of Andrew Jackson; how much does it use parallelism?

3. What does the second paragraph (lines 13–29) do?

4. What is the meaning of the Washington hostess's remark quoted
in lines 21–22?

5. Paragraphs three through five (lines 30–62) have a single purpose; what is it?

6. Why does the author make a paragraph division at line 42?

7. The author might well have omitted the paragraph division at
line 57; why?

8. The paragraph which begins at line 63 sums up what Professor

Schlesinger believes is the historically true view of Jackson, but it ends with a quotation from Franklin Roosevelt which, while it is relevant to this summary, has another purpose; what is that second purpose?

9. Why does Professor Schlesinger start a new section of his essay at line 74?

10. Why does he begin this section with two paragraphs on Jefferson (lines 74–95)? Has he prepared us for this discussion of Jefferson?

11. From line 96 to the end of this section (at line 151) Professor Schlesinger, though he is still talking about Andrew Jackson, is talking, not about his character, but about something else connected with him; what is that?

12. The opening sentence of Section III of this essay (line 152) ought to make us remember the last sentence of Section I (lines 69–73); why?

13. Section III of this essay deals with the major consequence, during Jackson's own time, of his victory in the controversy over the bank. What is that consequence?

14. Professor Schlesinger is particularly concerned with two aspects of this consequence; what are they?

15. The first part of Section IV of this essay (lines 191–242) explains why Professor Schlesinger is specially interested in Jackson's victory in the controversy over the bank; why is he?

16. The last paragraph of this essay (lines 232–242) explains why Professor Schlesinger is specially interested in our understanding the historically true view of Jackson; why is he?

SUGGESTED TOPICS

1. Write a paragraph in which you explain why Professor Schlesinger returns in the last paragraph (lines 232–242) to the subject of the first paragraph (lines 1–12).

2. Professor Schlesinger makes frequent comparisons between incidents in Jackson's time and incidents in our own time (e.g., lines 128–131). Point out other comparisons of this kind and explain the purpose of these comparisons.

3. Write a paragraph in which you summarize the argument by which Professor Schlesinger undertakes to show that "big government is . . . not the result of a wild-eyed radical conspiracy. It is the direct creation of big business" (lines 206–207).

13 / George Orwell and the Politics of Truth*

LIONEL TRILLING

O RWELL, by reason of the quality that permits us to say of him that he was a virtuous man, is a figure in our lives. He was not a genius, and this is one of the remarkable things about him. His not being a genius is an element of the quality that makes him what I am calling a figure. 5

If we ask what it is he stands for, what he is the figure of, the answer is: the virtue of not being a genius, of fronting the world with nothing more than one's simple, direct, undeceived intelligence, and a respect for the powers one does have, and the work one undertakes to do. We admire geniuses, we love them, but they 10 discourage us. They are great concentrations of intellect and emotion, we feel that they have soaked up all the available power, monopolizing it and leaving none for us. We feel that if we cannot be as they, we can be nothing. Beside them we are so plain, so hopelessly threadbare. How they glitter, and with what an imperi- 15 ous way they seem to deal with circumstances, even when they are wrong! Lacking their patents of nobility, we might as well quit. This is what democracy has done for us, alas—told us that genius is available to anyone, that the grace of ultimate prestige may be had by anyone, that we may all be princes and potentates, 20

* From *The Opposing Self* by Lionel Trilling. Copyright 1952 by Lionel Trilling. Reprinted by permission of The Viking Press, Inc., New York.

or saints and visionaries and holy martyrs, of the heart and mind.
And then when it turns out that we are no such thing, it permits
us to think that we aren't much of anything at all. In contrast with
this cozening trick of democracy, how pleasant seems the old, re-
25 actionary Anglican phrase that used to drive people of democratic
leanings quite wild with rage—"my station and its duties."

Orwell would very likely have loathed that phrase, but in a way
he exemplifies its meaning. And it is a great relief, a fine sight, to
see him doing this. His critical essays are almost always very fine,
30 but sometimes they do not fully meet the demands of their subject—as, for example, the essay on Dickens. And even when they
are at their best, they seem to have become what they are chiefly
by reason of the very plainness of Orwell's mind, his simple ability
to look at things in a downright, undeceived way. He seems to be
35 serving not some dashing daimon but the plain solid Gods of the
Copybook Maxims. He is not a genius—what a relief! What an
encouragement. For he communicates to us the sense that what
he has done any one of us could do.

Or could do if we but made up our mind to do it, if we but sur-
40 rendered a little of the cant that comforts us, if for a few weeks we
paid no attention to the little group with which we habitually exchange opinions, if we took our chance of being wrong or inadequate, if we looked at things simply and directly, having in
mind only our intention of finding out what they really are, not
45 the prestige of our great intellectual act of looking at them. He
liberates us. He tells us that we can understand our political and
social life merely by looking around us; he frees us from the need
for the inside dope. He implies that our job is not to be intellectual,
certainly not to be intellectual in this fashion or that, but merely
50 to be intelligent according to our lights—he restores the old sense
of the democracy of the mind, releasing us from the belief that
the mind can work only in a technical, professional way and that
it must work competitively. He has the effect of making us believe that we may become full members of the society of thinking
55 men. That is why he is a figure for us.

What concerned him was survival, which he connected with

the old simple ideas that are often not ideas at all but beliefs, preferences, and prejudices. In the modern world these had for him the charm and audacity of newly discovered truths. Involved as many of us are, at least in our literary lives, in a bitter meta- 60 physics of human nature, it shocks and dismays us when Orwell speaks in praise of such things as responsibility, and orderliness in the personal life, and fair play, and physical courage—even of snobbery and hypocrisy because they sometimes help to shore up the crumbling ramparts of the moral life. 65

We may say that it was on his affirmation of the middle-class virtues that Orwell based his criticism of the liberal intelligentsia. The characteristic error of the middle-class intellectual of modern times is his tendency to abstractness and absoluteness, his reluc- tance to connect idea with fact, especially with personal fact. I 70 cannot recall that Orwell ever related his criticism of the intel- ligentsia to the implications of *Keep the Aspidistra Flying*, but he might have done so, for the prototypical act of the modern in- tellectual is his abstracting himself from the life of the family. It is an act that has something about it of ritual thaumaturgy—at the 75 beginning of our intellectual careers we are like nothing so much as those young members of Indian tribes who have had a vision or a dream which gives them power on condition that they with- draw from the ordinary life of the tribe. By intellectuality we are freed from the thralldom to the familial commonplace, from the 80 materiality and concreteness by which it exists, the hardness of the cash and the hardness of getting it, the inelegance and in- tractability of family things. It gives us power over intangibles and imponderables, such as Beauty and Justice, and it permits us to escape the cosmic ridicule which in our youth we suppose is in- 85 evitably directed at those who take seriously the small concerns of the material quotidian world, which we know to be inadequate and doomed by the very fact that it is so absurdly *conditioned*— by things, habits, local and temporary customs, and the foolish errors and solemn absurdities of the men of the past. 90

The gist of Orwell's criticism of the liberal intelligentsia was that they refused to understand the conditioned nature of life. He

never quite puts it this way but this is what he means. He himself
knew what war and revolution were really like, what government
95 and administration were really like. From first-hand experience he
knew what communism was. He could truly imagine what nazism
was. At a time when most intellectuals still thought of politics as
a nightmare abstraction, pointing to the fearfulness of the nightmare as evidence of their sense of reality, Orwell was using the
100 imagination of a man whose hands and eyes and whole body were
part of his thinking apparatus. Shaw had insisted on remaining
sublimely unaware of the Russian actuality; Wells had pooh-
poohed the threat of Hitler and had written off as anachronisms
the very forces that were at the moment shaping the world—racial
105 pride, leader-worship, religious belief, patriotism, love of war. These
men had the trained political intelligence of the intelligentsia,
who now, in their love of abstractions, in their wish to repudiate the
anachronisms of their own emotions, could not conceive of directing upon Russia anything like the same stringency of criticism
110 they used on their own nations. Orwell observed of them that
their zeal for internationalism had led them to constitute Russia
their new fatherland. And he had the simple courage to point out
that the pacifists preached their doctrine under condition of the
protection of the British navy, and that, against Germany and
115 Russia, Ghandi's passive resistance would have been of no avail.

He never abated his anger against the established order. But a
paradox of history had made the old British order one of the still
beneficent things in the world, and it licensed the possibility of
a social hope that was being frustrated and betrayed almost every-
120 where else. And so Orwell clung with a kind of wry, grim pride
to the old ways of the last class that had ruled the old order. He
must sometimes have wondered how it came about that he should
be praising sportsmanship and gentlemanliness and dutifulness
and physical courage. But certainly the virtues he praised were
125 those of survival, and they had fallen into disrepute in a disordered
world.

QUESTIONS

1. This selection sets out to distinguish something Professor Trilling calls "not being a genius"—what we might perhaps call "genuineness"—from genius. It makes this distinction largely by examining the effect Orwell, as a merely genuine man, might have on intelligent people. In doing so, the selection divides into six fairly obvious parts. For instance, the first part (lines 1–10) establishes the subject, that Orwell was remarkable because he was not a genius; the second part (lines 11–26) shows how geniuses may discourage us. Can you point out the other four parts and describe in a sentence what each part does?

2. In his discussion of the way genius discourages us (lines 11–26) Professor Trilling uses a metaphor which is extremely important to what he has to say. It first becomes evident in line 12, but from there on it appears frequently until line 20. What is this metaphor? Indicate each point at which it shows itself.

3. Why does this metaphor give particular force to "This is what democracy has done for us, alas" in line 18?

4. It is this metaphor which leads Professor Trilling to make his final point by referring to "the old, reactionary Anglican phrase . . . 'my station and its duties' " (lines 24–26). How does it do so?

5. Professor Trilling concludes that the hierarchical organization of society represented by the idea of "my station and its duties" makes us less unhappy at not being geniuses than does a democratic society which plays this "cozening trick" on us (line 24). By what line of reasoning does Professor Trilling reach this conclusion?

6. In the fourth paragraph, beginning at line 39, Professor Trilling suggests that we could all do what Orwell did if we could make up our minds to be, not "intellectual," but "intelligent" (lines 48–50). Explain this distinction.

7. What is the meaning of the phrase, "the democracy of the mind" (line 51)?

8. How do you explain Professor Trilling's conviction that "the old sense of the democracy of the mind" can be restored to us by a man who exemplifies the meaning of an undemocratic idea such as "my station and its duties" (lines 24–26)?

9. In the two paragraphs which begin at line 66 and end at line

115, Professor Trilling outlines Orwell's criticism of "the liberal intelligentsia." The first of these two paragraphs points out the main fault of such people. What is it? Why are intellectuals tempted to commit it?

10. In the second of these paragraphs, Professor Trilling gives some examples of this fault in the thinking of famous intellectuals, and contrasts Orwell's attitude with theirs. How do these examples illustrate what he said in the first of these two paragraphs?

11. Orwell's remark about Shaw and Wells which is quoted in lines 110–112 is ironic. What makes it so?

12. Why did Orwell cling to the virtues of the established British order though it often angered him (lines 116–126)?

13. Does the final paragraph (lines 116–126) help us to understand more fully why Professor Trilling thinks Orwell exemplifies "the old, reactionary Anglican phrase" quoted in line 26?

SUGGESTED TOPICS

1. Write a paragraph in which you describe in your own words the way Orwell looked at the world.

2. Read Orwell's essay on Gandhi (pages 317–320) and choose from it some illustrations of the way Professor Trilling says Orwell's mind works.

3. Write a paragraph in which you demonstrate with examples of your own the way certain kinds of intellectuals escape from "the thralldom to the familial commonplace" (line 80).

14/ Thoughts on the Cause of the Present Discontents*

EDMUND BURKE

TO COMPLAIN of the age we live in, to murmur at the present possessors of power, to lament the past, to conceive extravagant hopes of the future, are the common dispositions of the greatest part of mankind; indeed the necessary effects of the ignorance and levity of the vulgar. Such complaints and humors ⁵ have existed in all times; yet as all times have *not* been alike, true political sagacity manifests itself in distinguishing that complaint which only characterizes the general infirmity of human nature, from those which are symptoms of the particular distemperature of our own air and season. ¹⁰

Nobody, I believe, will consider it merely as the language of spleen or disappointment, if I say, that there is something particularly alarming in the present conjuncture. There is hardly a man, in or out of power, who holds any other language. That government is at once dreaded and contemned; that the laws are ¹⁵ despoiled of all their respect and salutary terrors; that their inaction is a subject of ridicule, and their exertion of abhorrence; that rank, and office, and title, and all the solemn plausibilities of the world, have lost their reverence and effect; that our foreign politics are as much deranged as our domestic economy; that our ²⁰

* From Edmund Burke, "Thoughts on the Cause of the Present Discontents," 1770.

dependencies are slackened in their affection, and loosened from their obedience; that we know neither how to yield nor how to enforce; that hardly anything above or below, abroad or at home, is sound and entire; but that disconnection and confusion, in
25 offices, in parties, in families, in Parliament, in the nation, prevail beyond the disorders of any former time: these are facts universally admitted and lamented.

This state of things is the more extraordinary, because the great parties which formerly divided and agitated the kingdom are
30 known to be in a manner entirely dissolved. No great external calamity has visited the nation; no pestilence or famine. We do not labor at the present under any scheme of taxation new or oppressive in the quantity or in the mode. Nor are we engaged in unsuccessful war, in which our misfortunes might easily pervert our
35 judgment; and our minds, sore from the loss of national glory, might feel every blow of fortune as a crime in government.

It is impossible that the cause of this strange distemper should not sometimes become a subject of discourse. It is a compliment due, and which I willingly pay, to those who administer our affairs,
40 to take notice in the first place of their speculation. Our ministers are of opinion, that the increase of our trade and manufactures, that our growth by colonization, and by conquest, have concurred to accumulate immense wealth in the hands of some individuals; and this again being dispersed among the people, has rendered
45 them universally proud, ferocious, and ungovernable; that the insolence of some from their enormous wealth, and the boldness of others from a guilty poverty, have rendered them capable of the most atrocious attempts; so that they have trampled upon all subordination, and violently borne down the unarmed laws of a free
50 government; barriers too feeble against the fury of a populace so fierce and so licentious as ours. They contend that no adequate provocation has been given for so spreading a discontent; our affairs have been conducted throughout with remarkable temper and consummate wisdom. The wicked industry of some libelers,
55 joined to the intrigues of a few disappointed politicians, have, in

their opinions, been able to produce this unnatural ferment in the nation.

Nothing indeed can be more unnatural than the present convulsions of this country, if the above account be a true one. I confess I shall assent to it with great reluctance, and only on the compulsion of the clearest and firmest proofs; because their account resolves itself into this short but discouraging proposition, "That we have a very good ministry, but that we are a very bad people"; that we set ourselves to bite the hand that feeds us; that with a malignant insanity we oppose the measures, and ungratefully vilify the persons, of those whose sole object is our own peace and prosperity. If a few puny libelers, acting under a knot of factious politicians without virtue, partes, or character (such they are constantly represented by these gentlemen), are sufficient to excite this disturbance, very perverse must be the disposition of that people, amongst whom such a disturbance can be excited by such means. It is, besides, no small aggravation of the public misfortune, that the disease, on this hypothesis, appears to be without remedy. If the wealth of the nation be the cause of its turbulence, I imagine it is not proposed to introduce poverty as a constable to keep the peace. If our dominions abroad are the roots which feed all this rank luxuriance of sedition, it is not intended to cut them off in order to famish the fruit. If our liberty has enfeebled the executive power, there is no design, I hope, to call in the aid of despotism to fill up the deficiencies of the law. Whatever may be intended, these things are not yet professed. We seem, therefore, to be driven to absolute despair; for we have no other materials to work upon, but those out of which God has been pleased to form the inhabitants of this island. If these be radically and essentially vicious, all that can be said is, that those men are very unhappy, to whose fortune or duty it falls to administer the affairs of this untoward people. I hear it indeed sometimes asserted, that a steady perseverance in the present measures, and a rigorous punishment of those who oppose them, will in course of time infallibly put an end to these disorders. But this, in my opinion, is said without much observation of our present disposition, and

without any knowledge at all of the general nature of mankind. If the matter of which this nation is composed be so very fermentable as these gentlemen describe it, leaven never will be wanting to
95 work it up, as long as discontent, revenge, and ambition have existence in the world. Particular punishments are the cure for accidental distempers in the state; they inflame rather than allay those heats which arise from the settled mismanagement of the government, or from a natural indisposition in the people. It is of
100 the utmost moment not to make mistakes in the use of strong measures: and firmness is then only a virtue when it accompanies the most perfect wisdom. In truth, inconstancy is a sort of natural corrective of folly and ignorance.

I am not one of those who think that the people are never in
105 the wrong. They have been so, frequently and outrageously, both in other countries and in this. But I do say, that in all disputes between them and their rulers, the presumption is at least upon a par in favor of the people. Experience may perhaps justify me in going further. When popular discontents have been very prevalent,
110 it may well be affirmed and supported, that there has been generally something found amiss in the constitution, or in the conduct of the government. The people have no interest in disorder. When they do wrong, it is their error, not their crime. But with the governing part of the state, it is far otherwise. They certainly
115 may act ill by design, as well as by mistake. If this presumption in favor of the subjects against the trustees of power be not the more probable, I am sure it is the more comfortable speculation; because it is more easy to change an administration, than to reform a people.

QUESTIONS

This selection is a part of a much longer discussion of "The Cause of the Present Discontent." It consists of the part of that discussion in which Burke considers the view that seems to him wrong and that he must separate from his account of the cause before he can clearly explain the present discontents. This selection will stand by itself because, though Burke is fair in stating the arguments of those he disagrees with—that is with the government in power ("those who administer our affairs," line 39)—he implies very clearly throughout this statement his own opinion of what has caused the present discontents.

1. Burke does not get down to his discussion of the official explanation of the present discontents until paragraph four (starting at line 37), because he feels he must do something else first. What is it?

2. The first paragraph (lines 1–10) asserts that people always are discontented and complain of the age they live in. It might follow from this fact that in any particular age men need pay little attention to such complaints. But Burke thinks that such a conclusion is inadequate. Why?

3. In the second and third paragraphs Burke offers some reasons for thinking the situation in his own age is critical. List the reasons he offers in the second paragraph (lines 11–27). List the reasons he offers in the third paragraph (lines 28–36).

4. In the fourth paragraph Burke summarizes the government's explanation of the critical situation. List the reasons offered by the government.

5. In the fifth paragraph (lines 58–103), Burke comes to the heart of his argument, a statement of the difficulties which are inherent in the government's explanation of the critical situation. This paragraph consists of three sections. The point at which Burke moves from the first section to the second is indicated by a transition word ("besides," line 72); the point at which he moves from the second section to the third is also indicated by a transition word ("therefore," line 82). State in a sentence the point of each of these three sections and then explain why Burke makes the points in this order.

6. In the final paragraph of this selection, Burke brings into the open the assumption on which the explanation he is going to offer for the present discontents will be based. What is this assumption?

7. Go back through the fifth paragraph, and point out the places where you think Burke's specific comments on the government's explanation of the crisis have been influenced by what we now know is the assumption on which he plans to make his explanation of the crisis.

8. This selection was written just under two hundred years ago. As we did with Macaulay's essay, therefore, we must be sure we know

what Burke meant by some of the unusual words he uses. Be sure you know the meanings the following words have in Burke's sentences: levity, line 5; vulgar, line 5; infirmity, line 8; distemperature, line 9; spleen, line 12; conjuncture, line 13; contemned, line 15; plausibilities, line 18; industry, line 54; factious, line 67; excite, line 69; luxuriance, line 77; professed, line 81; radically, line 84; untoward, line 87.

9. Burke has a way of constructing his sentences that we have already observed in Macaulay, a writer who was influenced by the style of which Burke was one of the great masters. Burke wishes to keep the basic form of his sentences simple and clear; at the same time he wants to include in them everything that is important to the point he is making. Notice how he satisfies these two purposes in the very first sentence, for example (lines 1–5). The basic form of this sentence might well be represented by the formula, "to do A is B." But in the sentence Burke writes, there are actually four parts to A and these parts are in almost exact parallel; the exception is the third of these four parts which does not, as do the other parts, modify the object of the infinitive. If we write out each of these parts and indicate the grammatical function of every item in each, the nature of the parallel will be clear. "To complain of [infinitive] the age [object] which we live in [modifier of the object], to lament [infinitive] the past [object], to conceive [infinitive] extravagant hopes [object] of the future [modifier of the object]. . . ." In the same way B, the prediction of this sentence, has two parts which are in almost exact parallel (lines 3–5). This kind of careful parallelism is Burke's main way of making clear a large amount of complicated material, and it is, indeed, one of the main resources of the English language for doing so. You should therefore study Burke's method carefully, even though today we would not use the same vocabulary he does, and probably would not keep our sentences so minutely and exactly parallel. Notice how the important distinction Burke makes in lines 7–10 is made clearly by parallelism. Analyze the way the parallelism works in lines 14–27. In lines 74–80 there are three parallel sentences. Analyze them and then explain why Burke arranges them in the order he does. (The answer to this problem will be found in lines 40–51.)

SUGGESTED TOPICS

1. Take some general characteristic of your college, your home town, or some other place you know well and describe it in a sentence like the one with which this selection begins.

2. Write an explanation of the fact that, when Burke has spoken in lines 31–33 of a "scheme of taxation new or oppressive," he feels logically obligated to add "in the quantity or in the mode."

3. In the last paragraph (lines 104–119) Burke says it is reasonable to assume on general grounds that it is more likely the government will be to blame for discontents than that the people will be. Describe these general grounds.

15 / Sample Intelligence Test*

JAMES THURBER

T HE FUZZINESS that creeps into the thought processes of
those inspirationalists who seek to clarify the human scene
reaches an interesting point in Chapter XIV of "How to Develop
Your Personality," by Sadie Myers Shellow, Ph.D. Dr. Shellow
5 was formerly psychologist with the Milwaukee Electric Railway &
Light Company. These things happen in a world of endless
permutations. I myself was once connected with the Central Ohio
Optical Company. I was hired because I had a bicycle, although
why an optical company would want a bicycle might appear on
10 the face of it as inexplicable as why a railway-and-light company
would want a psychologist. My experience of motormen leads me
to believe that they are inarticulate to the point of never saying
anything at all, and I doubt if there is a motorman in all Wis-
consin who would reveal the story of his early childhood to a
15 psychologist. Dr. Shellow, of course, may have proceeded along
some other line, but most psychologists start with your childhood.
Or with your sex life. I somehow have never thought of motormen
as having sex lives, but this doesn't mean they don't have them. I
feel that this speculation is not getting us anywhere.
20   Let us return to Dr. Shellow's book. It was first published five
years ago, but her publishers have just brought out a dollar edition,
which puts the confusion of Chapter XIV within reach of every-

* From *Let Your Mind Alone!* by James Thurber. Permission of the author,
© 1937 The New Yorker Magazine, Inc.

onc. In 1932, the book went into six printings. The present edition was printed from the original plates, which means that the mistakes which appear in it have gone on and on through the years. 25 The book begins with a prefatory note by Albert Edward Wiggam, a foreword by Morris S. Viteles, and an introduction by Dr. Shellow herself. In Chapter I, first paragraph, Dr. Shellow gives the dictionary definition of "personality" as follows: "The sum total of traits necessary to describe what is to be a person." Unless 30 I have gone crazy reading all these books, and I think I have, that sentence defines personality as the sum total of traits necessary to describe an unborn child. If Dr. Shellow's error here is typographical, it looms especially large in a book containing a chapter that tells how to acquire reading skill and gives tests for efficiency in 35 reading. Dr. Shellow tells of a young woman who "was able to take in a whole page at a glance, and through concentrated attention relate in detail what she had read as the words flashed by." If Dr. Shellow used this system in reading the proofs of her book, the system is apparently no good. It certainly *sounds* as if it were 40 no good. I have started out with an admittedly minor confusion— the definition of personality—but let us go on to something so mixed up that it becomes almost magnificent.

Chapter XIV is called "Intelligence Tests," and under the heading "Sample Intelligence Test" twelve problems are posed. There 45 are some pretty fuzzy goings-on in the explanation of No. 11, but it is No. 12 that interests me most; what the Milwaukee motormen made of it I can't imagine. No. 12 is stated as follows: "Cross out the *one* word which makes this sentence absurd and substitute one that is correct: A pound of feathers is lighter than a pound of lead." 50 Let us now proceed to Dr. Shellow's explanation of how to arrive at the solution of this toughy. She writes, "In 12 we get at the critical ability of the mind. Our first impulse is to agree that a pound of feathers is lighter than a pound of lead, since feathers are lighter than lead, but if we look back, we will see that a *pound* of 55 feathers could be no lighter than a *pound* of lead since a pound is always the same. What one word, then, makes the whole sentence absurd? We might cross out the second pound and substitute

ounce, in which case we would have: A pound of feathers is heavier
60 than an ounce of lead, and that would be correct. Or we might cross
out the word heavier and substitute bulkier, in which case we
would have eliminated the absurdity."

We have here what I can only call a paradise of errors. I find,
in Dr. Shellow's presentation of the problem and her solution of
65 it, Transference, Wishful Thinking, Unconscious Substitution,
Psychological Dissociation, Gordian Knot Cutting, Cursory Enumeration, Distortion of Focus, Abandonment of Specific Gravity,
Falsification of Premise, Divergence from Consistency, Overemphasis on Italics, Rhetorical Escapism, and Disregard of the
70 Indefinite Article. Her major error—the conjuring up of the word
"heavier" out of nowhere—is enough to gum up any problem beyond repair, but there are other pieces of woolly reasoning in
No. 12. Dr. Shellow gets off on the wrong foot in her very presentation of the problem. She begins, "Cross out the *one* word which
75 makes this sentence absurd." That means there is *only* one word
which can be changed and restricts the person taking the test to
that one word, but Dr. Shellow goes on, in her explanation, to
change first one and then another. As a matter of fact, there are
five words in the sentence any one of which can be changed to
80 give the sentence meaning. Thus we are all balled up at the start.
If Dr. Shellow had written, "Cross out one word which makes this
sentence absurd," that would have been all right. I think I know
how she got in trouble. I imagine that she originally began, "Cross
out one of the words," and found herself face to face with that an-
85 cient stumbling block in English composition, whether to say
"which *makes* this sentence absurd" or "which *make* this sentence
absurd." (I don't like to go into italics, but to straighten Dr.
Shellow out you got to go into italics.) I have a notion that
Dr. Shellow decided that "make" was right, which of course it is,
90 but that she was dissatisfied with "Cross out one of the words
which make this sentence absurd" because here "words" dominates
"one." Since she wanted to emphasize "one," she italicized it and
then, for good measure, put the definite article "the" in front of it.
That would have given her "Cross out the *one* of the words which

make this sentence absurd." From there she finally arrived at what she arrived at, and the problem began slowly to close in on her.

I wouldn't dwell on this at such length if Dr. Shellow's publishers had not set her up as a paragon of lucidity, precision, and logical thought. (Come to think that over, I believe I would dwell on it at the same length even if they hadn't.) Some poor fellows may have got inferiority complexes out of being unable to see through Dr. Shellow's authoritative explanation of No. 12, and I would like to restore their confidence in their own minds. You can't just go batting off any old sort of answer to an intelligence test in this day when every third person who reads these books has a pretty firm idea that his mind is cracking up.

Let us go on to another interesting fuzziness in the Doctor's explanation. Take her immortal sentence: "We might cross out the second pound and substitute ounce," etc. What anybody who followed these instructions would arrive at is: "A pound of feathers is lighter than *a* ounce of lead." Even leaving the matter of weight out of it (which I am reluctant to do, since weight is the main point), you can't substitute "ounce" for "pound" without substituting "an" for "a," thus changing two words. If "an" and "a" are the same word, then things have come to a pretty pass, indeed. If such slipshoddery were allowed, you could solve the problem with "A pound of feathers is lighter than two pound of lead." My own way out was to change "is" to "ain't," if anybody is interested.

Let us close this excursion into the wonderland of psychology with a paragraph of Dr. Shellow's which immediately follows her explanation of No. 12: "If the reader went through this test quickly before reading the explanation, he may have discovered some things about himself. A more detailed test would be even more revealing. Everyone should at some time or other take a good comprehensive intelligence test and analyze his own defects so that he may know into what errors his reasoning takes him and of what faulty habits of thought he must be aware." I want everybody to file out quietly, now, without any wisecracks.

QUESTIONS

Mr. Thurber's essay offers us another example of taking some one apart. But, though it is not necessarily more profound than Burke's essay, it is more complicated in structure because Mr. Thurber is doing two other things: in the first place, he is suggesting that this psychologist is representative of psychologists in general and that psychologists represent a whole class of muddled minds in our society. In the second place, he is suggesting that it is particularly dangerous for such minds to be muddled because the job they make such a mess of is one that very much needs to be done well, as the personality of James Thurber shows. We ought, then, to be especially alert for three things in this selection: (1) How Mr. Thurber takes apart Dr. Shellow's argument; (2) How he suggests that Dr. Shellow is representative of a whole class of people; (3) How he suggests that the very existence of people like Dr. Shellow is likely to make disturbed minds worse rather than better. Since Mr. Thurber is doing all these things at once, he must be particularly careful to help us keep track of the main plan of his essay, and we ought to watch also for the means he uses to do so.

1. Mr. Thurber obviously thinks there is something comic about the name on the title page of *How to Develop Your Personality,* "Sadie Myers Shellow, Ph.D." (lines 3–4). Can you say why? Can you explain why his always referring to her as "Dr. Shellow" contributes to the second purpose mentioned above?

2. What purpose is served by Mr. Thurber's discussion of motormen (lines 11–15)?

3. Despite what Mr. Thurber says (lines 8–11), we do of course know why he was hired by the optical company; does this make the observation in lines 8–11 invalid? Has that observation the same purpose as Mr. Thurber's comment on Dr. Shellow's employment by the Milwaukee Electric Railway & Light Company (lines 10–11)?

4. Mr. Thurber's observation that "this speculation is not getting us anywhere" (lines 18–19) is certainly true in the sense that the sex life of motormen is somewhat remote from the subject with which the paragraph began, but it is nonetheless important to our understanding of what Mr. Thurber finds inexplicable about Dr. Shellow's job with the railway-and-light company (lines 10–11). Explain why.

5. In the second paragraph Mr. Thurber gives us an illustration of

the kind of confusion he finds in Dr. Shellow's book (lines 28–33). Explain why Dr. Shellow's sentence means, literally, what Mr. Thurber says it does.

6. What idea—much advocated by a certain kind of psychologist—is Mr. Thurber attacking in lines 33–40?

7. Why does Mr. Thurber say (line 30), "Unless I have gone crazy reading all these psychology books, and I think I have . . ."?

8. In paragraph three, which begins at line 44, Mr. Thurber comes to his main illustration of the "fuzzy goings-on" in Dr. Shellow's book. Why does he introduce the reference to "the Milwaukee motormen" in line 47?

9. In paragraph four Mr. Thurber begins to take apart Dr. Shellow's intelligence test. Why does he begin by listing a series of capitalized names of things he finds in Dr. Shellow's presentation and solution of the problem (lines 65–70)?

10. Some of the items listed in lines 65–70 are familiar psychological terms (e.g., "Wishful Thinking,") but many are not. Explain the inclusion in this list of each of the names which is not a familiar psychological term. (To answer this question, you must first read carefully Mr. Thurber's analysis of the faults in Dr. Shellow's intelligence test.)

11. Why is Mr. Thurber justified in saying that "Cross out the *one* word" means "there is *only* one word which can be changed" (lines 75–76)?

12. Mr. Thurber explains how Dr. Shellow got into this trouble by speculating about some of the pitfalls of the English language she might have been trying to avoid. Can you explain why he says Dr. Shellow was right in thinking that she ought to say "make," not "makes," and why she was right not to be satisfied with "one of the words which make" (lines 83–92)?

13. Why does Mr. Thurber insert the parenthesis in lines 99–100?

14. In lines 118–119, Mr. Thurber gives us his solution to the problem from Dr. Shellow's intelligence test. Why is Mr. Thurber's solution far more intelligent than any Dr. Shellow suggested?

15. Why does Mr. Thurber say his solution was to substitute "ain't" instead of saying it was to substitute "isn't"?

16. The passage Mr. Thurber quotes from Dr. Shellow's book in his last paragraph (lines 120–129) is a climactic example of all the faults he has been pointing out so far. How do you know this is his purpose in quoting the passage?

17. Point out the faults in the quotation from Dr. Shellow (lines 122–128) which aroused Mr. Thurber's ire.

18. Why does Mr. Thurber describe what we might say about this passage as "wisecracks"? Why does he write, "I want everybody to file out quietly, now . . ." (lines 128–129)?

SUGGESTED TOPICS

1. Write a paragraph in which you show the ways in which Mr. Thurber suggests to us that having muddled-headed psychologists around nowadays is particularly dangerous.

2. Write a paragraph in which you contrast the method of reading advocated by Dr. Shellow and the method of reading which you can deduce Mr. Thurber approves of.

3. Write a paragraph in which you make clear the reasons why Mr. Thurber's solution of question 12 is better than any solution suggested by Dr. Shellow.

16 / New York, New York*

ALISTAIR COOKE

A N ENGLISH NOVELIST came through New York a
little time ago and, as all travellers must, brooded
awhile about our ways. When he got home he did a radio talk
about it. Nothing more would have been heard about it if the script
of this talk had not been reprinted in the *New York Times*. It was   5
no sooner out than the ambulances were summoned to handle a
rush of high-blood-pressure cases, and the mail-trucks dumped bags
of protests on the *New York Times*. From these outcries you would
never have guessed that Mr. Priestley had just been a delegate to
the United Nations Educational, Scientific and Cultural Organiza-   10
tion, and that he was a man chosen to spread light and understanding among us.

Too bad, said Mr. Priestley, that New York's skyscrapers are not
dedicated 'to God or to some noble aspect of communal life' but
only to 'buying and selling dividends.' 'Is that so?' asked one cor-   15
respondent. 'Then let me tell him that the American Bible Society,
the American Association of Social Workers, the American Cancer
Society, the Medical Society of New York and the British Information Services, to name only a few,' don't buy or sell dividends.
Mr. Rockefeller of course might plead guilty, but his conviction   20
would carry the reminder that his skill in these things helped to
cure a lot of dysentery and scurvy in tropical places and helped a lot

* Reprinted from *One Man's America* by Alistair Cooke, by permission of
Alfred A. Knopf, Inc. Copyright 1952 by Alistair Cooke.

of Englishmen to come to the United States and have the leisure, after their work with microscopes, to share some of Mr. Priestley's
25 feelings about New York. Mr. Priestley conceded that this was 'just a passing thought.'

'It hardly seems worth while holding on to,' snapped this New Yorker.

As for the dismal state of the drama in these parts our man re-
30 ferred Mr. Priestley to the theatre pages of the newspapers, 'where he will note many plays he may later see in London.'

New York is overcrowded, complained Mr. Priestley. Granted, said the New Yorker, but New York takes to people and likes to crowd them in.

35   I creep into the argument at this point only because I possess a rather dog-eared but still unexpired credential. It is that I have lived in New York steadily—continuously, anyway—for nearly fifteen years; that I came here first as a transatlantic visitor, on money dished out from one of Mr. Harkness's skyscrapers; and that in
40 those days I saw New York much as Mr. Priestley sees it now. I think we were both wrong. And I hope it will throw light on more places than New York if I try to say why.

Neither a native nor a traveller can ever be objective about any place on the map. And all we can sensibly discuss is how true for
45 each of them are their feelings about the place. There is a special flow of moods in a traveller. And I think Mr. Priestley now, and I nineteen years ago, were talking more about ourselves than about New York. Because travellers are never the same at home and abroad. They always think they are, but the people you travel
50 among notice pretty soon that you have thrown off your responsibilities to your own country and don't have to take on any of theirs. This is the state of natural anarchy and for some grown-ups is the only time they know again the huge relief of kids when school's out. Travellers, however, once they are no longer young and
55 scampy, feel embarrassed, not to say guilty, about their freedom. They can express it in one of two ways. They can be secretly frightened by the alien life around them and retreat more tenaciously than ever into habits that belong to their country and nowhere else.

Hence the cricket clubs in Brazil and Hollywood, which, I have
noticed, manage to recruit some Britons who would not be playing 60
cricket at home. I have known Englishmen who in England can
take their tea or leave it but who get to insist on it in the United
States, precisely because afternoon tea is not a custom of the
country.

The other reflex looks like the opposite, but deep in the springs 65
of our childish fear it may be only another reaction to the same
threat. It is to go out and do with much bravery all the things you
do not do at home. Thus the Englishman who becomes a baseball
fan or learns to shudder at Brussels sprouts. This is a plucky show
that he is no longer bound by nostalgia or habit to the old life he 70
left behind him.

I believe there is a peculiar mythical appeal to Englishmen in the
distant prospect of America. It may go as far back as the Elizabethans, the travellers' tales of fat turkeys, gigantic oysters and succu-
lent fruits, the news of an Eldorado begging for settlement. 'Oh My 75
America, my new founde land!' cried Donne, though at that particular moment he wasn't thinking of leaving home. This myth has
been modified down the years, until there are at least two or three
generations of Britons conditioned by a whole childhood literature
about the West, and now by the glittering stereotypes of the 80
movies, and more regrettably by the solid tradition of reporting
back to England only what is corrupt or eccentric or scandalous.
From this there emerges a modern myth about America, some of
which is poetic and true, some of which is a punching-bag for stay-
at-homes. The city of New York has come to crystallize the night- 85
mare aspect of this dream country. It becomes a hard and hideous
place, with frightening canyons of skyscrapers. Its life is, in Mr.
Priestley's words, 'restless . . . in its nightly pursuit of diminishing
pleasures. Not a flower,' he moans, 'can blossom on these concrete
cliffs.' Well, I am told that in the granite veins of this city, on 90
Manhattan alone, they have found a hundred and seventy varieties
of semi-precious stones. Slit into the grey hunk of rock we inhabit
there are garnets and amethysts and opals and beryls and tourma-
lines, and other jewels even less pronounceable. There are still

95 about half as many trees as human beings. And the commonest
backyard tree is the ailanthus, which—I hate to tell Mr. Priestley—
the Chinese call the tree of heaven.

But this doesn't fit in with anything Europeans have been told,
and the heck with it. To more Europeans than would admit it,
100 there is always at the back of the mind this neon-lit image of New
York as Babylon, where innocence is banished, where anything
goes, where everything has its price, where—in the vivacious version
current among my schoolmates in England—you rode a perpetual
shoot-the-chutes and bounded the waves of pleasure, to the music
105 of Duke Ellington, while at your side snuggled a beautiful girl,
beautiful and up to no good.

If you think I am romancing about this, let me remind you that
the symbol of an island of pleasure, presided over by a beckoning
female, is almost a constant of the human imagination. It was
110 Circe in Greece, Izanami in Japan, Semiramis who built Babylon.
These, you may say, are only legends. But what is more real and
indispensable than the ideas that burst into life from men's im-
aginations precisely because they do not exist? They express the
permanent dissatisfactions of man with his lot, and this particular
115 one relieves the secret fear that, like Marley's ghost, we may be
wasting our days on earth weaving chains of bankbooks, files, ledgers, insurance policies.

When Mr. Priestley calls New York 'Babylon piled on Imperial
Rome,' I think he is the victim of this myth. Once you stay and
120 live in this city, you have to admit that it is nothing of the sort.
The intelligentsia will claim that New York tries to be the city
they would like to despise. But the intelligentsia is the same everywhere and is a poor guide to the real life of cities. And to the people
who live this life, the overpowering number of middle-class New
125 Yorkers, who have as much town pride as Leeds or Manchester,
there was one sentence of old Jeremiah Priestley's that really hurt:
'The lonely heart of man cannot come home here.'

No? On Manhattan Island alone (and Mr. Priestley was talking
about only one of the five boroughs) there are two million people
130 who won't live anywhere else and wouldn't want to, even after

three drinks. New York is their home town. It is not Babylon. It is the place where we rise in the mornings to the clicking of the radiator or the bawling of the downstairs brat. We take in the milk. We descend on the schools with a rush of kisses and a greeting of neighbors. We head for the subway. We hear a great bass rever- 135 berate over the island. It is not, as Mr. Priestley might suspect, the trump of doom. It is only the *basso profundo* of the *Queen Elizabeth* going downriver. We spend the day at work, restlessly perhaps to the extent of leaving home for a distant workshop and then at the end of the day reversing the process and leaving the workshop 140 to go home again. Maybe, if it is not slushy or damp, we decide to walk home and watch a copper sun sinking into an El Greco sky over against the Jersey shore. If the skies of New York often lift us, miserable ants that we are, into delusions of grandeur, we will often spot on the corner, as we turn to go in our building, something 145 casual or scurrilous that restores us to the affectionate human scale. On the wall of a bricked-up lot a tiny New Yorker scribbled a typical sentence. 'Nuts,' it said. 'Nuts to all the boys on Second Avenue'—a long struggling pause, then the concession, 'except between 68th and 69th Streets.'   150

We come in and we play with the children or bawl them out. We enjoy, if we have any sense, the variety of the people of our town, and there is often some crazy thing to tell. I have daily dealings with a score of Americans whom I shall only identify here as an Italian shoeshine man, a garrulous German elevator man, a 155 warm, wise-cracking Jewish newsagent, and a range of shopkeepers who span the gamut of New York names from Mr. O'Byrne De Witt to Circumstance H. Smith, a Negro with fine manners.

The thermometer dips overnight and we look forward to tomorrow, when the red ball goes up over Central Park—no signal for 160 revolution this, Mr. Priestley, or even retribution, but the City's cue to tell us there's going to be skating. Whenever we go to the Park and find, say, there's not enough sand in the sand box the children play in, we telephone the office of Mr. Moses, the Park Commissioner. Next morning two attendants come along with re- 165 plenishing boxes of sand. The city works pretty hard on the or-

ganizing of the citizen's play, and in summer there are handball courts to be repaired, there are city band concerts, city outdoor opera, city fish to be fed into the surrounding streams, and swim-
170 ming for thousands who leap the trains for the vast, city-sponsored lay-out of Jones Beach.

In the evening, what do we do? Well, I see from a city survey that only one in fifteen of us has ever been in a night-club. We sit and read, or have friends in, listen to the radio or go to lectures, or
175 a movie, play pinochle or checkers or poker, putter with this and that. And ninety-two in a hundred of us begin to go to bed about ten-thirty.

Our days and months are bound by work, and fun, and quarrels, and taxes, and movies and savings, and children and death and
180 friendship. When we are far from home we think of New York, and it is not Circe with a henna rinse bawling into a night-club microphone. We see in imagination the white steam hissing through the pavements. We smell the fishy smell of the Fulton market, or the whiff of chicory over Foley Square, or the malty
185 brew that hangs around the East Nineties. We recall the Bronx Zoo, and Mercury standing on his muscular thighs over the traffic lights on Fifth Avenue. We see in the mind's eye the magic dioramas of Africa and Hawaii in the Museum of Natural History, or the pink front page of the morning tabloids. We hear of a girl who
190 was loaded with furs and automobiles by a sharpie using absconded funds. Over the transatlantic wires they flash her confession: 'I never knew he was in an illegal business. He told me he was a gambler.' Glory be! We know her for our own.

Or some dank day in Brittany or Paris, we recall the one day
195 in three or four that is blindingly clear, brilliant as a knight in armour, the sun slashing down the avenues like a sword. On such a day, my cab-driver stopped for a red light at St. Patrick's. And so did a herd of young teen-agers before they turned in to say their prayers. Most of them, I should say, were in sweaters of every
200 colour. He leered at their faces and caught their twinkling shapes in the shafts of sunlight. He hit the steering-wheel with his open hand. And said to me, or perhaps to God: 'They come in all shapes

and sizes. Yes, sir. Great stuff. Whaddya say, Mac?' He laughed himself silly.

Restless we *are*, and very small, threading through our canyons. 205 But are we, as Mr. Priestley assures us we are, 'full of unease, disquiet, bewilderment'? Last summer Dr. Gallup found that over ninety per cent of us thought we were happy. Suppose we allow ten per cent for pride or bravado and another ten per cent for Mr. Priestley's transatlantic insight. That still leaves seventy per cent 210 who believe, maybe wrongly, that they are happy. Better let 'em wallow in their ignorance, Mr. Priestley, these placid dopes who don't even know when they're 'deeply bewildered and frustrated.' Whaddya say, Mac?

QUESTIONS

1. This essay, too, is a complicated example of the process of taking apart. Mr. Cooke's purpose is to show the inaccuracy of a myth about America, and especially about New York, which is widespread among Englishmen; he takes as his example the expression of this myth by the English novelist, J. B. Priestley. The first part of his essay outlines the myth, suggests how widespread it is, and gives an illustration of its absurdity. Where would you say this first part ends?

2. Explain why Mr. Cooke discusses the Elizabethans' "travellers' tales" about America in lines 73–77 and "the vivacious version" of the English myth about New York in lines 102–106.

3. There is an allusion in lines 72–73 to a famous poem by the author of the "Elegy in a Country Churchyard." What is the poem and why does Mr. Cooke allude to it?

4. Why does it seem ironic to Mr. Cooke that Mr. Priestley should have been "a delegate to the United Nations Educational, Scientific and Cultural Organization"?

5. Why does Mr. Cooke "hate to tell Mr. Priestley" that the Chinese call the ailanthus the tree of heaven (lines 96–97)?

6. Why does Mr. Cooke say "the heck with it" (line 99)?

7. What is Mr. Cooke suggesting about the Europeans' attitude toward the myth of New York, which they deplore so loudly, when he says it includes the vision of "a beautiful girl, beautiful and up to no good" (lines 105–106)?

8. Why does Mr. Cooke call Mr. Priestley, whose name is John Boynton Priestley, "Jeremiah Priestley" (line 126)?

9. In lines 131–177, Mr. Cooke takes us through a representative day of the middle-class New Yorkers for whom "New York is their home town." Why does he do so?

10. Is there anything in this account of a New Yorker's day which has special reference to what Mr. Cooke has quoted from Mr. Priestley?

11. Is there anything in Mr. Cooke's account of a New Yorker's day which would probably not be in it were not Mr. Cooke an Englishman, who has lived in America many years, writing about America for an English newspaper, the *Manchester Guardian?* Do you find evidence of this special purpose elsewhere in the essay?

12. Why is the scribbled sentence described in lines 148–150 particularly useful for making the point Mr. Cooke wishes to make in this passage about the life of New Yorkers?

13. In the paragraph beginning at line 178, Mr. Cooke tells us what a real New Yorker thinks of when he is homesick. He begins by saying that such a New Yorker does not think of "Circe with a henna rinse bawling into a night-club microphone" (lines 181–182). Why does he bother to deny this idea?

14. What have the things Mr. Cooke tells us a homesick New Yorker will remember in common (lines 180–193)?

15. Why is he specially amused that the girl described in lines 189–193 will be recognized by any New Yorker for "our own"?

16. In the paragraph beginning at line 194, Mr. Cooke tells us an anecdote about a New York cab-driver which he obviously feels sums up his feelings about New York; why does he begin this paragraph with a sentence about "some dank day in Brittany or Paris" (line 194)?

17. What is the cab-driver's feeling about the teen-agers (lines 202–204)?

18. Why is it particularly important that the cab-driver said, "Whaddya say, Mac" (line 203)?

19. Why does the anecdote about the cab-driver make Mr. Priestley's remark about the New Yorker's being "deeply bewildered and frustrated" (line 213) appear particularly silly? How does Mr. Cooke emphasize that silliness for us?

20. Has Mr. Cooke's quotation from Mr. Priestley at the end of

this essay (line 213) any connection with his reference to "the intelligentsia" (lines 121–123)? Has it any connection with the description of Mr. Priestley in the first paragraph of this selection (lines 1–12)?

SUGGESTED TOPICS

1. Write a paragraph which states the European view of New York which Mr. Priestley used in his broadcast.

2. This essay depends for its effect partly on a number of quiet but apt allusions. Write a set of notes which will make clear the point of these allusions to Eldorado (line 75); Babylon (line 101); *basso profundo* (line 137); El Greco (line 142); Circe (line 181); St. Patrick's (line 197).

3. Write a paragraph in which you summarize Mr. Cooke's defense of the New Yorker.

17/ Unemployment and "Wasteful" Expenditure*

JOHN MAYNARD KEYNES

WHEN involuntary unemployment exists, the marginal disutility of labour is necessarily less than the utility of the marginal product. Indeed it may be much less. For a man who has been long unemployed some measure of labour, instead
5 of involving disutility, may have a positive utility. If this is accepted, the above reasoning shows how "wasteful" loan expenditure may nevertheless enrich the community on balance. Pyramid-building, earthquakes, even wars may serve to increase wealth, if the education of our statesmen on the principles of the classical
10 economics stands in the way of anything better.

It is curious how common sense, wriggling for an escape from absurd conclusions, has been apt to reach a preference for *wholly* "wasteful" forms of loan expenditure rather than for *partly* wasteful forms, which, because they are not wholly wasteful, tend to be
15 judged on strict "business" principles. For example, unemployment relief financed by loans is more readily accepted than the financing of improvements at a charge below the current rate of interest; whilst the form of digging holes in the ground known as gold-mining, which not only adds nothing whatever to the real wealth
20 of the world but involves the disutility of labour, is the most acceptable of all solutions.

* From *The General Theory of Employment, Interest, and Money* by John Maynard Keynes. Reprinted by permission of Harcourt, Brace and Company, Inc.

If the Treasury were to fill old bottles with banknotes, bury them at suitable depths in disused coal-mines which are then filled up to the surface with town rubbish, and leave it to private enterprise on well-tried principles of *laissez-faire* to dig the notes up again (the right to do so being obtained, of course, by tendering for leases of the note-bearing territory), there need be no more unemployment and, with the help of the repercussions, the real income of the community, and its capital wealth also, would probably become a good deal greater than it actually is. It would, indeed, be more sensible to build houses and the like; but if there are political and practical difficulties in the way of this, the above would be better than nothing.

The analogy between this expedient and the gold-mines of the real world is complete. At periods when gold is available at suitable depths experience shows that the real wealth of the world increases rapidly; and when but little of it is so available, our wealth suffers stagnation or decline. Thus gold-mines are of the greatest value and importance to civilisation. Just as wars have been the only form of large scale loan expenditure which statesmen have thought justifiable, so gold-mining is the only pretext for digging holes in the ground which has recommended itself to bankers as sound finance; and each of these activities has played its part in progress —failing something better. To mention a detail, the tendency in slumps for the price of gold to rise in terms of labour and materials aids eventual recovery, because it increases the depth at which gold-digging pays and lowers the minimum grade of ore which is payable.

In addition to the probable effect of increased supplies of gold on the rate of interest, gold-mining is for two reasons a highly practical form of investment, if we are precluded from increasing employment by means which at the same time increase our stock of useful wealth. In the first place, owing to the gambling attractions which it offers it is carried on without too close a regard to the ruling rate of interest. In the second place the result, namely, the increased stock of gold, does not, as in other cases, have the effect of diminishing its marginal utility. Since the value of a house

depends on its utility, every house which is built serves to diminish the prospective rents obtainable from further house-building and
60 therefore lessens the attraction of further similar investment unless the rate of interest is falling *pari passu*. But the fruits of gold-mining do not suffer from this disadvantage, and a check can only come through a rise of the wage-unit in terms of gold, which is not likely to occur unless and until employment is substantially better.
65 Moreover, there is no subsequent reverse effect on account of provision for user and supplementary costs, as in the case of less durable forms of wealth.

Ancient Egypt was doubly fortunate, and doubtless owed to this its fabled wealth, in that it possessed *two* activities, namely, pyra-
70 mid-building as well as the search for the precious metals, the fruits of which, since they could not serve the needs of man by being consumed, did not stale with abundance. The Middle Ages built cathedrals and sang dirges. Two pyramids, two masses for the dead, are twice as good as one; but not so two railways from
75 London to York. Thus we are so sensible, have schooled ourselves to so close a semblance of prudent financiers, taking careful thought before we add to the "financial" burdens of posterity by building them houses to live in, that we have no such easy escape from the sufferings of unemployment. We have to accept them
80 as an inevitable result of applying to the conduct of the State the maxims which are best calculated to "enrich" an individual by enabling him to pile up claims to enjoyment which he does not intend to exercise at any definite time.

QUESTIONS

This brief but closely reasoned and witty selection is part of a long argument in Keynes' *General Theory of Employment, Interest, and Money* in which Keynes tries to show that the way to relieve a depression is for the government to make large expenditures of money which it borrows. He is very well aware that the economic ideas of conventional people will make this argument seem wilfully wrong and absurd and he has very cleverly observed that one illogical consequence of their attitude is that they are more willing to spend borrowed money in what he calls *"wholly* 'wasteful' " ways than in *"partly* wasteful" ways (lines 12–14). He sets out, therefore, to show both the value of even the most absurdly wasteful loan expenditure during a depression and the absurd wastefulness of the loan expenditures bankers and such people are willing to make, by choosing an illustration for his argument that will do both things at once. The basic form of this selection is, therefore, the same as the form of Becker's essay; its purpose is to show what is wrong with his opponent's view of a situation and what is right about his own view of it. But instead of taking these two things in order, it does them both at the same time. This takes great ingenuity and wit, which Keynes had in abundance, and means, too, that what he writes is complicated and requires very careful reading.

1. In the opening sentence of this selection, Keynes uses the phrase "marginal disutility" (lines 1–2) and in line 20 he speaks of the "disutility of labour." Be sure you look up in your dictionary the word "utility" and the phrase "marginal utility" and that you understand these two terms—and their opposites—as they are used in economics.

2. The first paragraph states the position Keynes is going to argue for in this selection. Why does he add to the last sentence of this paragraph the if-clause that begins in line 8?

3. Give an example of what Keynes thinks would be something "better" (line 10). You will find Keynes himself providing an example for you later on in the selection.

4. What are the "absurd conclusions" (line 12) that common sense wriggles to escape from?

5. In lines 18–19 Keynes calls gold-mining a "form of digging holes in the ground"; in what follows in this sentence he explains why he calls it that; show you understand this explanation by putting it in your own words.

6. What is Keynes seeking to suggest about the conventional attitude of "statesmen" (line 9) and other people of "common sense" (line 11) by saying that gold-mining is only "digging holes in the ground"?

7. In the paragraph that begins at line 22, Keynes suggests a fantastic expedient for curing unemployment. What is its relevance to what he has just said about gold mining?

8. How is Keynes being ironic in lines 26–27?

9. Explain the meaning of the assertion that "with the help of the repercussions, the real wealth of the community, and its capital wealth also, would probably become a good deal greater" (lines 28–30).

10. Explain the way in which Keynes means literally that "gold-mines are of the greatest value and importance to civilisation" (lines 38–39) and the way he means it ironically. The following sentence (lines 39–44) will help you here.

11. Why does Keynes say in line 44, "—failing something better"? has he said something like this before? He says something like it again within the next dozen lines; where?

12. Explain why an increase in the stock of gold does not "diminish its marginal utility" (line 57).

13. Why does this characteristic of gold-mining make it particularly important in a period of unemployment?

14. Keynes' last paragraph, which begins at line 68, sums up by a series of ironies his whole argument in this selection. Explain the irony in his assertion that "Ancient Egypt was doubly fortunate" because it was obsessed with pyramid-building and gold-mining.

15. What relation to these activities of the Egyptians have the building of cathedrals and the singing of dirges in the Middle Ages (lines 72–73)?

16. Why does Keynes not believe it is wrong to "to add to the financial burdens of posterity by building them houses to live in" when this will relieve unemployment (lines 77–78)?

17. Why does Keynes put the word "enrich" (line 81) in quotation marks?

18. Why does Keynes describe money in the bank as "claims to enjoyment which [the individual] does not intend to exercise at any definite time" (lines 82–83)?

SUGGESTED TOPICS

1. Explain in your own words why Keynes believes that during depressions the government ought to borrow money and spend it for the building of houses.

2. Explain why Keynes asserts that "pyramid-building, earthquakes, even wars may serve to increase wealth" (lines 7–8).

3. Explain why Keynes says that "the principles of the classical economics [stand] in the way of anything better" (lines 9–10). Notice in considering this topic what he says in lines 79–83.

FREDERICK LEWIS ALLEN

RALPH E. LAPP

PETER F. DRUCKER

HUNTER GUTHRIE

JONATHAN SWIFT

iii. Enumeration

18 / May 1919[*]

FREDERICK LEWIS ALLEN

I
F TIME were suddenly to turn back to the earliest days of the
Post-war Decade, and you were to look about you, what would
seem strange to you? Since 1919 the circumstances of American
life have been transformed—yes, but exactly how?

Let us refresh our memories by following a modern well-to-do 5
young couple of Cleveland or Boston or Seattle or Baltimore—it
hardly matters which—through the routine of an ordinary day in
May, 1919. (I select that particular date, six months after the
Armistice of 1918, because by then the United States had largely
succeeded in turning from the ways of war to those of peace, yet 10
the profound alterations wrought by the Post-war Decade had
hardly begun to take place.) There is no better way to suggest
what the passage of a few years has done to change you and me
and the environment in which we live.

From the appearance of Mr. Smith as he comes to the breakfast 15
table on this May morning in 1919, you would hardly know that
you were not in the nineteen-thirties (though you might, perhaps,
be struck by the narrowness of his trousers). The movement of
men's fashions is glacial. It is different, however, with Mrs. Smith.

She comes to breakfast in a suit, the skirt of which—rather 20
tight at the ankles—hangs just six inches from the ground. She
has read in Vogue the alarming news that skirts may become even

shorter, and that "not since the days of the Bourbons has the woman of fashion been visible so far above the ankle"; but six
25 inches is still the orthodox clearance. She wears low shoes now, for spring has come; but all last winter she protected her ankles either with spats or with high laced "walking-boots," or with high patent-leather shoes with contrasting buckskin tops. Her stockings are black (or tan, perhaps, if she wears tan shoes); the idea of flesh-
30 colored stockings would appall her. A few minutes ago Mrs. Smith was surrounding herself with an "envelope chemise" and a petti-coat; and from the thick ruffles on her undergarments it was ap-parent that she was not disposed to make herself more boyish in form than ample nature intended.

35   Strung across the front page of Mr. Smith's newspaper are head-lines telling of the progress of the American Navy seaplane, the NC-4, on its flight across the Atlantic *via* the Azores. That flight is the most sensational news story of May, 1919. (Alcock and Brown have not yet crossed the ocean in a single hop; they will do it
40 a few weeks hence, eight long years ahead of Lindbergh.) But there is other news too: of the Peace Conference at Paris, where the Treaty is now in its later stages of preparation; of the successful oversubscription of the Victory Loan ("Sure, we'll finish the job!" the campaign posters have been shouting); of the arrival of another
45 transport with soldiers from overseas; of the threat of a new strike; of a speech by Mayor Ole Hanson of Seattle denouncing that scourge of the times, the I. W. W.; of the prospects for the passage of the Suffrage Amendment, which it is predicted will enable women to take "a finer place in the national life"; and of Henry
50 Ford's libel suit against the Chicago *Tribune*—in the course of which he will call Benedict Arnold a writer, and in reply to the question, "Have there been any revolutions in this country?" will answer, "Yes, in 1812."

The sporting pages inform Mr. Smith that Rickard has selected
55 Toledo as the scene of a forthcoming encounter between the heavyweight champion, Jess Willard, and another future idol of the mob, Jack Dempsey. (They met, you may recall, on the Fourth of July, 1919, and sober citizens were horrified to read that 19,650

people were so depraved as to sit in a broiling sun to watch
Dempsey knock out the six-foot-six-inch champion in the third 60
round. How would the sober citizens have felt if they had known
that eight years later a Dempsey-Tunney fight would bring in more
than five times as much money in gate receipts as this battle of
Toledo?) In the sporting pages there may be news of Bobby Jones,
the seventeen-year-old Southern golf champion, or of William T. 65
Tilden, Jr., who is winning tennis tournaments here and there, but
neither of them is yet a national champion. And even if Jones were
to win this year he would hardly become a great popular hero; for
although golf is gaining every day in popularity, it has not yet become an inevitable part of the weekly ritual of the American busi- 70
ness man. Mr. Smith very likely still scoffs at "grown men who
spend their time knocking a little white ball along the ground";
it is quite certain that he has never heard of plus fours; and if he
should happen to play golf he had better not show his knicker-
bockers in the city streets, or small boys will shout at him, "Hey, 75
get some men's pants!"

Breakfast over, Mr. Smith gets into his automobile to drive to
the office. The car is as likely to be a Lexington, a Maxwell, a
Briscoe, or a Templar as to be a Dodge, Buick, Chevrolet, Cadillac,
or Hudson, and it surely will not be a Chrysler; Mr. Chrysler has 80
just been elected first vice-president of the General Motors Corporation. Whatever the make of the car, it stands higher than the
cars of the nineteen-thirties; the passengers look down upon their
surroundings from an imposing altitude. The chances are nine to
one that Mr. Smith's automobile is open (only 10.3 per cent of the 85
cars manufactured in 1919 were closed). The vogue of the sedan
is just beginning. Closed cars are still associated in the public
mind with wealth; the hated profiteer of the newspaper cartoon
rides in a limousine.

If Mr. Smith's car is one of the high, hideous, but efficient 90
model T Fords of the day, let us watch him for a minute. He
climbs in by the right-hand door (for there is no left-hand door
by the front seat), reaches over to the wheel, and sets the spark
and throttle levers in a position like that of the hands of a clock

95 at ten minutes to three. Then, unless he has paid extra for a self-
starter, he gets out to crank. Seizing the crank in his right hand
(carefully, for a friend of his once broke his arm cranking), he
slips his left forefinger through a loop of wire that controls the
choke. He pulls the loop of wire, he revolves the crank mightily,
100 and as the engine at last roars, he leaps to the trembling running
board, leans in, and moves the spark and throttle to twenty-five
minutes of two. Perhaps he reaches the throttle before the engine
falters into silence, but if it is a cold morning perhaps he does not.
In that case, back to the crank again and the loop of wire. Mr.
105 Smith wishes Mrs. Smith would come out and sit in the driver's
seat and pull that spark lever down before the engine has time to
die.

Finally he is at the wheel with the engine roaring as it should.
He releases the emergency hand-break, shoves his left foot against
110 the low-speed pedal, and as the car sweeps loudly out into the
street, he releases his left foot, lets the car into high gear, and is off.
Now his only care is for that long hill down the street; yesterday
he burned his brake on it, and this morning he must remember to
brake with the reverse pedal, or the low-speed pedal, or both, or all
115 three in alternation. (Jam your foot down on any of the three
pedals and you slow the car.)

One thing the Smiths certainly will not do this evening. They
will not listen to the radio.

For there is no such thing as radio broadcasting. Here and there
120 a mechanically inclined boy has a wireless set, with which, if he
knows the Morse code, he may listen to messages from ships at
sea and from land stations equipped with sending apparatus. The
radio-phone has been so far developed that men flying in an air-
plane over Manhattan have talked with other men in an office-
125 building below. But the broadcasting of speeches and music—well,
it was tried years ago by DeForest and "nothing came of it." Not
until the spring of 1920 will Frank Conrad of the Westinghouse
Company of East Pittsburgh, who has been sending out phono-
graph music and baseball scores from the barn which he has rigged
130 up as a spare-time research station, find that so many amateur wire-

less operators are listening to them that a Pittsburgh newspaper has had the bright idea of advertising radio equipment "which may be used by those who listen to Dr. Conrad's programs." And not until this advertisement appears will the Westinghouse officials decide to open the first broadcasting station in history in order to stimu- 135 late the sale of their supplies.

One word more about Mr. and Mrs. Smith. Not only have they never heard of radio broadcasting; they have never heard of Coué, the Dayton Trial, crossword puzzles, bathing-beauty contests, John J. Raskob, racketeers, Teapot Dome, Coral Gables, the *Ameri-* 140 *can Mercury*, Sacco and Vanzetti, companionate marriage, brokers' loan statistics, Michael Arlen, the Wall Street explosion, confession magazines, the Hall-Mills case, Radio stock, speakeasies, Al Capone, automatic traffic lights, or Charles A. Lindbergh.

The Post-war Decade lies before them. 145

COMMENTARY

THIS SELECTION is a clear-cut example of the way an author will pick out a number of items which are important to his subject and deal with them one at a time. As you will notice, Allen invents a framework within which to arrange his items, since the enumerative form he has chosen does not automatically provide an order. Sometimes, of course, the subject itself will provide some order, for example, when the items themselves are obviously arranged in a certain way, or when the writer discovers—and it is seldom an easy thing to discover—that taking up the items in a particular order is much the best way to make the subject clear. An obvious case of the last possibility occurs when the subject is an operation, as it is, for instance, in the two paragraphs of this essay which describe starting a model T Ford (lines 90–116).

But if, as is usually true, the subject the writer wishes to make clear to the reader does not itself suggest an arrangement, then the writer must provide one. The best one he can provide is usually the simplest, since such an arrangement is, under the best of circumstances, an artificial one, imposed on the material from outside rather than imposed from within by the relations of the items in the subject itself.

As we read Frederick Lewis Allen's essay, we quickly become aware that what he really wants to do is to give us an idea of what the life of the ordinary well-to-do American was like in 1919. He chose this date, he tells us, "because by then the United States had largely succeeded in turning from the ways of war to those of peace, yet the profound alteration wrought by the Post-war Decade had hardly begun to take place" (lines 9–12). It occurred to him that the best way to make us understand what life was like then would be to take up one by one the aspects of living with which most Americans, of one sex or the other, are likely to be concerned and to show what those aspects of living were like in 1919. Logically, therefore, he must have begun by thinking up a list of aspects. ("Logically," because it does not follow that an author will think of a certain thing first simply because it is, in the reader's eyes, logical that he should have done so; it is important for you to recognize that neither your mind nor the mind of any other writer always works completely logically and that you need not feel that there is something wrong with you or him if you discover that the way an essay was thought out was illogical; the important thing is that it should not be illogical when it is finished.) Allen's list included: 1) styles of dress; 2) the important news of the day, an item which he subdivides into a) what is on the front page, and b) what is on the sports page; 3) automobiles; 4) radio. But though Allen is well equipped—by considerable research—to tell us what was going on in these areas of daily living in May, 1919, he has —again, logically speaking—not yet devised a plan for arranging them in a reasonable order.

Logically speaking, then, it was at this point that a framework for these aspects of daily living occurred to him, the scheme of taking "the routine of an ordinary day in May, 1919," of "a modern well-to-do young couple" (lines 5–8) and arranging the aspects of living he wanted to tell us about in the order determined by this scheme. You will notice that this framework is not ideal for his purpose and that he has to "stretch" it, or go outside it, fairly often in order to tell us everything he wants to; for example, he begins his account of women's clothes within the framework by telling us how Mrs. Smith is dressed when she comes down to breakfast, but in this paragraph he has to move outside the framework twice in order to tell us things he thinks will interest us, that is, what kind of shoes (lines 25–28) and under-clothing (lines 30–32) women wore in the winter of 1919, neither of which would be visible as Mrs. Smith came to the breakfast table that May morning. Such stretching of a framework is almost unavoidable when the framework is not determined by the subject itself but imposed from outside, since only a plan which reflects the actual relations of the parts within the subject will be sure to allow the author to include all parts of the subject. Little harm is done by such stretching as long as the author closely connects the items which do not fit within the frame, as Allen does. His discussion of the shoes Mrs. Smith is wearing in May, 1919, makes it easy for him to slip in a reference to the shoes she was wearing last winter, and the fact that Mrs. Smith must have dressed just before she came down to breakfast makes it equally easy for him to mention the "envelope chemise." Another thing helps to keep us undisturbed by this stretching: we are perfectly aware from the start that the framework Allen is using is merely a convenience, that he is almost playing a game; that is clear from the way he sets his plan up for us (lines 5–8). For these reasons we are willing to let him tell us things that do not really fit his plan as long as he does not "lose" us or make his plan hard to follow. Notice for yourself how he moves outside his plan at lines 38–40, 50–53, 57–64, 64–67, 73–76, 80–82, 126–136.

This, then, is what Allen wants to do and the plan he has devised for doing it. We are now ready to see why this selection begins with two paragraphs that lead up to his account of a day in the lives of Mr. and Mrs. Smith (lines 1–14); the first of these paragraphs tells us his subject and the second his plan. Except for the one-sentence paragraph at lines 117–118—a newspaper trick of emphasis which probably does more harm than good in an essay—Allen's paragraphs are carefully fitted to the items in his list. There is one, brief paragraph for men's styles and a longer one for women's, one for the contents of the front page of Mr. Smith's newspaper and one for the contents of the sports page.

The most effective thing Allen does in these paragraphs is to use exact information, and to use it to bring the things he is talking about clearly, because precisely, before our minds. Thus, for example, we are told, not that an American plane has flown the Atlantic, but that a "Navy seaplane, the NC-4" has done so, and has gone laboriously "*via* the Azores," not "in a single hop," as Alcock and Brown and Lindbergh were to go. We are told, not that there was another war loan but that there was a Victory Loan and that it had a slogan which is bound to sound "period" to us now. We are told, not that Henry Ford was involved in a libel suit, but that he had brought "a libel suit against the Chicago *Tribune*"; and we are told some of the incredibly silly things he said during the trial of that suit. Details of this kind have a very special value for the kind of thing Allen is trying to do. For one thing, they give us a sense of how different our lives are from the lives of Americans in 1919. Perhaps our first impulse is to laugh at the people of 1919 for the not very good reason that they were different from us (human beings often suppose without thinking that anyone who is different from them is inferior and therefore absurd). There is not much harm in such laughter so long as it does not prevent our understanding the second and more important effect of such details. Any detail which strikes us as unusual will almost automatically set us to trying to imagine, to reconstruct in our minds, the surrounding circumstances of the times which made that detail seem, if not natural, at least not unexpected or impossible to people then. If an author picks such details skillfully, a very small number of them will create in our minds a remarkably full view of the period and will give us an often quite accurate sense of what it felt like to live then.

This effect will, of course, be particularly powerful for people who lived through the period the author is describing. It will be almost equally powerful, though in a somewhat different way, for people who have some interest in the aspects of life the author touches on. People interested in women's clothes will quickly imagine what it must have felt like to be dressed as Mrs. Smith was. People interested in the golden age of sports will be reminded of many things by one or two details about Willard and Dempsey, Bobby Jones and Tilden. People interested in old cars will respond by remembering what they look like when Allen names the Lexington, Maxwell, Briscoe, or Templar. Only the sad people with no interests at all and therefore no knowledge will be unaffected by any of these details.

When Allen comes to the third item on his list, he apparently feels that one aspect of it, the model T Ford, is so important to our sense of what things were like in May, 1919, that he must linger over it. Consequently, after he has written a paragraph on cars which is exactly like the paragraphs on dress, front-page news, and sports, he takes two paragraphs to give us a detailed account of exactly how one went about getting a model T Ford started (lines 90–116). It is, incidentally, worth comparing this account with Lee Strout White's on page 248). These two paragraphs really constitute a small essay within an essay and give us a very good example of how an author who is using the enumerative form selects and arranges his items when the subject itself determines the selection and arrangement. Assuming what is by no means always true (as any reader of directions on packages will have discovered), that the author understands what he is talking about, the selection of the items will be determined by the subject. Every move which it is necessary to make in order to accomplish the object must be mentioned and described in such a way as to make it possible for the reader to make the move. The arrangement of the items is also determined by the objective situation. Unless the reader is told the moves to make in the order in which he must make them, the explanation will be a failure.

Anyone who has ever tried to tell another person how to do something knows that this form of explanation is by no means easy. We all have a tendency to include in such an explanation items which are not necessary and will, if we are not careful, confuse the listener. We also have a tendency, especially if we know the subject well, to leave out important items, because we take them completely for granted ourselves, and then put them in later, at the wrong place in the explanation ("Oh, wait a minute; I should have said before that you must do so-and-so before you do so-and-so"); and some of us, because we are interested and perhaps because we are proud of our knowledge, tend to explain in detail things it is not necessary to understand in order to do the job successfully. In both the selection and the arrangement of his details, Allen makes none of these mistakes. But he is not giving a set of directions for a handbook to be distributed to owners of model T Fords, and consequently he adds something to his explanation which would be out of place in such a handbook, namely, something which will help us to feel what it was like to go through the process of starting a model T. Obvious examples of this kind of thing are the parenthesis in line 97 and expressions like "leaps to the trembling running board" (lines 100–101).

In line 117, Allen comes to his fourth item, radio, and writes a paragraph about it which is like the paragraphs he has already written on his other three items. But he ends his essay with a paragraph (lines 137–144) of a different kind. This paragraph consists of a list of things Mr. and Mrs. Smith will not have heard of in May, 1919. Now, the list of all the things Mr. and Mrs. Smith may be assumed not to have heard of would be almost immeasurably long. This is a list of a special kind of thing they have not heard of, namely, the things that will be important in the decade of the 1920's. Allen ends his essay with such a paragraph because this selection is actually the introduction to a book called *Only Yesterday: An Informal History of the 1920's,* and Mr. Allen has written this essay to prepare the reader to feel how different 1919 was, not from today, but from the 1920's. This paragraph, then, serves as a transition between the introduction of his book and its main part, as the last sentence-paragraph of the selection—"The Post-war Decade lies before them"—shows.

19 / Atomic Engines[*]

RALPH E. LAPP

S O MANY FABLES have been told about the miraculous feats which atomic power will perform in driving ships, planes, and rockets that one may easily be led to the conclusion that Buck Rogers and his interplanetary space ships are but a stone's throw away. Even without journeying into space the rumors about atomic energy have persuaded many that it will not be long before gasoline filling stations will be obsolete; all one will have to do is to flip a uranium pellet in the gas tank and drive around the world.

A pellet of pure U-235 the size of a small marble has enough energy in it to drive a modern automobile 100,000 miles or four times around the earth. But no scientists have yet discovered any way of getting any power from just one ounce of uranium. A single ounce of silvery-white U-235 has locked up in it the heat of 30,000 gallons of gasoline but the motor for generating atomic power, unlike a gasoline engine which can run with only a cupful of gasoline in the tank, requires a full charge of uranium before it will operate at all. An atomic engine has the peculiarity that it will not start unless its "gas tank" is full to the brim. Furthermore, the atomic engine must have a full supply of its uranium fuel or it will not continue to operate once started.

In the internal combusion engine, such as a gasoline-powered automobile, power is produced by the expansion of hot gases in

* From *The New Force* by Ralph E. Lapp. Copyright 1953 by Ralph Eugene Lapp. Reprinted by permission of Harper & Brothers.

the piston chamber. These hot gases produced by the ignition of
a gasoline-air mixture push against the piston forcing it down and
thus turning the drive shaft of the engine. This power is then trans-
mitted to the rear wheels of the car by means of gears. Comparing
this power conversion with the atomic engine we note that the
power produced is also heat but it cannot be used as in an internal
combustion engine. The heat must be removed from the core of
the nuclear reactor by means of some coolant which circulates
through it; this liquid is heated and may then be passed through
what is called a heat exchanger. In the latter steam can be produced
and this can be used to drive a turbine which in turn may generate
electricity. From this brief description it should be evident that
much of atomic power engineering is conventional in scope and
pertains to heat exchanges, pumps, turbines, and generators. The
core of the nuclear reactor serves as an intense source of heat and
this heat once produced must be handled in much the same way
as in a coal-fired boiler.

Atomic engines, however, have some important differences as
compared with conventional engines. In the first place, the matter
of controlling the nuclear reactor and changing its power is not
achieved as in a gasoline engine by opening up the carburetor and
feeding more gas into the engine. Instead, the heat generated in the
reactor core is controlled by moving control rods in and out of the
structure. The rods are specially coated so that elements in them
act as a wet blanket for the chain reaction, that is, they absorb
neutrons in the reactor and determine the rate at which the chain
reaction proceeds. Withdrawing a control rod from the reactor
increases the power for there is less of the rod inside the pile and
consequently few neutrons are robbed from the chain reaction.
Pushing the control rod back into the machine serves to decrease
the power and when all the way in the control rod completely
stops the chain reaction.

Controls for atomic engines have to be made foolproof so that
there is no chance for the chain reaction to "run away" and lead
to a disaster. The design must be such that there are safety pre-
cautions built into the reactor which will prevent the machine

from getting out of control. Were the chain reaction to get out of 60
hand the power in the machine would increase quickly, much
faster than heat could be taken from the machine, and the materials inside the reactor would melt and the whole engine would be
ruined. No atomic bomb explosion would result but the contents
of the reactor core might be melted and spewed out, thus con- 65
stituting a severe radioactive hazard. Proper design of reactors and
installation of adequate controls should make atomic power plants
as reliable as any modern steam power plant and there should be
no trouble about locating them in metropolitan areas.

Probably the biggest problem which nuclear engineers face in 70
designing atomic engines is the radioactive hazard. Once a nuclear
reactor is assembled and started up its core becomes intensely
radioactive due to the accumulation of split atoms within the
uranium fuel. These fissioned atoms or fission products are very
radioactive and some of them persist in emitting penetrating radia- 75
tion for months and even years. This means that once a nuclear
reactor goes into operation and some component within the core
fails you can't shut down the plant and send in repair men to replace the defective part. As far as possible all machinery within
the core of the machine must be made to function without failure 80
or in the event of trouble means must be provided to replace the
part without the human hand touching it. The latter calls for
great ingenuity and for what amounts to Rube Goldberg gadgetry.

If you visit the coal-fired steam plant which supplies your electricity you can see the heart of the plant right before your eyes 85
and see coal fed into the flames. If, someday, you are allowed to
visit an Atomic Energy Commission site and see a nuclear reactor you will note a very big difference between the two kinds of
power plants. The heart of the atomic power plant always has to
be kept covered up with a thick shield to protect personnel from 90
the penetrating rays emitted by the materials within the reactor
core. Very often this shield consists of seven feet of solid concrete,
and it envelops the reactor on all sides. Not only does the heart of
the nuclear power plant have to be so shielded but anything which
passes through the core, such as the coolant, has to be similarly 95

protected. This means that the circulating pumps and the heat exchanger must also be shielded. It is this massive shield which makes an atomic engine for an automobile out of the question for it would probably run the weight of the atomic motor up to forty
100 tons.

On your visit to your city's steam plant you would notice that the ashes from the burned coal have to be removed and you might wonder if there are any atomic ashes in the case of an atomic engine. The ashes from the fission of uranium are the two atoms
105 into which the single uranium atom splits. We have already noted that they are a great nuisance because of their great radioactivity which persists for a long time so that even if the power plant is shut down the radioactivity lingers. In fact, these radioactive ashes also produce some heat and make it impossible to completely shut
110 down a power plant very quickly. Like coal ash, the atomic ash must be periodically removed for it constitutes a kind of poison for the chain reaction. Some of the split atoms have a tremendous appetite for neutrons and if left in the reactor very long they would reduce the power output of the machine. To remove atomic
115 ashes from a reactor is much more difficult and costly than shaking some grates and carting off a bucket of clinkers. The split atoms stay right in the fuel rod with the original uranium so that the whole fuel rod must be discharged from the reactor and new ones inserted.

120 The discharged fuel from an atomic power plant cannot be thrown away because it contains a large proportion of valuable fissionable material. It would be ideal if the fuel could be kept cooking in the reactor until all of the U-235 or plutonium were used up but long before this happens the rod deteriorates under
125 the ceaseless bombardment of nuclear particles inside the reactor. Therefore, the discharged fuel has to be chemically processed to remove the objectionable atomic ashes or poisons and to produce pure fissionable material for use in the reactor. Such chemical processing is time-consuming and costly for it involves intensely
130 radioactive material which must be handled with the utmost caution.

There is a vexing problem present to health authorities in dealing with the atomic ashes and waste radioactive chemical solutions
from an atomic power plant and its chemical processing plant.
These cannot be dumped into a river or buried in the earth. Were 135
the radioactive wastes emptied into a river they would prove a
source of danger to fish and to any human beings who drew their
water from the river. Burying the wastes in the earth, even at an iso-
lated spot, runs the risk that they might contaminate the ground
water. It must be remembered that for every pound of uranium 140
fissioned there will be almost a pound of fission products produced
and if atomic power comes into widespread use the amount of
radioactivity will be prodigious. The first step in solving the problem is to concentrate the radioactive solutions so that one has to
deal with a small amount of material. Then this can be encased in 145
leakproof containers which can either be buried at sea or buried in
a suitable remote area designated as an official radioactive burial
ground.

QUESTIONS

1. The basic plan of this essay is to enumerate the typical difficulties involved in using atomic power, but at the very beginning the
author commits himself to a complication of this method by setting
up what we might call a subplan for contrasting each item he enumerates for the atomic engine with the comparable item for a conventional engine. He prepares the way for this subplan in the first paragraph (lines 1–9); how?

2. Why does the author begin by drawing our attention to the
"fables" which have been told about the "miraculous feats" atomic
power will perform (line 1)?

3. What is the first difficulty involved in using atomic power which
Mr. Lapp considers?

4. Why is it particularly advantageous to him to compare the
atomic engine with the internal combustion engine of an automobile
at this point (lines 13–21)?

5. What is the second difficulty in using atomic power the author
mentions?

6. Point out how the atomic engine resembles the conventional engine and how it differs from the conventional engine in respect to this second difficulty (lines 21–40).

7. Mr. Lapp gets at his third point about the atomic engine by suggesting that in this respect it differs markedly from the conventional engine (lines 41–55). How does it differ?

8. Why is this third point particularly important?

9. The items Mr. Lapp is going to enumerate from paragraph six (line 70) on are all related by one characteristic which they have in common; what is that characteristic?

10. What characteristic of the atomic engine does Mr. Lapp get at by mentioning the "coal-fired steam plant" (line 84)?

11. Why does Mr. Lapp suddenly bring up the automobile in the last sentence of this paragraph (lines 97–100)?

12. The last three paragraphs of Mr. Lapp's essay (lines 101–148) have to do with his final item, ashes or waste product. But he divides his discussion of this one item into three paragraphs. Why? Can you state in a sentence the main subject of each of these three paragraphs?

SUGGESTED TOPICS

1. Write a paragraph in which you state clearly but without explanation the items Mr. Lapp enumerates in this essay about atomic engines.

2. Write a paragraph on the nature of "atomic ash."

3. Write a paragraph explaining the problems which will have to be solved before atomic automobile engines will be practical.

20/ Henry Ford: Success and Failure*

PETER F. DRUCKER

HENRY FORD'S hold on America's imagination—indeed on the imagination of the world's masses—was not due to his fabulous financial success. And it can only partly be explained by the overwhelming impact of the automobile on our way of life. For Henry Ford was less the symbol and em- 5 bodiment of new wealth and of the automobile age than the symbol and embodiment of our new industrial mass-production civilization.

He perfectly represented its success in technology and economics; he also perfectly represented its political failure so far, its 10 failure to build an industrial order, an industrial society. The central problem of our age is defined in the contrast between the functional grandeur of the River Rouge plant, with its spotless mechanical perfection, and the formlessness and tension of the social jungle that is Detroit. And the two together comprise Henry 15 Ford's legacy.

Both his success and his failure can be traced to his being thoroughly representative of that most native and most dominant of all American traditions, the one which in Populism found its major political expression. Indeed, Henry Ford was both the last Populist 20

and perhaps the greatest one. He owed all his basic convictions to Bryan: pacifism, isolationism, hatred of monopoly and of "Wall Street" and of "international bankers," firm belief in a sinister international conspiracy, and so forth. He also made true the great
25 dream of the political crusaders of 1896: that industrial production might be made to serve the common man. This dream had obsessed the American people since Brook Farm and Robert Owen's New Lanark, half a century before Bryan.

The Populists had believed that a Jeffersonian millennium would
30 result automatically from eliminating "monopoly" and the "money power" and the "satanic mills" of crude industrialism—as these terms were understood in the nineteenth century. Ford fulfilled the dream. He succeeded without benefit of monopoly, he defied the big bankers, he gave his factories a clean and airy efficiency which
35 would have delighted nineteenth-century reformers. But in fulfilling the dream he dispelled it. And in the place of the old enemies which he vanquished we have today, in the industrial system which Ford did so much to develop, new problems to face: the long-term depression, and the political and social problems of in-
40 dustrial citizenship in the big plant. Henry Ford's solution of the industrial problems with which the nineteenth century had wrestled unsuccessfully constituted his success, his achievement. His inability to solve the problems of the new industrial system, his inability to see even that there were such problems, was the meas-
45 ure of his final and tragic failure.

It may seem paradoxical to interpret Henry Ford's importance in terms of a concept—especially a political concept such as Populism. He himself had nothing but contempt for concepts and ideas, and prided himself on being neither a theoretician nor a politician
50 but a "practical man." And the main criticism which has been leveled against him and against everything he stood for—the criticism embodied in, for instance, Charlie Chaplin's "Modern Times"—has been that he made mechanical perfection an end in itself. But even his contribution to technology was not really a
55 technical but a conceptual one—superb production man and engineer though he was. For he invented nothing, no new tech-

nique, no new machine, not even a new gadget. What he supplied was *the idea of mass production itself*—organization of man, machines, and materials into one productive whole.

In economics too Ford discovered no new facts; the data showing the effect of volume production on costs had all been collected and analyzed. But Ford was the first manufacturer to understand that these data disproved the traditional theory that restricted production and a high profit margin—that is, monopoly—provided the most profitable form of industrial production. He demonstrated that one could raise wages, cut prices, produce in tremendous volume, and still make millions.

Above all Ford himself regarded his technical and economic achievements primarily as means to a social end. He had a definite political and social philosophy to which he adhered to the point of doctrinaire absurdity. Concern with the social effects of his actions determined every one of his steps and decisions throughout his entire life. It underlay the break with his early partners who wanted to produce a luxury car for the rich rather than follow Ford's harebrained idea of a cheap utility car for the masses. It motivated the radical wage policy of the early Ford who in 1914 fixed his minimum wage at the then utopian figure of $5.00 a day for unskilled labor. It showed in Ford's lifelong militant pacifism, of which the tragicomic Peace Ship episode of 1915–16 was only one manifestation. It showed in his isolationism, in his hostility to Wall Street, and in the raucous pamphleteering of the Dearborn *Independent* in the twenties. This social philosophy explains the millions he poured into "chemurgy" or into utopian village communities of self-sufficient, sturdy, yeoman farmers. It was responsible for his belief in decentralization, and for his nostalgic attempt to recreate the atmosphere of an earlier and simpler America in a museum community right next door to the River Rouge plant.

It might almost be said that Henry Ford's life work, despite these moves of his, brought about the opposite kind of world from the one he hoped for and believed in. Thus Ford, the pacifist, built up one of the world's greatest armament plants and helped to make possible the mechanized warfare of our age. Ford, the

isolationist, more than any other man has made it impossible for this country to stay out of international politics and international
95 wars: for he made this country the most powerful industrial nation on earth. Ford, the agrarian decentralist, left as his life's work the River Rouge plant, the most highly centralized and most completely mechanized concentration of industrial power in the world. The enemy of finance-capital and bank credit, he made installment
100 buying a national habit. An orthodox Jeffersonian, he has come to stand for the extreme application of the assembly-line principle, with its subordination of the individual to the machine. And the very workers at the Ford Motor Company whose mass production was to give economic security and full industrial citizenship to all,
105 are today organized in the most class-conscious union in America —and in a Communist-dominated local at that.

Yet it would be wrong to argue from the failure of Ford's social ideas that they never were anything but "eccentric hobbies," as the obituaries rather condescendingly called them. The tragic irony
110 with which his every move turned against him in the end does not alter the fact that his was the first, and so far the only, systematic attempt to solve the social and political problems of an industrial civilization. There is also little doubt that Ford himself believed—certainly until 1941 when the Ford workers voted for
115 the CIO, and perhaps even afterward—that he had actually found the answer for which the American people had been searching for almost a century: the realization of the Jeffersonian society of independent equals through industrial technology and economic abundance.

120 Nor was he alone in this appraisal of the meaning of his work. It was shared by the American people as a whole in the years immediately following the first World War—witness Wilson's urging in 1918 that Ford run for the Senate, and the powerful "Ford for President" boom of 1923. The view was also held abroad, espe-
125 cially in the Europe of the early twenties and in Lenin's Russia— perhaps even more generally there than here. Indeed, it was the performance of Henry Ford's America which in 1918 and 1919 gave substance to Wilson's promise of the millennium of peace,

democracy, and abundance, and which established America's moral
and political authority in those years. And the Ford spell remained 130
potent long after Wilson's promise had faded under the cold light
of the international realities of the nineteen-twenties.

QUESTIONS

This essay is a good example of how easy it is to complicate the
enumerative form. Mr. Drucker dazzles us by the brilliance with
which he carries off a very complicated version of this form; he has
undertaken to enumerate the main items of Henry Ford's achievement and, at the same time, to show that each was the product of a
single intellectual tradition, "the one which in Populism found its
major political expression" (lines 19–20), and that each helps to
demonstrate one or the other aspect of the dual meaning of Henry
Ford's career which makes him a "symbol . . . of our new . . .
mass-production civilization" (lines 5–8).

1. Paragraph two of Mr. Drucker's essay (lines 9–16) begins with
two sentences which use parallelism and which are also parallel with
one another. What Mr. Drucker wishes to say clearly makes this
parallelism the right form for these sentences; why does it?

2. What is Populism (line 19)? What was Bryan's (line 22) connection with it?

3. The fourth paragraph of Mr. Drucker's essay (lines 29–45) is
made up of three logically distinguishable parts. The first two make
a contrast; what is it? Has Mr. Drucker made this contrast before?
What does the third part of this paragraph do?

4. Why does Mr. Drucker assert at the beginning of the fifth paragraph (lines 46–59) that "it may seem paradoxical to interpret Henry
Ford's importance in terms of a concept" (lines 46–47)?

5. What reasons does he give for thinking it is nonetheless right
to interpret Ford's importance in terms of a concept?

6. Why does Mr. Drucker spread his account of these reasons
(lines 54–87) over three paragraphs?

7. What evidence does Mr. Drucker offer that Henry Ford adhered
to a political and social philosophy "to the point of absurdity" (lines
70–71)?

8. Why does Mr. Drucker say "—right next door to the River Rouge plant" (line 87)?

9. Why does the plan to which Mr. Drucker committed himself at the start logically require him to move on from his account of Ford's adherence to his political and social philosophy to a paragraph which shows that Ford's "life work . . . brought about the opposite kind of world from the one he hoped for and believed in" (lines 88–90)?

10. What part of Ford's activity helped to make a world of the opposite kind from the one he hoped for?

11. Why does Mr. Drucker make the last point in this paragraph (lines 102–106)?

12. The last two paragraphs of this selection suggest that, though the world Ford helped to create failed to satisfy his ideals and created problems that everyone must recognize as difficulties, it nonetheless seemed to many people in America and abroad that Ford had contributed to "the realization of the Jeffersonian society of independent equals" (lines 117–118). What has Mr. Drucker said about Ford in this essay which suggests that he thinks so too?

SUGGESTED TOPICS

1. Look up Populism in a good encyclopedia or book of American history and write an essay of two or three paragraphs in which you show, somewhat more extensively than Mr. Drucker does, that Henry Ford was a Populist.

2. Analyze the relation between the seventh and eighth paragraphs.

3. Using the evidence Mr. Drucker gives you, write an essay on "Henry Ford's Failure."

21 / No More Football for Us[*]

HUNTER GUTHRIE

UNFORTUNATELY for research scholars in sports history, the birth of football at Georgetown in 1874 is not so well recorded as its demise in 1951. GEORGETOWN QUITS FOOTBALL was a headline which attracted nation-wide attention. Had the university burned to the ground the headlines would have been no bolder. Had the college faculty abandoned its traditional Jesuit philosophy the headlines would have shrunk to polite newsprint on the educational page of the Sunday editions.

Football is important. We at Georgetown began to think it was too important. No chairman of any department in the college received a salary comparable to that of the graduate manager of athletics. No professor, with a Ph.D., a dozen books to his credit and an international reputation for scholarship, could hope for the opulent salary received by the head coach of football. In fact, only after years of toil could the professor approach the income bracket of one of the four assistant coaches.

What brought that about? The inexorable logic of the dollar. The student pays a relatively small fee to be educated. The spectator pays a relatively large fee to witness that small portion of the student's education known as football. The college finds itself in possession of something which can have an important economic value, if it jazzes up the spectator-appeal element and gives the game a little professional flavor.

[*] From "No More Football For Us," *The Saturday Evening Post,* October 13, 1951.

That lays the ground for another split in the college's person-
25 ality. For the coaching staff's objective is not the objective of the
school administrators. The latter are looking for students capable
of benefiting from higher education, boys who will become responsible businessmen, statesmen, professional men. I do not mean
the football coaches are opposed to those objectives. It is simply
30 that they have found from bitter experience that recruits of that
type do not fill up the guard and tackle spots four-deep on both
sides of the line. So, other objectives in recruiting boys who are
to play football are inevitable.

Football is an educational problem and an economic problem.
35 Educationally, in its present professionalized, spectator-appeal
form, it is indefensible. It has as much reason to subsist on the
campus of an educational institution as a night club or a macaroni
factory.

So my first reason for stopping football at Georgetown Uni-
40 versity boils down to this: intercollegiate football as it is played
today is a big business exploiting a small number of "students" for
the benefit of paying spectators. It forms no part of an honest
educational system; it offers the students of a liberal-arts college
no exercise, no training or recreation which could not be given
45 them in a dozen better ways. Since Georgetown was founded to
benefit students and not spectators, I find it fulfills that purpose
better by offering its students forms of exercise other than intercollegiate football.

Conscious of its responsibilities for leadership, Georgetown had
50 to face squarely the educational menace of football. Part of its
dollar was invested in football under the guise of public relations
and advertising. Was it wisely invested? The first jolt to our false
security came from a student poll. In September, 1950, we asked
5330 students their reasons for coming to Georgetown. Only sev-
55 enty-two listed athletics as either a primary or a secondary factor.

To the educator that gives joy. To the football investor that
gives pause. How many advertising dollars were we expending to
garner seventy-two students? For us that was the nub of this phase
of the problem, because first of all, we did not pretend to be a foot-

ball college, and secondly, advertising is good only in proportion ⁶⁰
to the results it obtains.

At this point, let us say about the end of October, 1950, the university treasurer was called into the picture. Could we have a break-
down of our football expenditures over a ten-year period? No report was ever made out more swiftly nor handed to me with quite ⁶⁵
the glint-in-eye manner that this one was.

I had always thought the treasurer liked football. He certainly
attended all the home games. "I pay for them, don't I?" he said.
"I might as well get something for my money."

I have always been a bit slow finding out which end is up on ⁷⁰
financial reports. Patiently the treasurer explained that in a ten-
year period—I believe the years ran from 1930 to 1940—we had
taken in $1,000,000 from generous spectators eager to see our stu-
dents perform their educational exercises. But in the same period
we spent $2,000,000 to put the show on the road. It dawned on ⁷⁵
me then that football in that decade had been costing Georgetown
$100,000 a year.

I shall give you the full details on where the football money
goes, but meanwhile, you may say that money isn't everything.
Aren't there other kinds of values in football? ⁸⁰

Well, let's approach it that way. Conceivably, three principal
groups can benefit from football. First, there is the student group.
They started the game. It was a good, clean sport, gave a workout
to their muscles, furnished a welcome relief to the tedium of the
classroom, got them outdoors in the beautiful fall months before ⁸⁵
winter closed in and exercise was confined to the gymnasium. They
chose up sides or formed a league according to hall and dormitory
groupings. The benefit of this type of football for the student is
undeniable, and any sane educator would champion it.

Years pass, and we find more people watching the game than ⁹⁰
playing it. This introduces the second group—the spectator. The
game is now played for him instead of the student. Where every
autumn weekday afternoon used to witness several games among
the students, now there is practice—day after day, for one game a
week on Saturday afternoon, when the customers are free to at- ⁹⁵

tend. There is practice in the afternoon, blackboard diagramming of plays and study of films in the long evenings. This goes on from September to the end of November. For no good reason at all it starts up again in spring, and in the football colleges continues
100 through summer for the star players—with appropriate monetary compensation. Perhaps soon the gap of the winter months will be bridged.

This, of course, is no longer sport. It is big business in neon lights. The spectators love it, but what about the bewildered students who
105 started it! They are no longer around. Well, that's not exactly correct. They are now spectators. They are admitted to the games at cut rates, probably some kind of royalty arrangement in begrudging acknowledgement of their original authorship.

But they aren't out there on the field. The average student who
110 would love to kick a football and throw a forward pass has as much chance of breaking into this big-time monstrosity as your favorite saddle horse would have against Citation in the Kentucky Derby. Big-time football is open only to a sort of guild of finely conditioned young men. They join the fraternity in their high-school
115 years, and then work their way up. They eat, sleep and live football.

And that brings us to the third group, the one that puts on the show—in other words, the college. It also brings us back to money. Either football makes money or it doesn't make money. If it makes money, you have a singularly potent argument against your con-
120 science, a grand financial report to show your trustees—everything, in fact, but the slight inconvenience of an occasional cocktail party for the athletic branch of the fourth estate.

I have already told you that things did not work out this way at Georgetown, that the books showed we had been losing an average
125 of about $100,000 a year. On digging further, I found that this was just part of the financial story. The $100,000 figure applied only to visible expenses. There were hidden expenses which did not show on the ledgers. When these were added, our annual losses amounted to far more than $100,000.

130 Let me give you the hard facts about the 1950 football season—our last one. First, the visible expenses, consisting of items like

salaries, travel, printing, equipment, uniform cleaning, mainte-
nance, hospital insurance. These amounted to a total of $147,-
810.84. And those were expenses in an economy year. The gross
budget allotment for all sports for 1950–51 had been slimmed to 135
the unprecedented sum of $173,209.93. From the graduate man-
ager to the groundkeeper we were economy-conscious. Players
made one orange serve for two. Coaches split up scouting trips.

The publicity man beat behind every available bush for paying
spectators, trying to interest them in the spectacle that they, in the 140
last analysis, had created. When it was all over, the treasurer found
that we had taken in only $44,123.97. The customers had disowned
their own flesh and blood.

So our visible deficit was $103,686.87. Now come the hidden
costs. At Georgetown last year we had eighty-one football "scholar- 145
ships." There are no more contradictory and/or cynical terms in
the vernacular. These "scholars" received from Georgetown free
tuition, free lodging, free board, free books, free laundry and free
incidental fees. If you want to know what that would mean in
terms of money—a good Merchant of Venice expression—paid into 150
the university by eighty-one nonfootball-playing scholars, the answer is $134,865 plus. I say "plus" because I have figured according
to the usual college fees, which amount to $1665 per man. Some of
our football "scholars" were in the School of Foreign Service,
where the annual fee comes to $1790 per man, but why quibble 155
over $125 or so?

Hence the patient and long-suffering treasurer, in figuring out
Georgetown's 1950 contribution to the carnival of football for
the American spectator and sports-page reader, would be justified
in totaling up the figure of $238,551.87. 160

Am I stretching things? Does it really cost $134,865 to put eighty-
one athletes through Georgetown? Can't we get a little reduction
on that surprising figure?

The opposite is the case. Let's try it out on an individual student.
The actual cost of educating, lodging and boarding a college stu- 165
dent at Georgetown University is $1585. For the athlete, however,
it runs even higher. You must add a laundry bill of eighty dollars

and another sixty-five dollars for books, bringing the total to $1730
per athlete. Multiply this new figure by eighty-one and we have
170 $140,130, which, added to the operational loss, revises the deficit
upward to $243,816.87.

Things are not improving, are they? Each time we dig we seem
to turn up another shovelful of expense. Nor does it help much to
say that in the off seasons we put our athletes to work. Their earn-
175 ing capacities were generally of the unskilled variety, somewhere
in the dollar-per-hour class. A generous survey informs me that the
athlete averaged fifty man-hours at his appointed tasks. Hence,
eighty-one football players saved the university $4050 in wages, and
so reduced the football deficit for 1950 to $239,766.87.

180   The extravagances of football have forced us to re-examine our
educational, institutional and social objectives. On no count could
we see any justification for big-time football. We acted accord-
ingly. Georgetown University, mother of Catholic education in the
United States, will be the better for it.

QUESTIONS

1. This selection illustrates the way an author may select items to
support an argument rather than items to explain something. Father
Guthrie's argument has two aspects, which are indicated by his first
statement of his argument: "Football is important. We at Georgetown began to think it was too important" (lines 9–10). The way it
was important and the way it was too important are suggested by line
34. Can you put in your own words what these ways are?

2. The opening section of this selection (lines 1–16) glances
quickly at some of the obvious evidence that the football tail was
wagging the college dog at Georgetown. Father Guthrie offers three
points which suggest to him that football was too important at Georgetown; what are they?

3. In the two paragraphs that follow (lines 17–33) Father Guthrie
outlines his explanation of the situation he has just described. What
is the basic point of this explanation? How does he support it?

4. In lines 34–38 Father Guthrie repeats his thesis; why does he
do so here?

5. Football is very unlike a night club or a macaroni factory (lines 37–38) in a good many respects. What is the point of comparing them here?

6. In the following paragraph (lines 39–48) Father Guthrie makes two points about intercollegiate football; identify these two points and relate them to the two aspects of his argument already stated in lines 9–10 and 34–38.

7. In lines 49–77 Father Guthrie discusses what he has several times called the big-business aspect of intercollegiate football. He first considers the reason Georgetown had given itself for investing money in intercollegiate football, and then the amount of money it had invested. Why does he take these points in this order?

8. For what purpose does Father Guthrie stop in the middle of his account of what the treasurer's financial report told him ("I shall give you the full detail on where the football money goes, but meanwhile . . ." lines 78–80)?

9. Father Guthrie undertakes to discuss three groups in the section that begins at line 81. What are these groups? How does he arrange his discussion of the first two?

10. What aspect of his main thesis (lines 9–10 and 34–38) has Father Guthrie in mind when he compares the cut-rate prices of student tickets to "some kind of royalty arrangement" (lines 106–108)?

11. In line 116 Father Guthrie comes to his third group, the college. This group, he says, "also brings us back to money" (line 117). It thus brings us back to the subject that was dropped at what earlier point in the selection?

12. What is "the fourth estate" (line 122), and what is the origin of that name?

13. The last section of this selection, beginning at line 123, gives us further details of the treasurer's financial report and then considers a number of what Father Guthrie calls "hidden expenses" (line 127); how does Father Guthrie make it clear to us that he plans to arrange his material in this way?

14. Why does Father Guthrie divide his summary of the financial report into two paragraphs (lines 130–143)?

15. Explain what Father Guthrie means by calling "football scholarships" a "contradictory and/or cynical" term (lines 145–146).

16. Father Guthrie's account of the details of the football deficit (lines 144–179) is logically divided into three parts, though, like

Frederick Lewis Allen, he uses "dramatic" paragraphing several times and thus tends to conceal this fact. Show the points at which the logical divisions come and describe the subject of each of these three parts.

17. In his conclusion, Father Guthrie says, "The extravagances of football have forced" this re-examination on Georgetown (line 180). Plainly he means financial extravagance, but does he mean some other kind of extravagance too? In answering this question, remember the thesis with which he began.

SUGGESTED TOPICS

1. You are probably not in a position to try to answer the financial argument against intercollegiate football which Father Guthrie gives, but he makes two other arguments which you are in a position to answer, that intercollegiate football is irrelevant to education and that intercollegiate football does not play the part in student life that athletic exercise should. Write an answer to one of these arguments.

2. It is possible to argue that Father Guthrie has not arranged the points in his essay in the clearest way possible. Write a paragraph which includes, in summary, his major points and arrange them in a clearer order than his.

3. Take one of the standard arguments in favor of "athletic scholarships" (for example, that they provide educations for boys who would not otherwise have educations) and write an answer to this argument of the kind you think Father Guthrie might make.

22 / An Argument against Abolishing Christianity*

JONATHAN SWIFT

I T MAY PERHAPS be neither safe nor prudent to argue against
the abolishing of Christianity, at a juncture when all parties
appear so unanimously determined upon the point, as we cannot
but allow from their actions, their discourses, and their writings.
However, I know not how, whether from the affectation of singu-   5
larity, or the perverseness of human nature, but so it unhappily falls
out that I cannot be entirely of this opinion. Nay, although I were
sure of an order issued for my immediate prosecution by the At-
torney-General, I should still confess that in the present posture
of our affairs at home or abroad, I do not yet see the absolute   10
necessity of extirpating the Christian religion from among us.

This perhaps may appear too great a paradox even for our wise
and paradoxical age to endure; therefore I shall handle it with all
tenderness, and with the utmost deference to that great and profound majority which is of another sentiment.   15

I freely own that all appearances are against me. The system of
the Gospel, after the fate of other systems is generally antiquated
and exploded; and the mass or body of the common people, among
whom it seems to have had its latest credit, are now grown as
much ashamed of it as their betters; opinions, like fashions, always 20

* From An Argument against Abolishing Christianity by Jonathan Swift.

descending from those of quality to the middle sort, and thence to the vulgar, where at length they are dropped and vanish.

But here I would not be mistaken, and must therefore be so bold as to borrow a distinction from the writers on the other side, when they make a difference between nominal and real Trinitarians. I hope no reader imagines me so weak to stand up in the defence of real Christianity, such as used in primitive times (if we may believe the authors of those ages) to have an influence upon men's belief and actions. To offer at the restoring of that would indeed be a wild project; it would be to dig up foundations; to destroy at one blow all the wit and half the learning of the kingdom; to break the entire frame and constitution of things; to ruin trade, extinguish arts and sciences with the professors of them; in short, to turn our courts, exchanges, and shops into deserts; and would be full as absurd as the proposal of Horace, where he advises the Romans all in a body to leave their city, and seek a new seat in some remote part of the world, by way of cure for the corruption of their manners.

Therefore I think this caution was in itself altogether unnecessary, (which I have inserted only to prevent all possibility of cavilling) since every candid reader will easily understand my discourse to be intended only in defense of nominal Christianity, the other having been for some time wholly laid aside by general consent, as utterly inconsistent with our present schemes of wealth and power. But why we should therefore cast off the name and title of Christians, although the general opinion and resolution be so violently for it, I confess I cannot (with submission) apprehend the consequence necessary.

One great advantage proposed by the abolishing of Christianity is that there are, by computation, in this kingdom above ten thousand parsons, whose revenues added to those of my lords the bishops, would suffice to maintain at least two hundred young gentlemen of wit and pleasure and free-thinking, enemies of priestcraft, narrow principles, pedantry, and prejudice, who might be an ornament to the Court and Town. And then again, so great a number of able (bodied) divines might be a recruit to our fleet and armies.

This indeed appears to be a consideration of some weight. But then, on the other side, several things deserve to be considered likewise: As, first, whether it may not be thought necessary that in certain tracts of country, like what we call parishes, there shall be one man at least of abilities to read and write. Then it seems a wrong computation, that the revenues of the Church throughout that island would be large enough to maintain two hundred young gentlemen, or even half that number, after the present refined way of living; that is, to allow each of them such a rent as, in the modern form of speech, would make them easy. But still there is in this project a greater mischief behind; and we ought to beware of the woman's folly, who killed the hen that every morning laid her a golden egg. For, pray what would become of the race of men in the next age, if we had nothing to trust to besides the scrofulous, consumptive productions furnished by our men of wit and pleasure, when, having squandered away their vigour, health and estates, they are forced by some disagreeable marriage to piece up their broken fortunes, and entail rottenness and politeness on their posterity? Now, here are ten thousand persons reduced by the wise regulations of Henry the Eighth to the necessity of a low diet, and moderate exercise, who are the only great restorers of our breed, without which the nation would in an age or two become one great hospital.

Another advantage proposed by the abolishing of Christianity is the clear gain of one day in seven, which is now entirely lost, and consequently the kingdom one seventh less considerable in trade, business, and pleasure; besides the loss to the public of so many stately structures now in the hands of the clergy, which might be converted into playhouses, exchanges, market-houses, common dormitories, and other public edifices.

I hope I shall be forgiven a hard word, if I call this a perfect *cavil*. I readily own there hath been an old custom time out of mind, for people to assemble in the churches every Sunday, and that shops are still frequently shut, in order, as it is conceived, to preserve the memory of that ancient practice, but how this can prove a hindrance to business or pleasure, is hard to imagine. What

if the men of pleasure are forced, one day in the week, to game
at home instead of the chocolate-houses? Are not the taverns and
95 the coffeehouses open? Can there be a more convenient season for
taking a dose of physic? Is not that the chief day for traders to
sum up the accounts of the week, and for lawyers to prepare their
briefs? But I would fain know how it can be pretended that the
churches are misapplied. Where are more appointments and
100 rendezvous of gallantry? Where more care to appear in the foremost box with greater advantage of dress? Where more meetings
for business? Where more bargains driven of all sorts? And where
so many conveniences or incitements to sleep?

QUESTIONS

1. This selection shows how a writer, if he is brilliant enough, may
use ironically the form we are considering in this section. Swift's argument against abolishing Christianity is a mock argument, for in it he
poses as one of the intellectually fashionable rationalists of his day
(he was in fact a priest of the established Anglican Church) and
then offers a rationalist argument in defense of nominal Christianity.
He does so for two main purposes: (1) to show that the rationalist
can be only a nominal Christian and that nominal Christians are not
Christians in any real sense; (2) to give himself the chance to invent
arguments in favor of abolishing Christianity for his imagined opponents which, though no one ever actually made them, are, he feels
convinced, the real feelings of most people who solemnly pretend to
be serious rationalists. Since this selection was written nearly 250
years ago (in 1711), we must, as always with old selections, be specially careful about its vocabulary. Be sure you know what Swift
meant by the following words and phrases: singularity, lines 5–6; exploded, line 18; project, line 30; professors, line 33; courts, line 34;
exchanges, line 34; cavilling, lines 40–41; candid, line 41; recruit,
line 56; scrofulous, line 70; entail, line 74; to game, line 93; chocolate-
houses, line 94; rendezvous of gallantry, line 100; foremost box, lines
100–101.

2. Swift begins (lines 1–4) by asserting that we have to allow that

all parties appear unanimously determined to abolish Christianity. Does he assert that all parties *say* Christianity ought to be abolished? Explain the mockery in this sentence.

3. Swift's second sentence (lines 5–7) offers an apology for his singularity or perverseness in not being able to agree with the majority. Remind yourself of what he is failing to agree to and then explain why this apology is also mocking.

4. Does Swift in fact believe that his position will seem "too great a paradox" (line 12) to his age? If not, why does he say so?

5. In the third paragraph (lines 16–22) Swift is apparently admitting that the only sensible argument seems to be against his position, but the argument he sums up in this paragraph depends on the assumption that "the system of the Gospel" is an opinion and that opinions are like fashions. Does Swift believe this argument? Explain your answer.

6. What kind of people believe they have exploded the system of the Gospel (lines 16–22)?

7. In the next paragraph (lines 23–38) Swift says he means to defend only nominal Christianity. How does this assertion fit logically into the argument for Christianity that Swift as a pretended rationalist is making?

8. How does what Swift has to say in support of his assertion that he is defending only nominal Christianity serve as an attack on the rationalistic Christians of his day? What is the point, in this connection, of the particulars given in lines 30–33?

9. In lines 29–34 Swift pretends to be offering an explanation of why it would be absurd "to stand up in defense of real Christianity" in his day. But what he is really doing here is attacking the sincerity of most of the people in his day who called themselves Christians. How is he doing that?

10. What does Swift's comparison of the London of his day with the Rome of Horace's (lines 33–38) suggest is his opinion of London?

11. In what sense does Swift really think Horace's proposal was "absurd"; in what sense does he think it was not absurd?

12. At the start of the next paragraph, at line 39, Swift tells us the reason he thinks most people of his day who say they are Christians are hypocrites; what is that reason? Does it make clear for us the reason Swift referred to "real Christianity" as something that existed only in "primitive times" (lines 27–29)? Why does Swift suggest in

lines 27–28 that it is only by reading authors who wrote in primitive times that we can discover the nature of real Christianity?

13. Having asserted that no one but a fool would suppose he is defending real Christianity, Swift goes on, with a fine show of logical care, to say that he does not see why giving up real Christianity necessitates our giving up "the name and title of Christians, although the general opinion and resolution be so violently for it" (lines 45–48). Very few people in Swift's time actually said they were in favor of giving up the name and title of Christians; what, then, are Swift's grounds for saying most people are "violently for it"?

14. Swift now takes up two arguments which he pretends people make for the abolishing of nominal Christianity. Since no one ever actually made the argument given in lines 49–56, what grounds has Swift for implying that many people believe it?

15. Discuss, in the light of both the argument Swift is pretending to make and the purpose he really has in mind, the list of characteristics he gives for the young gentlemen who might be supported by the revenues of the Church (lines 52–55).

16. Taking into account the usual method of recruiting for the British Fleet in the eighteenth century, comment on Swift's suggestion of what might be done with "divines" whose income would be given to young gentlemen (lines 55–56).

17. Why does Swift refer to "tracts of country, like what we call parishes" (line 60)?

18. What is Swift suggesting by offering as an argument against abolishing parsons the point that there ought to be at least one man in every parish who could read and write (lines 59–61)?

19. What is the implication of Swift's argument that, if the parsons are abolished, England will become one great hospital (lines 69–79)?

20. What were "the wise regulations of Henry the Eighth" (lines 75–76)?

21. Why, according to Swift, will the abolishment of Christianity not produce a "clear gain of one day in seven" (lines 80–81)? What conditions would have had to exist for it to do so?

22. In the last paragraph (lines 87–103) Swift offers the kind of arguments likely to appeal to the kind of man he is pretending to be. What do these arguments show that is of real importance to Swift?

SUGGESTED TOPICS

1. Write a paragraph in which you state as directly and succinctly as you can what you understand to be Swift's real opinions of the Christianity of his time.

2. Write a paragraph in which you state as directly and succinctly as you can the attitude of fashionable rationalists (deists) in Swift's time, as far as you can deduce this attitude from Swift's essay.

3. Write a paragraph on the conception of the habitual life of a young gentleman of wit and pleasure which is implied in Swift's essay.

ERIC SEVAREID

CARL BECKER

JAMES THURBER

H. L. MENCKEN

GWEN RAVERAT

F. SCOTT FITZGERALD

VLADIMIR NABOKOV

iv. Autobiography

23 / The Politics of an Undergraduate*

ERIC SEVAREID

WE TRIED to apply our general ideas about human society to the specific world of the university. I doubt if our families and the public ever realized the deadly earnestness of "campus politics" and the appalling amount of time and energy students put into its practice. As in most state universities the authorities encouraged a modicum of "student government" as a kind of harmless training, always making sure to retain final control themselves. Hitherto, the machinery of student elections to various organizations and the organizations themselves had been the special preserve of the permanent fraternities and sororities, whose real leaders were frequently found among senior students in the law school. A small group of these men usually controlled all nominations by the dominant "party," which was essentially conservative, never dreaming of seriously challenging the university authorities on any real issue. They parceled out the elective honors to the Greek houses as a reward for party loyalty, arbitrarily deciding the class officers, for example, and which girls would have the honors of which places in line for the "grand march" of the class proms and balls. The award of these prerogatives was cause

---

* Reprinted from *Not So Wild A Dream* by Eric Sevareid, by permission of Alfred A. Knopf, Inc. Copyright 1946 by Eric Sevareid.

171

20 for endless conniving, bitter animosities, and the most acute heartburning imaginable. The most successful exponent of campus politics in years was a law student named Harold Stassen, who had
been graduated two or three years previously and whose name was
still a byword for political skill. But the coming of the new aca-
25 demic era with its intense concern over economic reform, over the
issue of military preparedness and peace, edged our wooden swords
with steel, and the battle seemed very real indeed. The Greek
houses suddenly discovered that while they had been immersed in
such matters as the class proms, other students by some diabolical
30 and mysterious means had overreached them and were controlling
the really vital instruments—the daily newspaper, the literary review, the law review, the board of publications, the student coun-
cil, and so on. At the bottom of all this was the Jacobin Club,
formed by ten or twelve of us who were in general revolt against
35 things as they were. The Greek houses first learned of our organized existence when we were included with the regular fraternities
in the quarterly list of academic standings, and they found us at
the top of the list with a scholastic average higher than any fraternity had established in thirty years. We became suspect among
40 the conventional conformists and very quickly feared by the university administration. We very nearly succeeded—we thought—in
making student government truly that, and did succeed in abolishing compulsory military training, the most important issue of all.
In the midst of this campaign, the authorities were forced to throw
45 over all pretense of being disinterested advisors of student affairs
and clamped a censorship on the daily newspaper. They sent their
young stooges from the publications board down to our printery,
and the editorial column of the paper carried the heading: "These
editorials have been approved by the board of publications." Then
50 followed a series of mock essays on the joys of springtime, the desirability of sprinklers that would throw water in squares instead of
circles, and the like. The embarrassed president and the dean of
men gave up this form of control, and tried other means, including
personal intimidation; but it was too late. We had the Governor of
55 the state on our side, he controlled some appointments to the

board of regents, and sixty years of compulsory military training came to an end at that university.

This battle and many others went on, however, and the next year the editor of the paper also was a member of the Jacobin Club. I was to follow him, by right of seniority and general agreement, as editor in my senior year. But the habit of success had relaxed our vigilance. As the election to the editorship drew near, the authorities worked steadily behind us. They had found a weak spot in the wavering convictions of my fellow Jacobin, the incumbent editor. They turned his head with a great deal of flattering attention—the president would call him in for "advice" very frequently—and convinced him that it was his duty to stand again for election and for the good of the university prevent Sevareid from taking over the paper, even though this meant that the boy would have to change his life plan and enter the law school in order to remain on the campus. It was a miniature example of a recognizable political pattern: the liberal, softened by success and propinquity with the rich and powerful, renouncing his comrades in revolt "for the good of all." When we discovered that this lad was "doing a Ramsay MacDonald" on us, the fight became intense and bitter. My friends pleaded with the boy for hours at a time, warning him that his victory would turn to ashes because not only would he lose all his friends, but his sponsors would despise him as their tool. It was too late. The military officers, we found, had been working for months on two or three members of the publications board to prevent my election, and the president did something he had never stooped to before—he ordered his own faculty representative on the board to vote as he desired regardless of that gentleman's convictions. After all, he had to keep his job. In sum, the administration in its own behavior betrayed all the principles of political uprightness that it insisted we be taught in our classes. As I later learned from my friends, some of the men and women in the Greek houses, who saw their chance to begin breaking down the power of the Jacobins, deliberately spread a rumor that I needed the editor's salary because I was in trouble and "had to get married." (I was engaged to a girl in the law school, an influential nonconformist herself.) The ferocity and vindictiveness of the campaign reached unbelievable heights. In the election by the board I lost by one vote. Tammany methods, when thus applied, were unbeatable.

95   Loevinger, who was president of the publications board, broke the news to me in the law review office next morning, and I was stunned. I had worked three years for this position and honor, and by every rule was entitled to it. I had never hidden anything nor worked behind anyone's back. I had assumed the opposition felt as 100 we did: that controversy was controversy, that a man's opinions were his own, and that, however anyone opposed them, he did not resort to calumny nor twist the very lives of his friendly enemies. I was the naïve liberal, still feeling somehow that truth could defeat a Hitler. Dimly I began to perceive the realities of political life. I 105 was unable to speak and walked down the stairs. Sherman Dryer caught up with me, put his arm over my shoulder, and solemnly said: "This changes my whole philosophy."

When the news got out there was an uproar. Although I was doing my major studies in political science and not in the journalism 110 department, all the members of the journalism faculty protested the decision, and about twenty-five of the thirty or so students on the newspaper staff signed an objection. They offered to strike, to refuse to publish, but—still clinging to the liberal's characteristic belief that the persuasion of truth would somehow suffice—I re-115 fused this drastic move. A second election was forced, but after an exhausting all-night battle, the board confirmed its vote and we gave up. I became a minor hero and martyr; my opponent was expelled from the Jacobin Club, formally censured for "conduct unbecoming a gentleman" by the journalistic honorary society of 120 which I was president, and continued as editor, a friendless, lonely boy. The pattern of power politics was carried out to its final orthodox step: I was called into the dean's office and with much flattery informed I had been chosen for membership in the senior honor society. This corresponded to a knighthood for an influential but 125 defeated opponent of the ruling system, which uses the glamorous apparatus of royal orders as a political weapon.

After that I buried myself in my books, earning bread and board by rising at five each morning and working in the university post office before classes, handling and distributing bundles of the newspaper which I had cherished and lost. It was many months before 130 the pangs of bitterness left me. I had one last fling. Every four years the students staged a mock political convention, of all parties instead of one, to nominate their choice for the presidency of the United States. As comic relief, I made a nominating speech for one Bernarr MacFadden, elderly exponent of vitamins and setting- 135 up exercises, at that time (1936) seriously trying to get the Republican nomination. I hired a bugler, a girl acrobatic dancer with a fulsome bust, and a football hero with sizable biceps, and paraded with them to the stand carrying a banner that depicted a muscular arm wielding a dumbbell. The speech began: "Fellow 140 Americans, are we men or mice?" and argued the need for a Strong Man in the White House. I was making a sarcastic attack on the preparedness program and warned with mock rhetoric of the imminent danger of the Japanese "invading the California coast in bathing suits." The mass of students in the field house screamed their 145 delight. Sherman, with glittering eye, made an impassioned attack on Governor Landon, "who would sacrifice the youth of the land on the altar of the balanced budget." We nominated Floyd B. Olson. The downtown political writers complimented us on our oratorical mastery and wondered in print why this level of plat- 150 form brilliance was unattained in state politics.

With this speech, with this message to my fellow students, I ended my university career. It was one year before the battle of Shanghai, two years before the *Anschluss*.

COMMENTARY

THIS IS A SELECTION from Eric Sevareid's autobiographical book, *Not So Wild a Dream*. It is an account of his undergraduate years during the middle 1930's. But this account does not exist for its own sake; we are not being told everything about young Sevareid that Mr. Sevareid remembers. The author has a subject other than himself for which his experience serves as an illustration. This subject is politics.

Moreover, he has a thesis or judgment about politics to offer us, at least by implication. Thus he wants to talk about his undergraduate experience only insofar as that experience is relevant to politics, and he wants to make us see how his undergraduate political experience suggests a particular conception of the nature of politics. These two purposes give him a standard for selecting from the mass of information he has about himself and a means for determining what aspect of the selected episodes he will emphasize.

Just how firmly he sticks to his subject and how drastically he eliminates anything that is not relevant to it may be measured by the fact that, though he was engaged during his undergraduate years and this engagement must have been a very important part of his undergraduate experience in general, he mentions it here only in a parenthesis, and only then because his subject logically requires him to tell us that his political opponents attacked him by spreading a rumor that he "was in trouble and 'had to get married' " (lines 86–91). The care with which he bears in mind the need to present his experience in such a way as to show us what he feels is its true meaning may be measured by the frequency with which his discussion comes back to two related —indeed, complementary—points, the point that in a crisis his opponents regularly resorted to an unscrupulous use of force and "betrayed all the principles of political uprightness that . . . [we were] taught in our classes" (lines 85–86), and the point that "I was the naïve liberal, still feeling somehow that truth could defeat a Hitler" (lines 102–104). The repetition of these two related judgments and the care Mr. Sevareid takes to state them so that they suggest we should apply them, not simply to his university experience, but to all political experience, is summed up in the generalization he makes about the first skirmish in his political battle, when the administration succeeded in winning over the editor of the university newspaper: "It was a miniature example of a recognizable political pattern" (lines 71–72).

Given this subject and this thesis about it, Mr. Sevareid saw that he would do well to focus our attention, somewhat in the manner of a classical dramatist, on the most important and the most revealing political battle of his undergraduate experience, the battle over the election of the editor of the newspaper; to this battle he subordinated the rest of his undergraduate political experience. You will notice that he is particularly careful to make the major political victory won by him and his friends—the abolishment of compulsory military training—a mere prelude (for them, a deceptive and weakening prelude) to the main battle (lines 41–57). It is perhaps slightly unfortunate—but this kind of misfortune is common when a writer is dealing with the stubborn facts of life instead of the invented details of fiction—that the final experience of his undergraduate political career, the mock political convention, is trivial in comparison to the main experience; it makes the end of his story a little anti-climactic, a consequence he tries to make up for by the powerful irony of the final paragraph (lines 152–154).

Like a good classical dramatist, too, Mr. Sevareid divides his story into five parts, or "acts," and an epilogue. The first act (lines 1–24) sets the scene and provides us with the information about the situation that we must have to understand the events to follow (this is what the theater calls "exposition"). The second act (lines 24–57) shows us how what Hamlet calls "the mighty opposites" of the drama acquire their power and take up their opposing positions. In the third act (lines 58–107), the battle is joined and reaches its first climax in Sevareid's defeat. In the fourth act (lines 108–126)—almost always a short one as here—this defeat is made final. The fifth act (lines 127–151) shows the hero adjusting himself again to ordinary life in the light of the new understanding he has acquired from his defeat. This final act is followed by a brief epilogue (lines 152–154) which drives home with great power what Mr. Sevareid has been suggesting all through his drama, that his undergraduate political experience, however insignificant in itself, was a real part of the larger political experience of his time and, in all of its main characteristics, "a miniature example" of that larger political experience. So great is the care with which Mr. Sevareid holds to the logic of his subject and his thesis in planning the structure of this selection that we could, if we wished, divide these "acts" into "scenes" (for example, the paragraph break at line 95 indicates a division of act three into two scenes), but this discussion of the structure of the selection has probably gone far enough to show how carefully and how logically it was planned. We must now consider some of the ways in which he uses the details of his experience to carry out the two purposes he has set himself here.

We are now ready, for instance, to see how purposeful the opening sentence of this selection is: "We tried to apply our *general* ideas about *human society* to the *specific world* of the *university"* (lines 1–2). Here at the very beginning of the selection is a clear indication of everything Mr. Sevareid plans to do in it, an indication that the specific world of the university is both a part and a miniature example of human society in general and that, in applying to it their general ideas, Sevareid and his fellow students will learn how wrong they were to believe that truth alone, unaided by force, "could defeat a Hitler"; and how wrong they also were to think that those who control the sources of force, either in the specific world of the university or in human society in general, "felt as we did . . . that . . . [one] did not resort to calumny nor twist the very lives of his friendly enemies" (lines 99–102).

The test of the integrity of a writer with a thesis is whether he can sum up the situation he is dealing with in a way that will be as acceptable to those who do not agree with his thesis as to those who do; Mr. Sevareid meets this test admirably, since a fair-minded member of the administration of the university or of a fraternity would probably say almost exactly the same things about "student government" that Mr. Sevareid does (in lines 1–24) (he would of course make a different judgment of their value). Mr. Sevareid does not achieve this result by resorting to some lifeless kind of "objectivity"; what he does is to keep very clear the distinction between what is, and what he feels about it. It is Mr. Sevareid's conviction that makes him say, in line 14, "never *dreaming* of *seriously* challenging the university authorities" and, in lines 16–17, *"arbitrarily* deciding the class officers." His opponents would use different words at these points because they would evaluate these actions differently. But they would probably not disagree with Mr. Sevareid that these actions were carried out. Notice also how Mr. Sevareid rounds off this "act" by referring again to the point with which he began—to the "endless conniving, bitter animosities, and . . . acute heartburning" of campus politics (lines 20–21); this is the point with which he began this section in lines 2–4: "I doubt if our families and the public ever realized the *deadly earnestness* of 'campus politics.' . . ."

In the second section of the selection, Mr. Sevareid begins with mild amusement at both his opponents and himself: "by some diabolical and mysterious means" (line 29) is a mild parody of the way the Greek houses would have described the Jacobin Club's method of achieving power; "in general revolt against things as they were" (lines

34–35) is a mild parody of the Jacobin Club's "revolutionary" prin-ciples. (Can you, incidentally, explain the name of this club?) But in the second part of this section, beginning at line 39, his tone becomes more serious. Notice that as Mr. Sevareid begins to describe the first moves in the battle he is careful to identify the two opponents, "the conventional conformists" (the Greek houses) and "the university administration" (lines 39–41). The first move (lines 41–57) is made entirely by the university administration, and the Jacobin Club defeats the administration—because, as Mr. Sevareid notes without hammer-ing the point home, the Club accidentally had real force behind it in the Governor (lines 54–57). It drove compulsory military train-ing off the campus—a year or two before the battle of Shanghai and the *Anschluss* (lines 153–154). (Make sure you know enough about these events to understand their significance in this context.)

In the third section of the selection, we come to the climax, the election to the editorship of the student newspaper. Notice that in dealing with the first move in the attack on the Jacobin Club's control of the paper, the administration's successful attempt to turn the in-cumbent editor's head, Mr. Sevareid is interested in two things, the way the actual political maneuver was worked (lines 65–71), and the exact way it represented a political pattern of society in general (lines 71–75). (Do you understand why the Jacobin Club called the incum-bent editor's conduct "doing a Ramsay MacDonald"?) We now hear in rapid succession the other moves of the Jacobin Club's opponents; they come upon us as rapidly as they must have come upon the Jac-obin Club itself. Notice that the account of these moves is divided according to the division of his opponents that Mr. Sevareid estab-lished at the beginning, the division into university administration and Greek houses (lines 39–41). Thus we are told here, first the things the administration did (lines 79–86) and then what the Greek houses did (lines 86–91). Again, Mr. Sevareid is interested in the political de-vices and in the way they were used—the application of flattery and of intimidation by the administration where they would work best, the use of scurrilous lies by some members of the Greek houses in an underhanded way which made them unanswerable. Again, he is in-terested in the way this campus situation represents the situation in society at large (lines 83–86): "Tammany methods, when thus ap-plied, were unbeatable" (lines 93–94).

Thus the real, inner climax of this central episode is the paragraph beginning at line 95. By all the rules that young Sevareid, a naïve liberal, understood, he was entitled to the editorship; and he had not got it. "Dimly I began to perceive the realities of political life" (line 104); as with his friend Dryer, this relatively insignificant campus experience initiated a change in his whole political philosophy (lines 105–107).

The fourth section (lines 108–126) describes the counter-attack mounted by the Jacobin Club and its friends and the way Sevareid frustrated it by "still clinging to the liberal's characteristic belief" (lines 113–114). It is, for Mr. Sevareid's purpose, a fine illustration of "the pattern of power politics" (line 121) that he was even made a member of the senior honor society. The final section (lines 127–151) describes Sevareid's "last fling" (line 131). The heart of this fling was an attack on the preparedness program (lines 142–145)— just as the beginning of his career in campus politics had been an attack on compulsory military training—and he argued that preparedness against Japan was particularly absurd. It is a very pretty closing illustration of Mr. Sevareid's thesis. Young Sevareid's liberalism was admirable; his assumption that his enemies, and his country's enemies, were honorable was gallant. But the historical truth was that, only a year after Sevareid made his attack on the preparedness program, the Japanese began the war which would reach its climax at Pearl Harbor and find Sevareid's country seriously unprepared. It is these implications of the fifth section of this selection which allow Mr. Sevareid to close with the apt and powerful conclusion of lines 152–154.

24 / Freedom and Responsibility*

CARL BECKER

MY FIRST CONTACT with the Cornell tradition occurred in December 1916, at the meeting of the American Historical Association at Cincinnati, where Professor Charles
Hull invited me to come to his room in the hotel to meet his colleagues of the history group. Intimations had reached me that I 5
was, as the saying is, being considered at Cornell for a position in
European history, so that I was rather expecting to be offered a
job, at a certain salary, on condition that I should teach a certain
number of courses, assume certain administrative duties, and the
like. I took it for granted that Cornell would handle these matters 10
in the same businesslike way that other universities did. But I
found that Professor Hull had a manner and a method all his own.
He did not offer me a job—nothing as crude as that; he invited me,
on behalf of his colleagues, to join the faculty of Cornell University. The difference may be subtle, but I found it appreciable. On 15
the chance that I might have formed a too favorable opinion of
Cornell, Professor Hull hastened to set me right by itemizing, in
great detail, the disadvantages which, from a disinterested point of
view, there might be in being associated with the institution, as
well as, more doubtfully, certain possible advantages. Among the 20
disadvantages, according to Professor Hull, was the salary; but he

* From *Cornell University: Founders & The Founding.* Reprinted by permission of the Cornell University Press.

181

mentioned, somewhat apologetically, a certain sum which I could surely count on, and intimated that more might be forthcoming if my decision really depended upon it. By and large, from Professor
25 Hull's elaborate accounting, I gathered that Cornell, as an educational institution, was well over in the red, but that, such as it was, with all its sins of omission heavy upon it, it would be highly honored if I could so far condescend to its needs as to associate myself with it.

30   There, apparently, so far as Professor Hull was concerned, the matter rested. Nothing was said of courses to be taught, minimum hours of instruction, or the like mundane matters. In the end I had to inquire what the home work would be—how many hours and what courses I would be required to teach. Professor Hull seemed
35 mildly surprised at the question. "Why," he said, "I don't know that anything is *required* exactly. It has been customary for the Professor of Modern History to give to the undergraduates a general survey course in modern history, and sometimes if he deems it advisable, a more advanced course in some part of it in which he is
40 especially interested, and in addition to supervise, to whatever extent may seem to him desirable, the work of such graduate students as may come to him. We had rather hoped that you would be disposed to do something of this sort, but I don't know that I can say that anything specific in the way of courses is really *required*. We
45 have assumed that whatever you found convenient and profitable to do would be sufficiently advantageous to the university and satisfactory to the students." Well, there it was. Such a magnification of the professor, such a depreciation of the university, had never before, in similar circumstances, come my way. After a de-
50 cent interval I condescended to join the faculty of Cornell University. And why not? To receive a good salary for doing as I pleased—what could be better? The very chance I had been looking for all my life.

And so in the summer of 1917 I came to Cornell, prepared to do
55 as I pleased, wondering what the catch was, supposing that Professor Hull's amiable attitude must be either an eccentric form of ironic understatement or else a super-subtle species of bargaining

technique. Anyway I proposed to try it out. I began to do as I pleased, expecting some one would stop me. No one did. I went on and on and still no one paid any attention. Personally I was cordially received, but officially no one made any plans to entertain me, to give me the right steer, to tell me what I would perhaps find it wise to do or refrain from doing. Professor Hull's attitude did seem after all to represent, in some idealized fashion, the attitude of Cornell University. There was about the place a refreshing sense of liberation from the prescribed and the insistent, an atmosphere of casual urbanity, a sense of leisurely activity going on, with time enough to admire the view, and another day coming. No one seemed to be in a hurry, except Mr. Burr, of course, and sometimes perhaps Mr. Ranum. But that was their affair—a response, no doubt, to the compulsion of some inner daemon. At least I saw no indication that deans or heads of departments were exerting pressure or pushing any one around. Certainly no head of the history department was incommoding me, for the simple reason, if for no other, that there didn't seem to be any history department, much less a head. There were seven professors of history, and when we met we called ourselves the "History Group," but no one of us had any more authority than any other. On these occasions Professor Hull presided, for no reason I could discover except that we met in his office because it was the largest and most convenient. Whatever the History Group was it was not a department. If there was any department of history, then there were six; in which case I was the sole member, and presumably the head, of the department of Modern European History. The only evidence of this was that twice a year I received a communication from the president: one requesting me to prepare the budget, which consisted chiefly in setting down the amount of my own salary, an item which the president presumably already knew more about than I did; the other a request for a list of the courses given and the number of students, male and female, enrolled during the year. I always supposed, therefore, that there were six departments of history, each manned by one professor, except the department of American history, which ran to the extraordinary number of two. I always sup-

posed so, that is, until one day Professor Hull said he wasn't sure
95 there were, officially speaking, any departments of history at all;
the only thing he was sure of was that there were seven professors
of history. The inner truth of the matter I never discovered. But
the seven professors were certainly members of the Faculty of
Arts, the Graduate Faculty, and the University Faculty since they
100 were often present at the meetings of these faculties. They were
also, I think, members of the Faculty of Political Science, a body
that seemed to have no corporeal existence since it never met, but
that nevertheless seemed to be something—a rumor, perhaps, a dis-
embodied tradition or vestigial remainder never seen, but lurking
105 about somewhere in the more obscure recesses of Goldwin Smith
Hall. I never had the courage to ask Professor Hull about the university—about its corporate administrative existence, I mean—for
fear he might say that he wasn't sure it had any: it was on the
cards that the university might turn out to be nothing more than
110 forty or fifty professors.

QUESTIONS

1. This selection is ostensibly a fragment of Becker's autobiography
in which he describes how he was hired by Cornell and how he began
his career there. But its real purpose is to describe what Professor
Becker feels is an essential characteristic of Cornell and to contrast
it (at least by implication) with other universities. He does these
things partly by enumeration and partly by implied comparison and
contrast. For instance, he is making a contrast in the first paragraph
when he tells us what he had expected when he went to the meeting
with Professor Hull and his colleagues (lines 7–12); what made him
expect these things?

2. What makes Becker surprised and amused that Professor Hull is
afraid he may "have formed a too favorable opinion of Cornell"
(lines 16–17)?

3. Why does it seem odd to Becker that Professor Hull "intimated
that more might be forthcoming if [his] decision really depended upon
it" (lines 23–24)? Why did this make Becker admire Cornell?

4. What is the point of Becker's elaborate way of describing the job offer (lines 27–29)?

5. In the paragraph beginning at line 30, Becker deals with his duties as a teacher at Cornell; this paragraph, too, uses an implied comparison. What is it?

6. Professor Hull's speech about the duties of the Professor of Modern History (lines 35–47) begins with "I don't know that anything is *required* exactly." Point out the phrases in the rest of the speech in which he is making it clear that nothing is "required."

7. Becker is of course aware that, in offering him "a good salary for doing as [he] pleased," Professor Hull is not simply mad but has some conception of what constitutes the best relation between a professor and a university. What is Professor Hull's conception?

8. Why does Becker say, "I condescended to join the faculty of Cornell University" (line 50)?

9. Lines 51–53 might be taken to mean that if we give a man a chance to do as he pleases he will do nothing useful; is that what they do mean? Explain your answer.

10. What would have been likely to make Becker think that there was a catch (line 55)?

11. Under what conditions would some one have told him the sort of things he mentions in lines 61–63?

12. What has Becker got in the back of his mind that makes the nature of the Cornell history "department" seem comic to him (lines 73–97)?

13. Does Becker make jokes about the incorporeality of the Faculty of Political Science (lines 100–106) and the "corporate administrative existence" of the university (lines 107–110) because he thinks it a bad thing for them to be incorporeal? If not, what is good about it?

SUGGESTED TOPICS

1. Becker was a very distinguished professor of history; write a paragraph in which you explain what he would have thought Cornell did to help him become so.

2. Take one of the passages in which Becker is apparently simply talking about himself and show how it contributes to his description

of what Cornell was like. Useful passages for this purpose are lines 49–53, 54–60, 106–108.

3. Becker's attitude toward Cornell throughout this selection is a kind of affectionate irony. Select a few passages where he shows this attitude clearly and explain, by analyzing them, why he takes this attitude.

25 / The Gentleman is Cold*

JAMES THURBER

IN THE FIRST chill days of November it was the subject of
sharp and rather nasty comment on the part of my friends and
colleagues that I went about the draughty streets of town without
a hat or overcoat. Once even a stranger who passed me in the street
snarled, "Put on your hat and coat!" It seemed to annoy people. ₅
They began to insinuate under their breath, and even come right
out and say, that I was simply trying to look strange and different
in order to attract attention. This accusation was made with increasing bitterness when my hair, which I always forgot to have
cut, began to get very long. It was obvious, my friends said, that I ₁₀
walked about the city cold and miserable in the hope that people
would nudge their companions and say, "There goes Jacob Thurman, the eccentric essayist."

There was, and is, no basis to these charges at all. I have reasons,
and good reasons, for not wanting to, for, in fact, not being able to, ₁₅
wear an overcoat. I have just as good reasons about the hat, but I
needn't go into them so fully. A week or so ago, however, the
smirking remarks and mean innuendoes of my associates forced me
one day to put on my overcoat (I couldn't find my hat and I
wouldn't buy a new one, because when I try one on and peer into ₂₀
the triplicate mirrors they have in hat shops, I catch unexpected
angles of my face which make me look like a slightly ill professor of

* From *The Middle-Aged Man on the Flying Trapeze* by James Thurber. Permission the author, © 1935 The New Yorker Magazine, Inc.

187

botany who is also lost). The overcoat, which I bought in 1930, after a brief and losing battle with a sharp-tongued clerk who was
25 taller than I am, does not fit me very well and never did fit me very well. That's one reason I don't like to wear it. Another is that it has no buttons (it didn't have any buttons after the first week) and is extremely difficult to manage in a head wind. In such a wind I used to grab for my hat with both hands, thus letting go the hold
30 I had on my coat to keep it together in front, and the whole thing would belly out all around me. Once, grabbing for my hat (and missing it, for I was a fraction of a second too late), I knocked my glasses off and was not only caught in a grotesque swirl of overcoat right at the corner of Fifth Avenue and Forty-fourth Street but
35 couldn't see a thing. Several people stopped and watched the struggle without offering to help until finally, when everybody had had his laugh, a woman picked up my glasses and handed them to me. "Here's your glasses," she tittered, grinning at me as if I were a policeman's horse with a sunbonnet. I put the glasses on, gathered
40 the coat together, and walked off with as much dignity as I could, leaving my hat swirling along the street under the wheels of traffic.

It was the twentieth of November this winter that I finally put on my overcoat for the first time. It is a heavy gray one, and looks a little like a dog bed because the strap on the inside of the collar
45 broke and the coat had been lying on the floor of my closet for almost a year. I carried it downstairs from my hotel room to the lobby, and didn't start to put it on until I had reached the revolving doors leading to the street. I had just got one arm into the sleeve when I was suddenly grabbed from behind, a hand shot up
50 under the coat, jerked my undercoat sharply down, and I fell backward, choking, into the arms of the hotel doorman, who had come to my assistance. He is a powerfully built man who brooks no denial of, or interference with, his little attentions and services. He didn't exactly throw me, but I took a pretty bad tossing around.
55 From the hotel, I went, in a badly disturbed state of mind, to my barber's, and I was just reaching into a pocket of the overcoat for my cigarettes and matches when the coat was whisked off me from behind. This was done with great firmness but no skill by the col-

ored porter and bootblack who sneaks up behind people at Joe's
barbershop and tears their coats off their backs. This porter is not 60
so powerfully built as the doorman at my hotel, but he is sinewy
and in excellent condition. Furthermore, he is not wearing an overcoat himself, and the man who *is* wearing an overcoat is at a great
disadvantage in a struggle. This porter is also a coat-tugger, be-
longing to that school of coat-tuggers who reach up under your 65
overcoat after they have helped you on with it and jerk the back
of your suit jacket so savagely that the collar of the jacket is pulled
away from its proper set around the shoulders and makes you feel
loutish and miserable. There is nothing to do about this except
give the man a dime. 70

It wasn't, however, until I went with some fine acquaintances of
mine to an excellent restaurant that night that I got into my old
familiar plight with the ripped lining of the left sleeve. After din-
ing, the gentlemen in the party were helped on with their coats by
one of those slim, silent waiters with the cold and fishy eye of an 75
art critic. He got me adroitly into the right sleeve of my overcoat,
and then I stuck my left arm smoothly into the lining of the other
sleeve. Running an arm into the ripped lining of an overcoat while
people, both acquaintances and strangers, look on and the eye of
the struggling waiter gets colder and colder, is one of the most hu- 80
miliating experiences known to the American male. After it was finally straightened out and I got my arm through the sleeve, I
couldn't find any money for the tip; I couldn't even find a dime. I
don't like to dwell on that incident.

After leaving the restaurant, we went to a theatre, and there an- 85
other reason I do not like to wear an overcoat and never will wear
an overcoat again reared its terrifying head. In taking off my overcoat to hand it to the unsympathetic hat-check boy, I took off with
it the jacket to my dinner clothes and was left standing in the
crowded and well-dressed lounge in my shirt sleeves, with a section 90
of my suspenders plainly visible through the armhole of my waist-
coat. So speedily do hat-check boys work that my overcoat and
jacket had been whisked to the back of the hat-check room and
hung up under a couple of other overcoats before I could do any-

95 thing about it. The eight or ten seconds that went by before I recovered my dinner jacket were among the worst moments of my life. The only worse experience I can think of was the time my suitcase flopped open on the Madison Avenue car tracks when I was hurrying to make a train at Grand Central.

100 I tried to pass off the episode of the dinner jacket nonchalantly, but succeeded only in lapsing into that red-faced fixed grin which no truly well-poised man-about-town ever permits himself to lapse into. I reached for my cigarettes, but I found that I had left them in a pocket of my overcoat, so in order to have something to do 105 with my hands—for people were still staring and leering—I gracefully pulled a neatly folded handkerchief from the breast pocket of my dinner jacket, only to discover when I shook it out that it was a clean white silk sock. The last time I had dressed for dinner, I had been unable to find a fresh handkerchief, and after considerable ef-110 fort had finally folded the sock and tucked it into the pocket of my jacket in such a way that it looked like a handkerchief. Of course, on that occasion, I had remembered not to pull the handkerchief out. I had remembered this by grimly repeating it to myself all evening, but that had been several nights before and I had completely 115 forgotten about the sock.

I would never have brought out all these humiliating revelations had it not been for the fact that even those persons who know me best, for a modest, unassuming man, had really come to believe that I went around town without an overcoat in order to make the 120 same kind of impression that Oscar Wilde made with his sunflower or Sean O'Casey with his brown sweater. I simply want to be mentally at ease, and I have found out after years of experience that I cannot be mentally at ease and at the same time wear an overcoat. Going without an overcoat in bitter weather has, God 125 knows, its special humiliations, but having a kindly old lady come up to me on the street and hand me a dime is nothing compared to the horrors I went through when I wore an overcoat, or tried to wear one.

QUESTIONS

1. The main part of this selection consists of three episodes in Mr. Thurber's life, all of which took place on the same day. What are they, and what section of the essay does each occupy?

2. Because Mr. Thurber is recounting these episodes in his life for a particular purpose, he begins with an introductory section in which he explains that purpose. Why does he divide this introduction into two paragraphs? What method of explanation is he using in this introduction?

3. Like all Mr. Thurber's work, the first paragraph (lines 1–13) is very carefully constructed and very skillfully phrased. The arrangement of its ideas is particularly interesting. One might start a summary of them somewhat as follows: Friends commented very nastily on my not wearing a hat and coat; once even a stranger spoke to me about it; it seemed, in fact, to annoy everyone, and as a result, people began to insinuate. . . . Continue this summary to the end of the paragraph.

4. What leads Mr. Thurber to say the stranger "snarled" (line 5); what leads him to make the people his friends imagine say, "There goes *Jacob Thurman*" (lines 12–13); what makes him describe his associates' remarks as "smirking" and "mean" (line 18)?

5. Paragraph two (lines 14–41) has two purposes, to eliminate the hat from the discussion and to indicate some of the defects of the coat. At what point does the paragraph shift from one point to the other?

6. Why does Mr. Thurber say, in explaining why he does not buy a new hat, that triplicate mirrors make him look "like a slightly ill professor of botany who is also lost" (lines 22–23)? Clearly this joke does not depend on any literal resemblance; explain what it does depend on.

7. Describe the human characteristics, not usually taken account of in manuals of salesmanship, which operated when Mr. Thurber bought his overcoat (lines 23–25).

8. Explain why Mr. Thurber says his coat is "difficult to manage *in a head wind*" (line 28), instead of simply on a windy day?

9. To what extent would you say that Mr. Thurber's account of the people who surrounded him when he lost his glasses (lines 35–41) is influenced by what these people really were, and to what extent by his feelings? What were his feelings?

10. What is Mr. Thurber implying about the woman who grinned "as if I were a policeman's horse with a sunbonnet" (lines 38–39)? Would it have been better if he had said that she "laughed, smiling at me . . ."?

11. Instead of saying that his coat was very rumpled, Mr. Thurber says it looked "a little like a dog bed" (line 44); why?

12. Why does Mr. Thurber conclude his description of how the hotel doorman helped him on with his coat by saying the doorman "had come to my assistance" (lines 51–52)?

13. What is the purpose of combining the phrase "brooks no denial" with the phrase "his little attentions and services" (lines 52–53)?

14. Notice the verbs in the description of the porter at Joe's barbershop (lines 57–60) and explain why Mr. Thurber uses them.

15. "In excellent condition" (line 62) is an expression usually associated with what kind of people? Why does Mr. Thurber use it here?

16. What ideas about the waiter lead Mr. Thurber to compare his "cold and fishy eye" to that of "an art critic" (lines 75–76)?

17. Why does Mr. Thurber say he stuck his left arm *"smoothly* into the lining of the other sleeve" (lines 77–78)?

18. Mr. Thurber has carefully prepared us for the climactic humiliation of his not being able to find a tip for the waiter, and he does something to remind us that he has (lines 81–84). Show how.

19. What does Mr. Thurber gain by adding the apparently trivial detail about the way a section of his suspenders showed (lines 90–92) to his description of his appearance without a jacket?

20. How does the fact that Mr. Thurber's loss of his jacket occurred at a theater make his reference to a "well-poised man-about-town" particularly apposite?

21. All through this selection, Mr. Thurber has been making jokes which depend on the discrepancy between what a philosopher might call The Ideal and The Actual; explain how the episode of the white sock (lines 105–115) depends on this discrepancy.

22. Recall the first paragraph of this selection (lines 1–13) and then explain Mr. Thurber's references to Oscar Wilde and Sean O'Casey (lines 120–121).

23. Explain why the kindly old lady handed Mr. Thurber a dime (lines 124–126).

SUGGESTED TOPICS

1. Select one of Mr. Thurber's jokes that depends on the discrepancy mentioned in Question 21 and explain how this joke works.

2. Write a paragraph which explains the feelings which lead Mr. Thurber to describe as he does the doorman's helping him on with his coat (lines 48–54).

3. Write a paragraph in which you explain why it is important to this selection that there is nothing wrong with Mr. Thurber's coat which has not, at one time or another, been wrong with nearly everyone's coat.

26 / Larval Stage of a Bookworm*

H. L. MENCKEN

MONG MY FATHER'S BOOKS I found a series of eight or ten volumes cheek by jowl, and it appeared on investigation that the whole lot had been written by a man named Mark Twain. I had heard my father mention this gentleman once
5 or twice in talking to my mother, but I had no idea who he was or what he had done: he might have been, for all I knew, a bartender, a baseball-player, or one of the boozy politicoes my father was always meeting in Washington. But here was evidence that he was a man who wrote books, and I noted at once that the pictures in
10 those books were not of the usual funereal character, but light, loose and lively. So I proceeded with my inquiry, and in a little while I had taken down one of them, a green quarto, sneaked it to my bedroom, and stretched out on my bed to look into it. It was, as smarties will have guessed by now, "Huckleberry Finn."

15 If I undertook to tell you the effect it had upon me my talk would sound frantic, and even delirious. Its impact was genuinely terrific. I had not gone further than the first incomparable chapter before I realized, child though I was, that I had entered a domain of new and gorgeous wonders, and thereafter I pressed on
20 steadily to the last word. My gait, of course, was still slow, but it became steadily faster as I proceeded. As the blurbs on the slipcovers of murder mysteries say, I simply couldn't put the book

---

* Reprinted from *The Days of Mencken* by H. L. Mencken, by permission of Alfred A. Knopf, Inc. Copyright 1939, 1947 by Alfred A. Knopf, Inc.

down. After dinner that evening, braving a possible uproar, I took
it into the family sitting-room, and resumed it while my father
searched the *Evening News* hopefully for reports of the arrest, 25
clubbing and hanging of labor leaders. Anon, he noticed what I
was at, and demanded to know the name of the book I was reading. When I held up the green volume his comment was "Well,
I'll be durned!"

I sensed instantly that there was no reproof in this, but a kind of 30
shy rejoicing. Then he told me that he had once been a great
reader of Mark Twain himself—in his younger days. He had got
hold of all the volumes as they came out—"The Innocents" in
1869, when he was still a boy himself; "Roughing It" in 1872, "The
Gilded Age" in 1873, "Tom Sawyer" in 1876, "A Tramp Abroad" 35
in 1880, the year of my birth, and so on down to date. (All these
far from pristine firsts are still in the Bibliotcca Menckeniana in
Hollins street, minus a few that were lent to neighbor boys and
never returned, and had to be replaced.) My father read them in
the halcyon days before children, labor troubles and Grover Cleve- 40
land had begun to frazzle him, and he still got them down from
the shelf on quiet evenings, after the first-named were packed off to
bed. But a man of advancing years and cares had to consider also
the sorrows of the world, and so he read in Mark less than afore-
time.   45

As for me, I proceeded to take the whole canon at a gulp—and
presently gagged distressfully. "Huckleberry Finn," of course, was
as transparent to a boy of eight as to a man of eighty, and almost
as pungent and exhilarating, but there were passages in "A Tramp
Abroad" that baffled me, and many more in "The Innocents," and 50
a whole swarm in "A Gilded Age." I well recall wrestling with the
woodcut by W. F. Brown on page 113 of the "Tramp." It shows
five little German girls swinging on a heavy chain stretched between two stone posts on a street in Heilbronn and the legend under it is "Generations of Bare Feet." That legend is silly, for all the 55
girls have shoes on, but what puzzled me about it was something
quite different. It was a confusion between the word *generation* and
the word *federation*, which latter was often in my father's speech

in those days, for the American Federation of Labor had got under
60 way only a few years before, and was just beginning in earnest to
harass and alarm employers. Why I didn't consult the dictionary
(or my mother, or my father himself) I simply can't tell you. At
eight or nine, I suppose, intelligence is no more than a small spot
of light on the floor of a large and murky room. So instead of seek-
65 ing help I passed on, wondering idiotically what possible relation
there could be between a gang of little girls in pigtails and the Haymarket anarchists, and it was six or seven years later before the
"Tramp" became clear to me, and began to delight me.

   It then had the curious effect of generating in me both a great
70 interest in Germany and a vast contempt for the German language.
I was already aware, of course, that the Mencken family was of
German origin, for my Grandfather Mencken, in his care for me as
Stammhalter, did not neglect to describe eloquently its past glories
at the German universities, and to expound its connections to the
75 most remote degrees. But my father, who was only half German,
had no apparent interest in either the German land or its people,
and when he spoke of the latter at all, which was not often, it was
usually in sniffish terms. He never visited Germany, and never signified any desire to do so, though I recall my mother suggesting,
80 more than once, that a trip there would be swell. It was "A Tramp
Abroad" that made me German-conscious, and I still believe that
it is the best guidebook to Germany ever written. Today, of course,
it is archaic, but it was still reliable down to 1910, when I made my
own first trip. The uproarious essay on "The Awful German Lan-
85 guage," which appears at the end of it as an appendix, worked the
other way. That is to say, it confirmed my growing feeling, born
of my struggles with the conjugations and declensions taught at
F. Knapp's Institute, that German was an irrational and even in-
sane tongue, and not worth the sufferings of a freeborn American.
90 These diverse impressions have continued with me ever since. I am
still convinced that Germany, in the intervals of peace, is the most
pleasant country to travel in ever heard of, and I am still convinced
that the German language is of a generally preposterous and malignant character.

"Huck," of course, was my favorite, and I read it over and over. 95
In fact, I read it regularly not less than annually down to my for-
ties, and only a few months ago I hauled it out and read it once
more—and found it as magnificent as ever. Only one other book,
down to the beginning of my teens, ever beset me with a force
even remotely comparable to its smash, and that was a volume 100
called "Boys' Useful Pastimes," by "Prof. Robert Griffith, A.M.
principal of Newton High School." This was given to me by my
Grandmother Mencken at Christmas, 1889, and it remained my
constant companion for at least six years.

[But] the influence of "Huck Finn" was immensely more pow- 105
erful and durable. It not only reinforced my native aversion to the
common run of boys' books; it also set me upon a systematic ex-
ploration of all the volumes in the old secretary, and before I finished with them I had looked into every one of them, including
even Brother Schultz's sombre history of Freemasonry in Mary- 110
land. How many were actually intelligible to a boy of eight, nine,
ten? I should say about a fourth. I managed to get through most of
Dickens, but only by dint of hard labor, and it was not until I discovered Thackeray, at fourteen, that the English novel really began to lift me. George Eliot floored me as effectively as a text in 115
Hittite, and to the present day I have never read "Adam Bede" or
"Daniel Deronda" or "The Mill on the Floss," or developed any
desire to do so. So far as I am concerned, they will remain mere
names to the end of the chapter, and as hollow and insignificant as
the names of Gog and Magog.   120

But I plowed through Chambers' Encyclopedia relentlessly, beginning with the shortest articles and gradually working my way
into the longer ones. The kitchen midden of irrelevant and incredible information that still burdens me had its origins in those
pages, and I almost wore them out acquiring it. I read, too, the 125
whole of Lossing, nearly all of Charlotte M. Yonge, and even some
of Duyckinck, perhaps the dullest historian ever catalogued by
faunal naturalists on this or any other earth. My brother Charlie
and I enjoyed "Our Living World" chiefly because of the colored
pictures, but I also read long stretches of it, and astonished my fa- 130

ther by calling off the names of nearly all the wild beasts when the circus visited Baltimore in 1889. Finally, I recall reading both "Life Among the Mormons" and "One Thousand Proofs That the Earth Is not a Globe."

135　　Thus launched upon the career of a bookworm, I presently began to reach out right and left for more fodder. When the Enoch Pratt Free Library of Baltimore opened a branch in Hollins street, in March, 1886, I was still a shade too young to be excited, but I had a card before I was nine, and began an almost daily harrying of
140 the virgins at the delivery desk. In 1888 my father subscribed to *Once-a-Week*, the predecessor of *Collier's*, and a little while later there began to come with it a long series of cheap reprints of contemporary classics, running from Tennyson's poems to Justin M'Carthy's "History of Our Own Times"; and simultaneously
145 there appeared from parts unknown a similar series of cheap reprints of scientific papers, including some of Herbert Spencer. I read them all, sometimes with shivers of puzzlement and sometimes with delight, but always calling for more. I began to inhabit a world that was two-thirds letter press and only one-third trees,
150 fields, streets and people. I acquired round shoulders, spindly shanks, and a despondent view of humanity. I read everything that I could find in English, taking in some of it but boggling most of it.

　　This madness ran on until I reached adolescence, and began to
155 distinguish between one necktie and another, and to notice the curiously divergent shapes, dispositions and aromas of girls. Then, gradually, I began to let up.

　　But to this day I am still what might be called a reader, and have a high regard for authors.

QUESTIONS

1. This selection from H. L. Mencken's autobiography, *Happy Days,* describes how Mencken became a book-lover, and this subject is always the center of his discourse. But Mencken is an ebullient

writer and cannot resist the temptation to work in a certain number of related but not strictly necessary matters. For instance, while he is discussing how he discovered Mark Twain, he works up, on the side, an amused and affectionate account of his father's attitude toward life. Point out another example of the same kind of thing.

2. Like the construction, the style of this selection is lively and often comically extravagant. For instance, when Mencken wishes to convey to us the fact that all he knew about Mark Twain was that his father had mentioned Twain in his hearing, he says, "[Twain] might have been, for all I knew, a bartender, a baseball-player, or one of the boozy politicoes my father was always meeting in Washington." This is comic extravagance; it is unlikely that an eight-year-old's speculations as to a man's identity would lead him first to thoughts of bartenders and baseball-players. But having launched himself on this joke, Mencken carries it out. What does it tell us about his opinion of politicians that he adds them to this list? Why does he call them "boozy politicoes" (line 7)? Does this joke have anything to do with his calling Twain "this gentleman" (line 4)?

3. The eight-year-old Mencken clearly feared his father might disapprove of his reading Mark Twain ("braving a possible uproar, I took it into the family sitting-room," lines 23–24). Does this fear show in a previous passage?

4. Do you believe that Mencken's father was really hopeful of finding in the newspaper reports of the clubbing and hanging of labor leaders (lines 25–26)? What was his attitude? What is Mencken's point in describing it this way?

5. What would be plain English for "Biblioteca Menckeniana" (line 37)? Why does Mencken use these words for it?

6. How does Mencken feel about his father's motives for now reading Twain less than he did in the early years of his life (lines 39–45)? How do you know?

7. How does Mencken feel about his father's fear of the American Federation of Labor (lines 58–61)? How do you know?

8. Who were "the Haymarket anarchists" (lines 66–67) and why is it particularly ludicrous for the eight-year-old Mencken to confuse with them "a gang of little girls"?

9. What is a *"Stammhalter"* (line 73) and how does Mencken's use of the word here help to convey what he feels about his grandfather's attitude?

10. Why does Mencken describe his dislike of the German language as a feeling that it "was not worth the sufferings of a freeborn American" (lines 88–89)?

11. Why does Mencken compare George Eliot's novels to "a text in Hittite" and "the names of Gog and Magog" (lines 115–116 and 120)?

12. Why does Mencken call his general knowledge a "kitchenmidden of . . . information" (lines 123–124)?

13. What leads Mencken to call his search for more reading matter a reaching out for "more fodder" (lines 135–136)?

14. What does Mencken mean by saying he inhabited "a world that was two-thirds letter-press" (lines 148–149)?

15. What leads Mencken to mention neckties and girls together (lines 155–156)?

16. Why does Mencken say that he is still "what might be called a reader" (line 158)?

SUGGESTED TOPICS

1. Select a passage of ten or a dozen lines from this essay and analyze the comic extravagance of its style.

2. Write a paragraph on the extent to which Mencken's comic exaggeration depends on the use of incongruous metaphors.

3. All his life Mencken was a political conservative, and he certainly had no sympathy with the Haymarket rioters and no special tenderness toward the American Federation of Labor. Write a paragraph in which you explain why he does not agree with his father's feelings about such people and institutions.

27 / Religion in Childhood*

GWEN RAVERAT

HE FIRST RELIGIOUS experience that I can remember
is getting under the nursery table to pray that the dancing
mistress might be dead before we got to the Dancing Class. I was
about half-way through the exasperating business which dancing
class entailed: being changed right down to my skin, and washed   5
and brushed, and having the comfortable dirt taken out of my fin-
gernails. Margaret was sitting on the table, while Nana made her
hair into long sausage-curls, with a wet brush round her finger. We
thought the sausages very ugly, but Nana admired them, and we
all loved Nana so much that we would do anything she liked. So   10
Margaret bore it as well as she could, and only gave a little snarl
when a drop of cold water fell on her bare neck. Charles was carefully washing his hands without any soap, the usual expression of
philosophic calm on his round face. I think that he sometimes
washed without any water either, for I well remember the smooth   15
and permanent pale grey texture of his fingers.

When I was about half dressed, as I said, in my white flannel
petticoat to be exact, I considered my costume suitable, and I got
under the table for religious seclusion, and took up an attitude
modelled on Sir Joshua Reynolds' 'Infant Samuel kneeling in   20
Prayer,' as the correct position for divine transactions. We knew

* Reprinted from *Period Piece* by Gwendolyn Mary Raverat. By permission
of W. W. Norton & Company, Inc. Copyright 1952 by Gwendolyn Mary
Raverat.

the Infant Samuel very well, from the picture-card game of National Gallery, which we often played.

It was not that I had any grudge against that particular dancing
25 mistress, who was called, I think, Miss Ratcliffe. Of course, all dancing mistresses were affected jades. Hamlet's words perfectly described them, when I read them later on: *"You jig, you amble, you lisp and nickname God's creatures and make your wantonness your ignorance."* But that would not have mattered to me if only
30 they had kept their jigging and ambling to themselves and left me in peace. But as it was, we were forced to go, and I really could think of no other weapon of self-defense except prayer. Not that I believed in that much; still, perhaps it was worth trying.

But, of course, prayer did not succeed. Prayers, at least *my*
35 prayers, never did. So far as I can remember, none of the dancing mistresses from whom I suffered ever had so much as a cold in the head in all the time I knew them. There they always were, that scourge of the human race; and we always had to go through the whole degrading ritual, from the first March Past with its ele-
40 gant bows to Miss Ratcliffe, right down to the bitter end of the waltz or the lancers.

I have sometimes wondered what would have been my reaction if the dancing mistress had fallen down dead, as I came into the classroom. I suppose I should have felt rather guilty; but after all it
45 would have been God's doing, not mine; and that He should have done such a thing at my request would have destroyed my respect for Him, once and for all.

For the only virtue God had, to my mind, was that of impartiality; and so prayer itself seemed to me to be an immoral proceed-
50 ing. It was as if you were trying to bribe the Judge. My idea of prayer was: "Please God, if you will let there be Chocolate Pudding for lunch, I will be very good to-day." I am now told that this is not the right idea of prayer, but it was mine then. Well, now: could it be right that God should suddenly put Chocolate Pudding into
55 the head of the cook, when she had intended to make Marmalade Pudding, which I hated, but which other people liked? No, it would be exceedingly unjust. In fact, it would be a shabby thing

for me to try to do a deal for myself in that way; and most unfair of God to agree to my terms. But, anyhow, He never did; God simply never did what I asked Him; so that on the whole I thought Him incorruptible, which was just as well. There remained the possibility that prayer might work as magic. But even as magic it never succeeded. It was altogether a bad idea. After that, prayer became synonymous for me with giving up hope; if ever I prayed again, it was only in a final frenzy of despair, and was the first step toward resignation at not getting what I wanted.

God had a smooth oval face, with no hair and no beard and no ears. I imagine that He was not descended, as most Gods are, from Father Christmas, but rather from the Sun Insurance Office sign. Even now this hairless, earless, egg-shaped face gives me a sort of holy feeling in my stomach. He sat up in the night sky like that, sending out Good Things with one hand, and Bad Things with the other hand. This was somehow connected with not letting your right hand know what your left hand was doing. There were probably an equal number of Good Things and Bad Things, and they were probably sent out with fair impartiality; at least, I was willing to give God the benefit of the doubt about it—though certainly it did seem as if the Bad Things had a strong tendency to go to the Good people; and vice versa. For from my earliest childhood I knew very well that Being Good did not pay. It was just a thing that you might—or might not—like for its own sake; and the verse about the wicked flourishing like the green bay tree was one of the few texts that went home to me with a click. God was not good and kind; at best, He was indifferent and the world was beautiful but quite pitiless.

Prayer was not the only idea of the grown-ups which seemed to me wrong in itself. They had a complete set of values for Badness and Goodness, which I will call System A; and this only partly coincided with my own private set of values: System B. I was always troubled by the confusion of trying to reconcile the two incompatible codes. System A and System B overlapped and agreed in disapproving of dishonesty, cruelty and cowardliness; but otherwise they had little on common; and there might often be very different

points of view about what constituted dishonesty or cowardliness.
95 For instance, when I had been obliged to steal some sugar, I felt
that it made it perfectly honest if I put my head through the
drawing-room door and shouted: "I've taken three lumps of sugar
out of the pantry," and then ran away. My conscience was quite
clear after that, and it did not prevent me from doing it again.
100 This is the principle of Confession. I should have minded very
much if I had felt myself to be dishonest; but I did not mind if
they scolded me for disobedience. Obedience, though important in
System A, had no place at all in System B.

Of course all kinds of goodness, in both systems, were hampered
105 by being, by definition, something which you did not want to do.
If you did want to do it, then it wasn't goodness. Thus being kind
to a person you liked didn't count at all, because you wanted to do
it; and being kind to a person you didn't like was no use either; because—as I thought then—the person always knew perfectly
110 well that you disliked them, and so of course the kindness could not
please them. So kindness was no use anyway. Nor were other efforts
at Goodness more successful. For one thing Goodness never made
me feel nice afterwards; I must be abnormal, for the reputed afterglow of virtue simply did not occur. Goodness-against-the-grain
115 simply made me feel mean, hypocritical and servile; so that Goodness only resulted in a weight on my conscience; a weight often
heavier than if I had been Bad on purpose; and nearly as heavy
as if I had been Bad by accident.

For the most muddling thing of all was that the Badnesses you
120 did *by accident* were what made you feel most guilty. Of course,
this was all wrong by System A. The grown-ups pretended that it
was what you did *on purpose* that mattered. This was, and is,
quite untrue. No one ever really regrets doing a Badness on purpose. For instance, if you were rude or disobedient to Miss X, a
125 governess you rightly despised, you felt rather pleased with yourself
afterwards; or if you paddled without asking leave, anyhow you had
had the paddling, and no one could ever take it away from you
again.

But if you were unkind or rude by mistake to someone you loved

—Ah, then you just wished you were dead. Once when Nana was ill in hospital, and my mother wanted to take me to see her, I refused to go, in all innocence. I could not bear the idea of seeing her changed, and sick, and surrounded by strangers. What could I say to her in public? We could only look at each other from far off, so what was the use of going? If I could possibly have believed that she would have liked to see me, I would willingly have gone; but that never occurred to me at all. This is the sort of thing one is sorry for afterwards, just because one did not do it on purpose.

My own code of virtue, System B, took this strange fact into account, but the grown-ups' System A was not realistic enough to do so. Yet if they could only be honest, even old people would admit that when they forget an appointment or are cross on purpose, they don't feel sorry at all; whereas, if they did the same things by accident, they would feel thoroughly guilty. Can it be called anything but Remorse, the anguish which pierces your breast when you discover that you have thrown away your return ticket, or lost your latchkey, by your own carelessness?

Anyhow, whether by accident or on purpose, by being Good or by being Bad, System A or System B, I always had a weight on my conscience of many pounds—if conscience weight is measured in pounds? Guiltiness was a permanent condition, like rheumatism; and one just had to learn to disregard it, and to carry on under it, as best one could. Huckleberry Finn has the last word on conscience—and I was as conscience-ridden as poor Huck himself.

"It don't make no difference whether you do right or wrong, a person's conscience ain't got no sense, and just goes for him anyway. If I had a yaller dog that didn't know more than a person's conscience, I would pison him. It takes up more room than all the rest of a person's insides, and yet ain't no good, nohow."

This is most terribly TRUE.

QUESTIONS

1. This selection is a good deal richer in content and suggestion than is perhaps evident at first glance; its deceptive air of casualness comes partly from its apparently—but not actually—off-hand organization and from the unusual attitude of the writer toward the feelings and convictions of childhood. We are never allowed to forget that what she is describing are the feelings of childhood, but the writer at the same time enters into these feelings with such completeness and has such sympathy with the kind of rightness a child's feeling has that, despite the evident limitations of these feelings, we take them with an unaccustomed seriousness. Moreover, the writer suggests, in her unobtrusive way, that the child is right and the grownups wrong (for example, in lines 122–123) and, frequently, that, though the child is not completely right, she is righter than we may at first think (for example, lines 53–59). In structure, the selection falls into four logically distinct parts, which might be described as 1) Prayer, 2) The Nature of God, 3) Morality, 4) Conscience. At which point does the author move from one to the other of these topics?

2. The arrangement of what the author has to say about the first topic is particularly skillful, for she has committed herself to talking about a particular exercise of prayer—about Dancing Class—and therefore about a particular occasion in her life, with all its attendant details about her sister and brother and Nana. Notice that the first sentence indicates all these subtopics to us by mentioning prayer, the Dancing Class, and the nursery table. Which of these three subtopics is dealt with in the first paragraph (lines 1–16) and how does the author arrange what she tells us of this subtopic? With which subtopic does the second paragraph (lines 16–23) deal? At what point does the author come back finally to her main subject, praying that the dancing mistress might be dead?

3. What is the author suggesting by saying that Margaret gave a snarl, but "only gave a little snarl," when the cold water fell on her neck (lines 11–12)?

4. What is the author suggesting about the child by mentioning the child's concern for a suitable costume, religious seclusion, and a position for divine transactions (lines 18–21)? Is this suggestion intensified by the diction ("religious seclusion," "divine transactions")?

What is the effect of the author's saying, "We knew the Infant Samuel very well" (lines 21–22); notice that she is not referring here to Reynolds' picture but to Samuel himself.

5. The child thinks of prayer as a "weapon of self-defense" (lines 31–32); does this conception fit with the child's general conception of prayer which is outlined in lines 48–61?

6. In line 39 the author describes the child's Dancing Class as a "degrading ritual." Where has she shown us why the child thought it degrading? To what extent do you think the author shares the child's feelings about Dancing Class?

7. Having described the child's conception of the nature of God and the conception of prayer which logically follows from it (lines 48–52), the author observes, "I am now told that this is not the right idea of prayer, but it was mine then" (lines 52–53). Why does she not say, "I now know that this is not the right idea of prayer"?

8. Given the child's conception of God and of prayer, prayer became immoral, both from the point of view of God and from the point of view of the suppliant (lines 48–50); why?

9. At lines 67–74, the author describes the child's conception of the appearance of God. ("Father Christmas" is the English name for the person we call "Santa Claus.") This passage of course reminds us that we are dealing with the primitive mind of a child, but it also serves as a transition. This transition is not really completed until line 86. What topics does it connect and how does it do so?

10. To what extent do you think the author sympathizes with the child's conviction that "Being Good did not pay" (line 80)? What do you think of the child's belief about Goodness, that "it was just a thing you might—or might not—like for its own sake" (lines 80–81)?

11. What does the author mean by saying in line 100 that the anecdote about the three lumps of sugar illustrates "the principle of Confession"?

12. When the author tells us that the child felt that "if you did want to do it, then it wasn't goodness" (line 106), she is telling us something about the child's way of feeling, of the child's actual experience of things rather than her abstract ideas. What does this feeling have to do with what she calls Conscience in the last section of the selection?

13. Badness *by accident,* the author tells us, is what bothered the

child's conscience (lines 119–120). Consider the illustration about Nana ill in the hospital (lines 130–138) and then describe exactly what the author means by the phrase "by accident."

14. Of this curious phenomenon—accidental Badness—the author remarks, "yet if they could only be honest, even old people would admit that" it is the real cause of remorse (lines 141–143). Is she speaking here as that "old person," the author, or as the young person, the child the author is describing? Explain your answer.

15. It was the reality of the child's experience that "Guiltiness was a permanent condition" (line 151); has anyone else ever thought this —in addition to Huck Finn?

16. There is irony in Mark Twain's making Huck say that "conscience ain't got no sense" (line 156), and no doubt the author understands and shares this irony. That is to say, she feels that conscience does *not* make sense and that its not doing so is a very serious matter. At the same time she feels that at some point of understanding deeper than commonsense, conscience is nonetheless right, as if conscience were profounder in its grasp of human experience than any rational system of right and wrong. In which places has the child's insight led her to see this more clearly than the grownups? In which places does the child's failure to see make her depend on logic and commonsense in a way which is ludicrously out of accord with men's usual conclusions about experience?

17. Is there some special point in making it a child—the one described by the author or Huck Finn—who sees that conscience is not sensible and yet is very powerful?

SUGGESTED TOPICS

1. Write two paragraphs in which you show the way the author of this essay makes children seem wiser than grownups.

2. Write a paragraph in which you state clearly the child's reasons for thinking that conscience "ain't got no sense."

3. Write two paragraphs in which you discuss the question of the extent to which the author shares the child's convictions and the extent to which she does not.

28 / Handle with Care[*]

F. SCOTT FITZGERALD

NOW THE STANDARD cure for one who is sunk is to consider those in actual destitution or physical suffering—this is an all-weather beatitude for gloom in general and fairly salutary day-time advice for everyone. But at three o'clock in the morning, a forgotten package has the same tragic importance as a death sentence, and the cure doesn't work—and in a real dark night of the soul it is always three o'clock in the morning, day after day. At that hour the tendency is to refuse to face things as long as possible by retiring into an infantile dream—but one is continually startled out of this by various contacts with the world. One meets these occasions as quickly and carelessly as possible and retires once more back into the dream, hoping that things will adjust themselves by some great material or spiritual bonanza. But as the withdrawal persists there is less and less chance of the bonanza—one is not waiting for the fade-out of a single sorrow, but rather being an unwilling witness of an execution, the disintegration of one's own personality . . .

Unless madness or drugs or drink come into it, this phase comes to a dead-end, eventually, and is succeeded by a vacuous quiet. In this you can try to estimate what has been sheared away and what is left. Only when this quiet came to me, did I realize that I had gone through two parallel experiences.

The first time was twenty years ago, when I left Princeton in junior year with a complaint diagnosed as malaria. It transpired, through an X-ray taken a dozen years later, that it had been tuberculosis—a mild case, and after a few months of rest I went back to college. But I had lost certain offices, the chief one was the presidency of the Triangle Club, a musical comedy idea, and also I dropped back a class. To me college would never be the same. There were to be no badges of pride, no medals, after all. It seemed on one March afternoon that I had lost every single thing I had wanted—and that night was the first time that I had hunted down the spectre of womanhood that, for a little while, makes everything else seem unimportant.

Years later I realized that my failure as a big shot in college was all right—instead of serving on committees, I took a beating on English poetry; when I got the idea of what it was all about, I set about learning how to write. On Shaw's principle that "If you don't get what you like, you better like what you get," it was a lucky break—at the moment it was a harsh and bitter business to know that my career as a leader of men was over.

Since that day I have not been able to fire a bad servant, and I am astonished and impressed by people who can. Some old desire for personal dominance was broken and gone. Life around me was a solemn dream, and I lived on the letters I wrote to a girl in another city. A man does not recover from such jolts—he becomes a different person and, eventually, the new person finds new things to care about.

The other episode parallel to my current situation took place after the war, when I had again over-extended my flank. It was one of those tragic loves doomed for lack of money, and one day the girl closed it out on the basis of common sense. During a long summer of despair I wrote a novel instead of letters, so it came out all right, but it came out all right for a different person. The man with the jingle of money in his pocket who married the girl a year later would always cherish an abiding distrust, an animosity, toward the leisure class—not the conviction of a revolutionist but the smouldering hatred of a peasant. In the years since then I have never been

able to stop wondering where my friends' money came from, nor
to stop thinking that at one time a sort of *droit de seigneur* might 60
have been exercised to give one of them my girl.

For sixteen years I lived pretty much as this latter person, dis-
trusting the rich, yet working for money with which to share their
mobility and the grace that some of them brought into their lives.
During this time I had plenty of the usual horses shot from under 65
me—I remember some of their names—*Punctured Pride, Thwarted
Expectation, Faithless, Show-Off, Hard Hit, Never Again.* And
after awhile I wasn't twenty-five, then not even thirty-five, and
nothing was quite as good. But in all these years I don't remember
a moment of discouragement. I saw honest men through moods of 70
suicidal gloom—some of them gave up and died; others adjusted
themselves and went on to a larger success than mine; but my
morale never sank below the level of self-disgust when I put on
some unsightly personal show. Trouble has no necessary connection with discouragement—discouragement has a germ of its own, 75
as different from trouble as arthritis is different from a stiff joint.

When a new sky cut off the sun last spring, I didn't at first relate it to what had happened fifteen or twenty-five years ago. Only
gradually did a certain familiar resemblance come through—an
over-extension of the flank, a burning of the candle at both ends; 80
a call upon physical resources that I did not command, like a man
over-drawing at his bank. In its impact this blow was more violent
than the other two but it was the same kind—a feeling that I was
standing at twilight on a deserted range, with an empty rifle in my
hands and the targets down. No problem set—simply a silence with 85
only the sound of my own breathing.

In this silence there was a vast irresponsibility toward every obligation, a deflation of all my values. A passionate belief in order, a
disregard of motives or consequences in favor of guess work and
prophecy, a feeling that craft and industry would have a place in 90
any world—one by one, these and other convictions were swept
away. I saw that the novel, which at my maturity was the strongest
and supplest medium for conveying thought and emotion from one
human being to another, was becoming subordinated to a me-

95 chanical and communal art that, whether in the hands of Hollywood merchants or Russian idealists, was capable of reflecting only the tritest thought, the most obvious emotion. It was an art in which words were subordinate to images, where personality was worn down to the inevitable low gear of collaboration. As long
100 past as 1930, I had a hunch that the talkies would make even the best selling novelists as archaic as the silent pictures. People still read, if only Professor Canby's book of the month—curious children nosed at the slime of Mr. Tiffany Thayer in the drugstore libraries—but there was a rankling indignity, that to me had become
105 almost an obsession, in seeing the power of the written word subordinated to another power, a more glittering, a grosser power . . .

I set that down as an example of what haunted me during the long night—this was something I could neither accept nor struggle
110 against, something which tended to make my efforts obsolescent, as the chain stores have crippled the small merchant, an exterior force, unbeatable.

So there was not an "I" any more—not a basis on which I could organize my self-respect—save my limitless capacity for toil that it
115 seemed I possessed no more. It was strange to have no self—to be like a little boy left alone in a big house, who knew that now he could do anything he wanted to do, but found that there was nothing that he wanted to do.

QUESTIONS

1. In this selection the subject the author wishes to explain has become so important that the material is no longer arranged chronologically, as it almost certainly would be in the ordinary biographical essay. Fitzgerald's primary concern is to make us understand a state of mind; for this purpose he has selected three occasions from his life which he tells us he now sees were similar. What were these three occasions? What did they have in common?

2. Why does the author describe the advice mentioned in the first sentence as "day-time advice" (line 4)?

3. Since it is literally impossible for the time to be "always three o'clock in the morning, day after day," (lines 7–8) what does Fitzgerald mean by saying it is?

4. In the rest of the paragraph (lines 8–17), Fitzgerald is defining the difference between "a single sorrow" and "the disintegration of one's own personality" (lines 15–17). This second phrase embodies the central idea of the selection. How is it illustrated by the two episodes from his early life which follow (lines 23–61)? Where does he define "the disintegration of one's own personality" in more detail? Why does he wait to give this detailed definition?

5. In lines 38–40 Fitzgerald says the experience he has just described was "a lucky break"; but in lines 30–32 he says it cost him "every single thing I had wanted." How do you reconcile these two statements? Does your explanation fit what Fitzgerald says in the paragraph which begins at line 42?

6. Why did *life around him* seem like "a solemn dream" (line 45) in his last year in college?

7. What kind of comparison is being used in the phrase "over-extended my flank" (line 50)? Does this kind of comparison occur elsewhere in the selection? Why?

8. Why does Fitzgerald say, "The man with the jingle of money in his pocket who married the girl a year later . . ." lines 54–55) instead of something like "We were married a year later, but . . ."?

9. What is the difference between the attitudes of a revolutionist and a peasant (lines 57–58)? What does the expression *"droit de seigneur"* (line 60) mean? Why is it specially appropriate here? To what actual possibility does it refer?

10. With the phrase "For sixteen years I lived . . ." (line 62) Fitzgerald brings us back to "the present"—or, to be exact, to "last spring." If you know that this selection was originally published in March, 1936, what date would you assign to the two episodes Fitzgerald has just described? At what point in the selection did Fitzgerald leave "the present" to which he here returns?

11. What is Fitzgerald's distinction between "trouble" and "discouragement" (lines 74–76)? With what earlier distinction do you connect it?

12. Why does Fitzgerald say, *"a new sky* cut off the sun last spring" (line 77)?

13. Would you say Fitzgerald does or does not believe the theory

about the obsolescence of the novel which he describes in lines 92–107?

14. The comparison in the last paragraph, beginning at line 113, has two aspects. The little boy looks forward to being left alone in a big house so that he can do anything he wants to do; but when he is so left, he finds there is nothing he wants to do. Explain the two aspects of the author's situation to which these two aspects of the little boy's situation apply.

SUGGESTED TOPICS

1. Write a paragraph on Fitzgerald's attitude toward wealth, as far as you can deduce it from this selection.

2. Write two paragraphs in which you explain, first, the chronological arrangement of the material in this selection, and, second, the reasons for this arrangement.

3. Choose one of the many metaphors in this selection which is being used to tell us how it feels to be in this state of mind, and explain how the metaphor conveys this feeling.

29 / A Russian Childhood*

VLADIMIR NABOKOV

THE KIND of Russian family to which I belonged—a kind now extinct—had, among other virtues, a traditional leaning toward the comfortable products of Anglo-Saxon civilization. Pears's Soap, tar-black when dry, topaz-like when held to the light between wet fingers, took care of one's morning bath. Pleasant was the decreasing weight of the English collapsible tub when it was made to protrude a rubber underlip and disgorge its frothy contents into the slop-pail. "We could not improve the cream, so we improved the tube," said the English toothpaste. At breakfast, golden syrup imported from London would entwist with its glowing coils the revolving spoon from which enough of it had slithered on to a piece of Russian bread-and-butter. All sorts of snug, mellow things came in a steady procession from the English Shop on Nevski Avenue: fruit cakes, smelling salts, playing cards, picture puzzles, striped blazers, talcum-white tennis balls.

I learned to read English before I could read Russian. My first English friends were four simple souls in my grammar—Ben, Dan, Sam and Ned. There used to be a great deal of fuss about their identities and whereabouts—"Who is Ben?" "He is Dan," "Sam is in bed," and so on. Although it all remained rather stiff and patchy (the compiler was handicapped by having to employ—for the initial lessons, at least—words of not more than three letters), my imagination somehow managed to obtain the necessary data. Wan-faced, big-limbed, silent nitwits, proud in the possession of 25 certain tools ("Ben has an axe"), they now drift with a slow-motioned slouch across the remotest backdrop of memory; and, akin to the mad alphabet of an optician's chart, the grammar-book lettering looms again before me.

The schoolroom was drenched with sunlight. In a sweating glass 30 jar, several spiny caterpillars were feeding on nettle leaves (and ejecting interesting barrel-shaped pellets of olive-green frass). The oil-cloth that covered the round table smelled of glue. Miss Clayton smelled of Miss Clayton. Fantastically, gloriously, the blood-coloured alcohol of the outside thermometer would rise to 24° 35 Réaumur (86° Fahrenheit) in the shade. Through the window one could see kerchiefed peasant girls weeding a garden path on their hands and knees or gently raking the sun-mottled sand. Golden orioles in the greenery emitted their four brilliant notes.

Ned lumbered past the window in a fair impersonation of the 40 gardener's mate. On later pages longer words appeared; and at the very end of the brown, ink-stained volume, a real, sensible story unfolded its adult sentences—the little reader's ultimate triumph and reward. I was thrilled by the thought that some day I might attain such proficiency. The magic has endured, and whenever a 45 grammar book comes my way, I instantly turn to the last page to enjoy a forbidden glimpse of the laborious student's future, of that promised land where, at last, words are meant to mean what they mean.

Summer *soomerki*—the lovely Russian word for dusk. Time: 50 a dim point in the first decade of this unpopular century. Place: latitude 59° north from your equator, longitude 100° east from my writing hand. The day would take hours to fade, and every-thing—sky, tall flowers, still water—would be kept in a state of in-finite vesperal suspense, deepened rather than resolved by the dole-55 ful moo of a cow on a distant meadow or by the still more moving cry that came from some bird beyond the lower course of the river, where the vast expanse of a misty-blue sphagnum bog, because of its mystery and remoteness, was called America.

In the drawing room of our country house, before going to bed, I would often be read to in English by my mother. As she came to a particularly dramatic passage, where the hero was about to encounter some strange, perhaps fatal, danger, her voice would slow down, her words would be spaced portentously, and before turning the page she would place upon it her hand, with its familiar pigeon-blood ruby and diamond ring (within the limpid facets of which, had I been a better crystal-gazer, I might have seen a room, people, lights, trees in the rain—a whole period of émigré life for which that ring was to pay).

There were tales about knights whose terrific but wonderfully aseptic wounds were bathed by damsels in grottoes. From a windswept cliff top, a medieval maiden with flying hair and a youth in tights gazed at the round Isles of the Blessed. In "Misunderstood," the fate of Humphrey used to bring a more specialized lump to one's throat than the one Hollywood now commercializes, while a shamelessly allegorical story, "Beyond the Blue Mountains," dealing with two pairs of little travellers—good Clover and Cowslip, bad Buttercup and Daisy—contained enough exciting details to make one forget its message.

There were also numerous glossy picture books. I particularly liked the blue-coated, red-trousered, coal-black Golliwog, with underclothes buttons for eyes, and his meagre harem of five wooden dolls. By the illegal method of cutting themselves frocks out of the American flag (Peg taking the motherly stripes, Sarah Jane the pretty stars) two of the dolls acquired a certain soft femininity once their neutral articulations had been clothed. The Twins (Meg and Weg) and the Midget remained stark naked and, consequently, sexless.

We see them in the dead of night stealing out of doors to sling snowballs at one another until the chimes of a remote clock ("But Hark!" comments the rhymed text) send them back to their toybox in the nursery. Another time they went on a bicycle journey and were captured by cannibals; our unsuspecting travellers had

been quenching their thirst at a palm-fringed pool when the tom-
toms sounded. Over the shoulder of my past I admire again the
95 crucial picture: the Golliwog, still on his knees by the pool but no
longer drinking; his hair stands on end and the normal black of his
face has changed to a weird ashen hue. There was also the motor-
car book (Sarah Jane, always my favorite, sporting a long green
veil), with the usual (circa 1906) sequel—crutches and bandaged
100 heads.

And, yes—the airship. Yards and yards of yellow silk went to
make it, and an additional tiny balloon was provided for the sole
use of the fortunate Midget. At the immense altitude to which the
ship reached, the aeronauts huddled together for warmth while the
105 lost Midget, still the object of my intense envy notwithstanding
his plight, drifted into an abyss of frost and stars—alone.

QUESTIONS

1. This selection is ostensibly concerned with telling us how a boy
who lived in Russia "in the first decade of this unpopular century"
(line 50) learned English. But we quickly discover that the author is
interested in much more than that. By the second sentence we are
aware that he would like to make us see and feel the boy's experience;
the qualities and characteristics that excited the boy are the things he
describes for us, not the mere undifferentiated facts. But this essay is,
at the same time, not what is sometimes called "the stream of consciousness" of the boy; the whole adult intelligence of the author is
present to us, and what he has learned during the rest of his life is included. A simple illustration of this range of awareness occurs in the
first two sentences when the author tells us, first, that the kind of
family he grew up in is extinct (lines 1–2) and immediately afterwards
exactly what Pears's soap looked like (line 4). Describe some of the
feelings that are induced by this combination.

2. What activity, very characteristic of a small child, are we made
to think of by Mr. Nabokov's telling us of the two different colors of
the soap (line 4)? Why is it just right for him to tell us that it is
"topaz-like when held to the light *between wet fingers*" (lines 4–5)?

3. Why does he tell us the advertising slogan that was on the tooth-paste tube (lines 8–9)?

4. What is the connection between the first paragraph (lines 1–15) and the account of the boy's learning to read English which begins at line 16?

5. Why does Mr. Nabokov describe Ben, Dan, Sam and Ned as his "English friends" and "simple souls" and why does he say that there "used to be a great deal of fuss" about their identities (lines 16–19)?

6. How did the boy know about these characters the things Mr. Nabokov remembers in lines 24–25?

7. Why did the grammar-book lettering look to him like "the mad alphabet of an optician's chart" (line 27)?

8. The paragraph which begins at line 29 gives us a number of details which the author apparently remembers from a particular day. In a sense they are random details. What holds them together? Why are they so precise (the glass jar "sweating," the pellets "barrel-shaped" and "olive-green," the thermometer alcohol "blood-colored," the temperature exactly "24° Réaumur," and the orioles' song just "four brilliant notes")?

9. Explain Mr. Nobokov's statement, that "Ned lumbered past the window in a fair impersonation of the gardener's mate" (lines 39–40)?

10. The first part of this selection is mainly about the boy's learning to read in the literal sense. With what is the part that begins at line 49 primarily concerned?

11. What is the relation between the paragraph that begins at line 49 and the rest of this section of the selection?

12. Why does Mr. Nabokov insert the parenthesis which begins at line 65? Why does this parenthesis include the reference to "a room, people, lights, trees in the rain" (lines 66–67)?

13. In the paragraph about the stories he has read, beginning at line 69, why does the author speak of the knights' wounds as "wonderfully aseptic" (lines 69–70)?

14. In the first paragraph about the Golliwog (lines 79–87) the author combines two ways of seeing the characters in this book; at one moment he is telling us that they were "wooden dolls" or had "under-clothes buttons for eyes," and at another he is speaking of them as a "harem" and as having "a certain soft femininity." Why does he use this combination?

15. What is gained by the parenthesis in lines 89–90?

16. Why does Mr. Nabokov write, in line 94, "Over the shoulder of my past I admire again"?

17. Why does Mr. Nabokov call the travellers "aeronauts" (line 104)?

18. Why does Mr. Nabokov end this selection with a statement about the fate of the Midget (lines 104–106)?

SUGGESTED TOPICS

1. Take any paragraph of this selection and explain as clearly as you can the purpose behind each of the sharply distinct details in it.

2. Take the paragraph which begins at line 69, indicate what words and phrases in it reflect the adult opinion of the writer rather than the child-like opinion of the boy he is remembering, and explain why you think they do.

3. In the light of the author's discussion of learning English, write a paragraph on "words [which] are meant to mean what they mean" (lines 47–48).

A. J. LEIBLING

EDMUND WILSON

E. B. WHITE

LEE STROUT WHITE

SALLY CARRIGHAR

ROBERT PENN WARREN

v. Feeling and Attitude

30/ Apology for Breathing*

A. J. LEIBLING

P EOPLE I KNOW in New York are incessantly on the point
of going back where they came from to write a book, or of
staying on and writing a book about where they came from. Back
where they came from, I gather, is the American scene (New York,
of course, just isn't America). It is all pretty hard on me because I 5
have no place to go back to. I was born in an apartment house at
Ninety-third Street and Lexington Avenue, about three miles from
where I now live. Friends often tell me of their excitement when
the train on which they are riding passes from Indiana into Illi-
nois, or back again. I am ashamed to admit that when the Jerome 10
Avenue express rolls into Eighty-sixth Street station I have absolutely no reaction.

I always think of back where my friends came from as one place,
possessing a homogeneous quality of not being New York. The
thought has been well expressed by my literary adviser, Whitey 15
Bimstein, who also trains prize-fighters. I once asked him how he
liked the country. He said, "It is a nice spot." I have been to the
country myself. I went to college in New Hampshire. But I seldom
mention this, because I would like to be considered quaint and regional, like Jesse Stuart or Kenneth Roberts. 20

The finest thing about New York City, I think, is that it is like
one of those complicated Renaissance clocks where on one level an

* From A. J. Leibling's *Back Where I Came From*, reprinted by permission
of A. J. Leibling and Sheridan House.

allegorical marionette pops out to mark the day of the week, on
another a skeleton death bangs the quarter hour with his scythe,
25 and on a third the Twelve Apostles do a cakewalk. The variety of
the sideshows distracts one's attention from the advance of the
hour hand. I know people who say that, as in the clock, all the ex-
hibits depend upon the same movement. This they insist is economic. But they are the sort of people who look at a fine woman
30 and remind you that the human body is composed of one dollar
and sixty-two cents worth of chemicals.

I like to think of all the city microcosms so nicely synchronized
though unaware of one another: the worlds of the weight-lifters,
yodelers, tugboat captains and sideshow barkers, of the book-
35 dutchers, sparring partners, song pluggers, sporting girls and religious painters, of the dealers in rhesus monkeys and the bishops of
churches that they establish themselves under the religious corporation law. It strengthens my hold on reality to know when I
awake with a brandy headache in my house which is nine blocks
40 due east of the Empire State, that Eddie Arcaro, the jockey, is gal-
loping a horse around the track at Belmont while Ollie Thomas, a
colored clocker of my acquaintance, is holding a watch on him. I
can be sure that Kit Coates, at the Aquarium, is worrying over the
liverish deportment of a new tropical fish, that presently Whitey
45 will be laying out the gloves and headguards for the fighters he
trains at Stillman's gymnasium, while Miss Ira, the Harlem
modiste, will be trying to talk a dark-complexioned girl out of buying herself an orange turban and Hymie the Tummler [1] ruminates
a plan for opening a new night club. It would be easier to predicate
50 the existence of God on such recurrences than on the cracking of
ice in ponds, the peeping of spring peepers in their peeperies and
the shy green sprigs of poison ivy so well advertised by writers like
Thoreau.

The language of New York is a regional tongue imported from
55 the British Isles, as is the dialect spoken by the retarded inhabitants

---

[1] A "tummler" is a small-scale Broadway operator. Later in the book from
which this selection is taken, Mr. Leibling describes a "tummler" named Hymie Katz. " 'Hymie is a tummler,' the boys at the I. & Y. say. ' Hymie is a
man what knows to get a dollar.' "

of the Great Smoky mountains back where *they* come from. Being spoken by several million people, it has not been considered of any philological importance. Basically, New Yorkese is the common speech of early nineteenth century Cork, transplanted during the mass immigration of the South Irish a hundred years ago. Of this Cork dialect Thomas Crofton Croker in 1839 wrote: "The vernacular of this region may be regarded as the ancient cockneyism of the mixed race who held the old city—Danes, English, and Irish. It is a jargon, whose principal characteristic appears in the pronunciation of the *th*, as exemplified in *dis, dat, den, dey*—this, that, then, they; and in the dovetailing of words as, 'kum our rish' for 'come of this.' " New York example, "gerradahere" for "get out of here." The neo-Corkonian proved particularly suited to the later immigrants who came here from continental Europe—the *th* sound is equally impossible for French, Germans and Italians. Moreover, it was impressed upon the late-comers because it was the talk of the police and the elementary school teachers, the only Americans who would talk to them at all.

It is true that since the diaspora the modern dialects of Cork and New York have diverged slightly like Italian and Provencal, both of which stem from vulgar Latin. Yet Sean O'Faolain's modern story of Cork, "A Born Genius," contains dialogue that might have come out of Eleventh Avenue: "He's after painting two swans on deh kitchen windes. Wan is facin' wan way and d'oder is facin' d'oder way.— So dat so help me God dis day you'd tink deh swans was floatin' in a garden! And deh garden was floatin' in trough deh winda! And dere was no winda!"

There are interesting things about New York besides the language. It is one of the oldest places in the United States, but doesn't live in retrospect like the professionally picturesque provinces. Any city may have one period of magnificence, like Boston or New Orleans or San Francisco, but it takes a real one to keep renewing itself until the past is perennially forgotten. There were plenty of clipper ships out of New York in the old days and privateers before them, but there are better ships out of her today. The Revolution was fought all over town, from Harlem to Red Hook and back again, but that isn't the revolution you'll hear New Yorkers discussing now.

Native New Yorkers are the best mannered people in America; 95 they never speak out of turn in saloons, because they have experience in group etiquette. Whenever you hear a drinker let a blat out of him you can be sure he is a recent immigrant from the south or the middle west. New Yorkers are modest. It is a distinction for a child in New York to be the brightest on one block; he acquires 100 no exaggerated idea of his own relative intelligence. Prairie geniuses are raced in cheap company when young. They are intoxicated by the feel of being boy wonders in Amarillo, and when they bounce off New York's skin as adults they resent it.

New York women are the most beautiful in the world. They have 105 their teeth straightened in early youth. They get their notions of chic from S. Klein's windows instead of the movies. Really loud and funny New Yorkers, like Bruce Barton, are invariably carpetbaggers. The climate is extremely healthy. The death rate is lower in Queens and the Bronx than in any other large city in the United 110 States, and the average life expectancy is so high that one of our morning newspapers specializes in interviewing people a hundred years old and upward. The average is slightly lowered, however, by the inlanders who come here and insist on eating in Little Southern Tea Roomes on side streets.

115   The natives put up with a lot back here where I came from. If the inhabitants of Kentucky are distrustful of strangers, that is duly noted as an entertaining local trait. But if a New Yorker says that he doesn't like Kentuckians he is marked as a cold churl. It is perennially difficult for the New Yorker who subscribes to a circu- 120 lating library to understand how the city survived destruction during the Civil War. When he reads about those regional demigods haunted by ancestral daemons and festooned in magnolia blossoms and ghosts who composed practically the whole Confederate Army, he wonders what happened to them en route. I asked 125 Whitey Bimstein what he thought about that one. He said: "Our guys must have slapped their ears down." Whitey does not know that we have been paying a war indemnity ever since in the form of royalties.

COMMENTARY

THIS SELECTION provides a clear example of the form of essay this section will include. This form often looks like autobiography (all but two of the selections here are written in the first person), but it actually uses personal experience merely as illustration and the first person—when it does use it—as a convenient device: the first person allows the author to speak with the authority of first-hand information, to include the homely and often impressive kind of illustration which cannot be used in a more formal kind of essay, and, above all, to speak freely of his feelings about his subject. Mr. Leibling, for example, manages to convey to us a fairly complicated set of feelings about New York.

It is part of his New-York character, a character he is proud of, to be superior to the provincial sentimentality which he calls being "quaint and regional" (line 19). At the same time, he loves New York as he thinks only a real, dyed-in-the-wool New Yorker can (Alistair Cooke has this feeling about New York, too, in selection 16). It therefore irritates him when people from other parts of the country—especially people from the South—boast about the special regional merits of the place they come from and take a superior attitude toward New York, as if it had no characteristic life of its own. He is aware that his attitude will seem absurd to people who are not from New York; he has heard all too often that New York is only a place to visit, that no one there has any roots, that it is all hard glitter, pavement, and sky-scrapers. He is genuinely belligerent in his feeling that such people are wrong, but he knows well enough that their feeling is the common one, and therefore he attacks them, not directly but by irony because he is on the defensive: even his title, "Apology for Breathing," shows this attitude: the real New Yorker must say, "Excuse me for living," because most Americans are convinced that there is no such person.

These are the feelings which dominate the essay and they are particularly Mr. Leibling's concern in the first two paragraphs, where he is setting up his subject for us. Notice the irony of the first sentence; all these people are in New York and obviously are going to remain in New York, but they keep insisting that the "real" America is some place else. Mr. Leibling reduces this habit to an absurdity by the parenthesis at the end of the sentence (lines 4–5). In the same way, in the last sentence of the paragraph (lines 10–12), he makes the reported excitement of his friends seem either faked or ridiculous by comparing it to his feeling when the "Jerome Avenue express rolls into Eighty-sixth Street station." He is, of course, only pretending to be "ashamed" of this feeling; he thinks it is the sensible feeling and that his friends ought to be—though they are not—the ones who feel ashamed, because they are absurdly sentimental. Of this sentimentality he provides a parody in the second paragraph (lines 13–20) by showing us how a New Yorker would talk if he had the same exaggerated feeling about all the rest of the country that people from the South or the West have. The only thing such a person would know about any place else would be that it was not New York; he would, of course, like professional Southerners and Westerners, be quite kind about it and indicate that he had been there and found it "a nice spot."

Having made these feelings clear, Mr. Leibling needs only to suggest them in the rest of the essay to keep us aware of them. He is now ready to tell us what is really fine about New York to a man who knows it well but is neither provincial nor sentimental about it. Actually, he is expressing a strong and carefully defined love of New York, but this feeling is not at all the same sort of sentiment as the second-hand, calendar-art love of quaintness which he associates with regionalists from other parts of the country. We are made clearly aware of how much feeling there is in his attitude when, at the end of the third paragraph (lines 21–31), he compares people who think the articulation of New York life is merely mechanical (that is, economic determinists) to "people who look at a fine woman and remind you that the human body is composed of one dollar and sixty-two cents worth of chemicals." Mr. Leibling does not deny this fact, any more than he overlooks the fact that the articulated variety of New York—perhaps he would say of all of life—depends on a social organization that is in many ways, like the organization of a clock, mechanical. He is only asserting that this view is partial and leaves out what matters most: a magnificent Renaissance clock (like the one on the Piazza San Marco in Venice, for example) is not the same kind of thing as a Baby Ben. Apart from the merely mechanical beauty of the clockwork itself, what it actuates is not merely a timepiece but a beautiful and meaningful allegory which "distracts one's attention from the advance of the hour hand." This comparison makes it clear that the New York Mr. Leibling loves is particularly suited to be the home town of people who share with him a certain view of life.

In the next paragraph (lines 32–53) Mr. Leibling shows us in some detail how this view of New York "strengthens [one's] hold on reality" (line 38), if one shares this philosophy with Mr. Leibling. What is most important in this paragraph is Mr. Leibling's sense of the way New York coordinates an enormous variety of people with widely varied occupations, all of whom carry on those occupations in a very ordinary and human way, solemnly making themselves bishops of churches they have invented, worrying over a tropical fish as if it were a new baby, ruminating over a new night club with the self-importance of a real-estate tycoon contemplating a new Rockefeller Center. It would be easier for him, he concludes (lines 49–53), to be convinced of the existence of God by all this than by what people like Thoreau think of as the beauties of nature—not, as we can tell from phrases like "shy green sprigs of poison ivy," beautiful to Mr. Leibling. (Do you know enough about the attitude of the eighteenth-century Deists toward the universe and God to see the resemblance of Mr. Leibling's view to theirs? If you do, do you then see a resemblance between Mr. Leibling's attitude and that held by Mr. Wilson in selection 31?) Mr. Leibling's ability to recall an apparently inexhaustible number of particulars about the daily lives of New Yorkers has a great deal to do with his ability to convince us that he really does feel as he says he does. The ability to summon up particulars in this way is the best evidence an author can give us of the strength of his feeling for his subject; it is also the only means he has for making us share his feeling.

Mr. Leibling now comes to the heart of his essay, a series of paragraphs on a carefully selected list of characteristics, namely, language, the sense of the past, manners, the beauty of the women, the healthiness of the climate. There is something almost sly about this selection of topics; it bears a considerable resemblance to the selection of topics one might find in a conventional guidebook to a famous and self-approving city. Something of this slyness controls the way Mr. Leibling deals with these topics, too. It is all part of his mockery of the self-conscious regionalist of other parts of America. But he is quite serious in dealing with these aspects of New York. Indeed, he obviously thinks New York has something to show in these respects that is much more important and interesting than what can be shown by other parts of the United States. Back where *they* come from, the *"retarded* inhabitants of the Great Smoky mountains" speak a dialect; in New York where he comes from, they speak a language of considerable antiquity and interest (lines 54–58). Do you see how the ending of this paragraph (lines 71–73) fits in with Mr. Leibling's feeling that the provincialism of other regions is often a bad kind of provincialism? Mr. Liebling is half-joking with his reference to "the diaspora" (line 74) and his comparison of the dialects of Cork and New York with Italian and Provencal (lines 75–76); these are very elevating comparisons. But he is partly serious, too, for he thinks it less foolish to talk this way about New York speech than to talk with solemn folklore seriousness about mountain dialects. In the same way, he makes a virtue of New York's up-to-dateness, its unwillingness to live in the past (lines 83–93); he feels that cities which still talk about clipper ships and Revolutionary battles do so because they have had nothing of equal importance in their lives since. New York had all these things—and more of them than other cities—but it has more interesting ones now.

Notice how, in making similar points about New York manners, Mr. Leibling deliberately resorts to the language of New York ("Whenever you hear a drinker let a blat out of him. . . . Prairie geniuses are raced in cheap company . . ."), as if to mock the habit of people from other parts of the country whose speech becomes more markedly their native dialect when they are praising their home towns in the presence of outlanders. It is characteristic of the feelings of this essay that Mr. Leibling uses this language half-jokingly, as if to say, "if you people from other parts of the country want to know how you sound to us, listen a minute." The same motive dictates what he has to say about the beauty of New York's women. S. Klein's is not Bergdorf's, but if you do not know how much better its taste is than Hollywood's, Mr. Leibling, as a New Yorker, has nothing but scorn for you. As a New Yorker, too, he is clearly convinced by his experience with people from other parts of the country that the straightening of people's teeth when they are young is a practice largely limited to New York. The remark about Little Southern Tea Roomes with which the paragraph closes (lines 113–114) is a deliberately obvious display of prejudice (the statistics obviously reveal no such thing) used to make us aware of the extent to which Mr. Leibling is joking.

Having completed his guidebook account of some of the characteristic features of New York, Mr. Leibling returns for his conclusion to his opening idea, a comparison of New Yorkers and people from other regions. Note how he deliberately reverses the usual language and calls the New Yorkers "natives," the Kentuckians merely "inhabitants" (lines 115–116). He pretends to be puzzled that the heroic Southerners of Civil-War romances failed to conquer the North and he consults his friend Whitey Bimstein, who gave him such good advice about the country in line 17, and, in the language of his profession, Whitey provides us with what Mr. Leibling really thinks— except for the last indignant grumble about the way the South has outmaneuvered New York with books in praise of its unique virtues and superiorities. With this final grumble, Mr. Leibling returns to the half-comic indignation at the regional pride of other parts of the country with which he began.

31 / Miami*

EDMUND WILSON

*C**OTTON BLOSSOM EXPRESS*: I went to sleep in the winter darkness, and wake up to a dazzle of golden light on green palms and low-growing pines that drip with Florida moss. An extraordinary pageant of bird-life presents itself outside the window: snowy egrets, several kinds of heron—some bluish, some beige—and other darker long-winged birds that I take to be buzzards—all looking as if they had flown straight out of Audubon: how excited he must have been when he came here. There are also some smaller birds that fly in flocks with quick twinkling wing-beats, and one experiences a pleasure that has something in common with the pleasure derived from music in following the contrasts of tempo between these and the slower rhythms of the larger birds that hover. They all fly quite close to the train and not far from the endless pale swamps and plains. It is wonderful to watch an egret alighting and folding its wings, deliberately, with dignity and grace.

Miami: I have never been here before and am astounded and appalled by this place. It is not that it is particularly different from other American seaside resorts, from Asbury Park to Coronado Beach, but that here both the cheap and the expensive aspects have been developed on a scale that I have never elsewhere seen equalled. You have acres of nougat-like shops, mountain ranges of

---

* From *Red, Black, Blond and Olive* by Edmund Wilson (Oxford Press, 1956). Reprinted by permission of Edmund Wilson.

232

vanilla ice-cream hotels. Miami Beach goes on for miles, with its monotonous lines of palms, its thousands of hotels and houses which seem to have had imposed on them, by the exigency of a city-planning board, a blanched and insipid uniformity. It even makes one feel more kindly toward Southern California, with its elements of lunatic fantasy. What draws people down to this vacuum? How do they amuse themselves here?

These vacationists look soft and vapid. You rarely see a really pretty girl, and the men do not give the impression of doing much fishing or swimming. You find them at the movies in the evening. The American ideal of luxury is in Miami carried to lengths that I have never encountered before. At my hotel, I had the annoyance of removing encasements of cellophane from the toilet seat and the drinking tumbler. In the movie-house, the seats are the kind that swing noiselessly back and forth to let people get in and out, and their cushions melt beneath one like a featherbed. A subdued indirect lighting, like the sweet creamy liquid of an ice-cream soda, bathes a dove-gray and shrimp-pink interior, the walls of which are ornamented with large cameo-like white seashells framing naked mythological figures that seem to have been badly imitated from the bas-reliefs of Paul Manship in Rockefeller Center, and with branching white plaster exfoliations that remind one of the legs and defensive antennae of the crawfish in the Miami aquarium. The film—*Oh, You Beautiful Doll*—was a technicolor that covered the whole surface of a high and overpowering screen with a routine sentimental romance, trumped up to manufacture glamor from the career of an American song-writer whose songs were widely sung in my college days. They were commonplace enough then, and today they are simply sickly. These attempts on the part of Hollywood to exploit the immediate past—in which the fashions of the eighties and nineties are sometimes confused with those of the twenties—show the precipitous decline of the movies as purveyors of entertainment, since the producers, after wrecking such contemporary talent as their salaries have tempted to Hollywood, have now been obliged to fall back on the favorites, first, second or third rate, of the day before yesterday and yesterday,

when it was possible for a producer or an actor, a composer or a
60 dancer, to perfect an art of his own and create for himself a reputation. Yet this product has its steady customers: one finds oneself
among them here. Comfortably padded in the muffled atmosphere
that seems to smell of scented face-powder—one cannot tell
whether the theater has been perfumed or the women are all using
65 the same cosmetics—this inert and featureless drove that have been
drifting through the bleached sunny streets now sit watching ster-
eotyped characters that are made to appear impressive by being
photographed in very bright colors and gigantically magnified. The
three shorts that follow the first showing of the film all happen to
70 deal with animals: a hunting number, an animated cartoon that
gets some not ill-deserved laughs, and a picture about racing whippets. The commentator seems slightly embarrassed at the spectacle
of the uniformed attendants who have a full-time job grooming the
whippets. "You may think they work as hard as the dogs," he pro-
75 pounds, with his microphone emphasis that gropes through time
and space and can never drive any nails. "Well, they work a lot
harder!" The truth is that so many Americans, specialized in operating machines or in transacting long-distance business, have de-
teriorated as animal organisms, that we now have a special pleasure
80 in watching almost any agile animal. What the audience gets out
of these animal shorts is the same thing that I have been getting
out of looking out the window at the birds and contrasting them
with the Miami vacationers.

This is all the kind of thing, I realize, that strikes foreigners who
85 visit this country, but that I have long ago arranged my life in such
a way as to avoid or ignore, so that I am likely to be shocked by
and to discount the uncomplimentary reports of visitors. Miami is
a rude revelation: I had not really known this was going on. I read
uneasily of President Truman's recent arrival in Florida for one of
90 a long series of sunlit holidays. This is the place where he seems
most at home. It is only when I get to the airfield that my national
self-respect picks up. It is a feat to have conceived, to have built
and to navigate these passenger planes. We humans have contrived
our wings by deliberate calculations, out of inorganic materials,

instead of growing them out of our bodies, and this does leave us 95
less hardy than the buzzard, less graceful than the white egret; but
we have, after all, by our planes, in other ways surpassed the birds,
and there had been moments in Miami when I was doubtful of
that before I took off for Haiti. And those disparate rhythms of
flight that I found so delightful to watch, Walt Disney, in his film 100
Snow White, where deer and rabbits and other animals are shown
running together at different speeds and gaits, has rendered them
for the first time in plastic art. The multiplied drawings of the
studio that turns out the Disney cartoons are as anonymous as the
hundreds of parts that go to make up a plane. I couldn't myself 105
have invented the simplest of these mechanisms or processes; but
the current prestige of the United States is partly derived from
these, and I cannot help feeling a pride in them.

QUESTIONS

1. Here is another selection which appears at first glance to be
autobiographical but which is seen, on inspection, to be focussed with
beautiful precision on an aspect of American life. The first paragraph,
with its description of birds, is very important to the plan of this selection, despite its casual air. At what places, later in the selection,
does Mr. Wilson make clear to us his reasons for starting with this
description of birds (lines 1–16)?

2. Who was Audubon, that the birds could all look "as if they had
flown straight out of" him (line 7)?

3. Mr. Wilson has a good reason for every adverb and adjective
he uses to describe the egret's landing in lines 14–16, but we do not
know what it is until we come to lines 30–32. Explain the connection?
Point out another place in the selection where he uses a similar
contrast.

4. What is Mr. Wilson suggesting about the people who like Miami
when he describes the colors of the shops and hotels as "nougat-like"
and "vanilla ice-cream" (lines 22–23)? Where else in the selection
does he do the same thing?

5. Obviously the "blanched and insipid uniformity" of Miami was

not imposed "by the exigency of a city-planning board" (lines 25–26). How was it imposed?

6. Why does Mr. Wilson prefer the "lunatic fantasy" of Southern California—little as he evidently likes it—to Miami (lines 26–28)?

7. Explain why Mr. Wilson ends the second paragraph with the two questions in lines 28–29.

8. The adjective "soft" (line 30) refers to what Mr. Wilson says in the next sentence (lines 30–32); what does "vapid" refer to?

9. In lines 34–36 Mr. Wilson takes it for granted that the hotel's reason for encasing things in cellophane is nonsense; explain why he thinks so.

10. Mr. Wilson speaks of the "American ideal of luxury" (lines 33–34) as if he were a foreigner and uninvolved with this ideal; what does he tell us elsewhere in this selection which shows this is at least partly true?

11. One of the most effective things about Mr. Wilson's description of the theater (lines 38–46) is the way he makes us feel that he is neither indulging a preconceived prejudice nor inventing unfavorable comparisons afterwards but that he really looked closely at the theater and the film and felt at the time the things he tells us. What are some of the things in his description that make us feel this?

12. Why does *Oh, You Beautiful Doll* make Mr. Wilson feel that Hollywood is artistically sterile (lines 51–61)?

13. Explain why Mr. Wilson inserts a reference to the audience (lines 61–68) between his description of the feature and his description of the shorts?

14. Why does Mr. Wilson dwell on the animals in the shorts (lines 68–72)?

15. What does Mr. Wilson mean by saying the commentator's "emphasis . . . gropes through time and space" and that it "can never drive any nails" (lines 75–76)?

16. Why does Mr. Wilson compare the planes with the buzzard and "the white egret" (lines 95–96)?

17. The conclusion of this selection is a very brilliant piece of construction and should be read with special care. Explain the special aptness of Mr. Wilson's statement that "there had been moments in Miami" when he doubted that we were superior to the birds in any way (lines 98–99).

18. What has Mr. Wilson said earlier that gives special point to

his reference to the delight of watching the rhythm of animals running at different speeds (lines 101–102)?

19. Why is the rhythm of the running animals in Walt Disney's cartoon, *Snow White,* particularly apt at this point in the discussion (lines 101–102)?

20. Earlier (lines 85–86), Mr. Wilson had dissociated himself from the American ideal of luxury that is reflected in Miami; does that help to explain why he is careful to tell us here that he could not have invented "the simplest of these mechanisms or processes" he has just been describing (lines 105–106)?

SUGGESTED TOPICS

1. Write a paragraph in which you describe what there is about "the American ideal of luxury" (lines 33–34) that distresses Mr. Wilson; see if you can think of examples from American life other than the ones Mr. Wilson uses.

2. Write a paragraph in which you explain the way Mr. Wilson uses throughout the selection the description of the birds which he gives in the first paragraph (lines 1–16).

3. Write a paragraph in which you show how Mr. Wilson, without using any specifically derogatory words, makes us feel that the kind of luxury represented by the theater he describes in lines 38–46 is vapid and second-rate.

32 / Once More to the Lake*

E. B. WHITE

August, 1941

ONE SUMMER, along about 1904, my father rented a camp on a lake in Maine and took us all there for the month of August. We all got ringworm from some kittens and had to rub Pond's Extract on our arms and legs night and morning, and
5 my father rolled over in a canoe with all his clothes on; but outside of that the vacation was a success and from then on none of us ever thought there was any place in the world like that lake in Maine. We returned summer after summer—always on August first for one month. I have since become a salt-water man, but
10 sometimes in summer there are days when the restlessness of the tides and the fearful cold of the sea water and the incessant wind which blows across the afternoon and into the evening make me wish for the placidity of a lake in the woods. A few weeks ago this feeling got so strong I bought myself a couple of bass hooks and a
15 spinner and returned to the lake where we used to go, for a week's fishing and to revisit old haunts.

I took along my son, who had never had any fresh water up his nose and who had seen lily pads only from train windows. On the journey over to the lake I began to wonder what it would be like.
20 I wondered how time would have marred this unique, this holy spot—the coves and streams, the hills that the sun set behind, the

camps and the paths behind the camps. I was sure that the tarred
road would have found it out and I wondered in what other ways
it would be desolated. It is strange how much you can remember
about places like that once you allow your mind to return into 25
the grooves which lead back. You remember one thing, and that
suddenly reminds you of another thing. I guess I remember clearest
of all the early mornings, when the lake was cool and motionless,
remembered how the bedroom smelled of the lumber it was made
of and of the wet woods whose scent entered through the screen. 30
The partitions in the camp were thin and did not extend clear to
the top of the rooms, and as I was always the first up I would dress
softly so as not to wake the others and sneak out into the sweet
outdoors and start out in the canoe, keeping close along the shore
in the long shadows of the pines. I remembered being very careful 35
never to rub my paddle against the thwart for fear of disturbing the
stillness of the cathedral.

The lake had never been what you would call a wild lake. There
were cottages sprinkled around the shores, and it was in farming
country although the shores of the lake were quite heavily wooded. 40
Some of the cottages were owned by nearby farmers, and you would
live at the shore and eat your meals at the farmhouse. That's what
our family did. But although it wasn't wild, it was a fairly large
and undisturbed lake and there were places in it which, to a child
at least, seemed infinitely remote and primeval.   45

I was right about the tar: it led to within half a mile of the
shore. But when I got back there, with my boy, and we settled into
a camp near a farmhouse and into the kind of summertime I had
known, I could tell that it was going to be pretty much the same
as it had been before—I knew it, lying in bed the first morning, 50
smelling the bedroom, and hearing the boy sneak quietly out and
go off along the shore in a boat. I began to sustain the illusion that
he was I, and therefore, by simple transposition, that I was my
father. This sensation persisted, kept cropping up all the time we
were there. It was not an entirely new feeling, but in this setting it 55
grew much stronger. I seemed to be living a dual existence. I would
be in the middle of some simple act, I would be picking up a bait

box or laying down a table fork, or I would be saying something, and suddenly it would be not I but my father who was saying the
60 words or making the gesture. It gave me a creepy sensation.

We went fishing the first morning. I felt the same damp moss covering the worms in the bait can, and saw the dragonfly alight on the tip of my rod as it hovered a few inches from the surface of the water. It was the arrival of this fly that convinced me beyond
65 any doubt that everything was as it always had been, that the years were a mirage and there had been no years. The small waves were the same, chucking the rowboat under the chin as we fished at anchor, and the boat was the same boat, the same color green and the ribs broken in the same places, and under the floorboards the
70 same fresh-water leavings and debris—the dead helgramite, the wisps of moss, the rusty discarded fish-hook, the dried blood from yesterday's catch. We stared silently at the tips of our rods, at the dragonflies that came and went. I lowered the tip of mine into the water, tentatively, pensively dislodging the fly, which darted two
75 feet away, poised, darted two feet back, and came to rest again a little farther up the rod. There had been no years between the ducking of this dragonfly and the other one—the one that was part of memory. I looked at the boy, who was silently watching his fly, and it was my hands that held his rod, my eyes watching. I felt
80 dizzy and didn't know which rod I was at the end of.

We caught two bass, hauling them in briskly as though they were mackerel, pulling them over the side of the boat in a businesslike manner without any landing net, and stunning them with a blow on the back of the head. When we got back for a swim before
85 lunch, the lake was exactly where we had left it, the same number of inches from the dock, and there was only the merest suggestion of a breeze. This seemed an utterly enchanted sea, this lake you could leave to its own devices for a few hours and come back to, and find that it had not stirred, this constant and trustworthy body
90 of water. In the shallows, the dark, water-soaked sticks and twigs, smooth and old, were undulating in clusters on the bottom against the clean ribbed sand, and the track of the mussel was plain. A school of minnows swam by, each minnow with its small individual

shadow, doubling the attendance, so clear and sharp in the sunlight. Some of the other campers were in swimming, along the shore, one of them with a cake of soap, and the water felt thin and clear and unsubstantial. Over the years there had been this person with the cake of soap, this cultist, and here he was. There had been no years.

Up to the farmhouse to dinner through the teeming, dusty field, the road under our sneakers was only a two-track road. The middle track was missing, the one with the marks of the hooves and the splotches of dried, flaky manure. There had always been three tracks to choose from in choosing which track to walk in; now the choice was narrowed down to two. For a moment I missed terribly the middle alternative. But the way led past the tennis court, and something about the way it lay there in the sun reassured me; the tape had loosened along the backline, the alleys were green with plantains and other weeds, and the net (installed in June and removed in September) sagged in the dry noon, and the whole place steamed with midday heat and hunger and emptiness. There was a choice of pie for dessert, and one was blueberry and one was apple, and the waitresses were the same country girls, there having been no passage of time, only the illusion of it as in a dropped curtain— the waitresses were still fifteen; their hair had been washed, that was the only difference—they had been to the movies and seen the pretty girls with the clean hair.

Summertime, oh summertime, pattern of life indelible, the fade-proof lake, the woods unshatterable, the pasture with the sweet-fern and the juniper forever and ever, summer without end; this was the background, and the life along the shore was the design, the cottagers with their innocent and tranquil design, their tiny docks with the flagpole and the American flag floating against the white clouds in the blue sky, the little paths over the roots of the trees leading from camp to camp and the paths leading back to the outhouses and the can of lime for sprinkling, and at the souvenir counters at the store the miniature birch-bark canoes and the post cards that showed things looking a little better than they looked. This was the American family at play, escaping the city

130 heat, wondering whether the newcomers in the camp at the head
of the cove were "common" or "nice," wondering whether it was
true that the people who drove up for Sunday dinner at the farmhouse were turned away because there wasn't enough chicken.

It seemed to me, as I kept remembering all this, that those times
135 and those summers had been infinitely precious and worth saving.
There had been jollity and peace and goodness. The arriving (at
the beginning of August) had been so big a business in itself, at the
railway station the farm wagon drawn up, the first smell of the
pine-laden air, the first glimpse of the smiling farmer, and the great
140 importance of the trunks and your father's enormous authority in
such matters, and the feel of the wagon under you for the long ten-
mile haul, and at the top of the last long hill catching the first view
of the lake after eleven months of not seeing this cherished body
of water. The shouts and cries of the other campers when they
145 saw you, and the trunks to be unpacked, to give up their rich
burden. (Arriving was less exciting nowadays, when you sneaked
up in your car and parked it under a tree near the camp and took
out the bags and in five minutes it was all over, no fuss, no loud
wonderful fuss about trunks.)

150 Peace and goodness and jollity. The only thing that was wrong
now, really, was the sound of the place, an unfamiliar nervous
sound of the outboard motors. This was the note that jarred, the
one thing that would sometimes break the illusion and set the years
moving. In those other summertimes, all the motors were inboard;
155 and when they were at a little distance, the noise they made was a
sedative, an ingredient of summer sleep. They were one-cylinder
and two-cylinder engines, and some were make-and-break and some
were jump-spark, but they all made a sleepy sound across the lake.
The one-lungers throbbed and fluttered, and the twin-cylinder ones
160 purred and purred, and that was a quiet sound too. But now the
campers all had outboards. In the daytime, in the hot mornings,
these motors made a petulant, irritable sound; at night, in the still
evening when the afterglow lit the water, they whined about one's
ears like mosquitoes. My boy loved our rented outboard, and his
165 great desire was to achieve singlehanded mastery over it, and au-

thority, and he soon learned the trick of choking it a little (but
not too much), and the adjustment of the needle valve. Watching
him I would remember the things you could do with the old one-
cylinder engine with the heavy flywheel, how you could have it
eating out of your hand if you got really close to it spiritually. 170
Motor boats in those days didn't have clutches, and you made a
landing by shutting off the motor at the proper time and coasting
in with a dead rudder. But there was a way of reversing them, if
you learned the trick, by cutting the switch and putting it on again
exactly on the final dying revolution of the flywheel, so that it 175
would kick back against compression and begin reversing. Ap-
proaching a dock in a strong following breeze it was difficult to
slow up sufficiently by the ordinary coasting method, and if a boy
felt he had complete mastery over his motor, he was tempted to
keep it running beyond its time and then reverse it a few feet from 180
the dock. It took a cool nerve, because if you threw the switch a
twentieth of a second too soon you would catch the flywheel when
it still had speed enough to go up past center, and the boat would
leap ahead, charging bull-fashion at the dock.

We had a good week at the camp. The bass were biting well and 185
the sun shone endlessly, day after day. We would be tired at night
and lie down in the accumulated heat of the little bedrooms after
the long hot day and the breeze would stir almost imperceptibly
outside and the smell of the swamp drift in through the rusty
screens. Sleep would come easily and in the morning the red squir- 190
rel would be on the roof, tapping out his gay routine. I kept remembering everything, lying in the bed in the mornings—the small
steamboat that had a long rounded stern like the lip of a Ubangi,
and how quietly she ran on the moonlight sails, when the older
boys played their mandolins and the girls sang and we ate dough- 195
nuts dipped in sugar, and how sweet the music was on the water
in the shining night, and what it had felt like to think about girls
then. After breakfast we would go up to the store and the things
were in the same place—the minnows in a bottle, the plugs and
spinners disarranged and pawed over by the youngsters from the 200
boys' camp, the fig newtons and the Beeman's gum. Outside, the

road was tarred and cars stood in front of the store. Inside, all was just as it had always been, except there was more Coca Cola and not so much Moxie and root beer and birch beer and sarsaparilla.
205 We would walk out with a bottle of pop apiece and sometimes the pop would backfire up our noses and hurt. We explored the streams, quietly, where the turtles slid off the sunny logs and dug their way into the soft bottom; and we lay on the town wharf and fed worms to the tame bass. Everywhere we went I had trouble
210 making out which was I, the one walking at my side, the one walking in my pants.

One afternoon while we were there at that lake a thunderstorm came up. It was like the revival of an old melodrama that I had seen long ago with childish awe. The second-act climax of the
215 drama of the electrical disturbance over a lake in America had not changed in any important respect. This was the big scene, still the big scene. The whole thing was so familiar, the first feeling of oppression and heat and a general air around camp of not wanting to go very far away. In midafternoon (it was all the same) a curious
220 darkening of the sky, and a lull in everything that had made life tick; and then the way the boats suddenly swung the other way at their moorings with the coming of a breeze out of the new quarter, and the premonitory rumble. Then the kettle drum, then the snare, then the bass drum and cymbals, then crackling light against
225 the dark, and the gods grinning and licking their chops in the hills. Afterward the calm, the rain steadily rustling in the calm lake, the return of light and hope and spirits, and the campers running out in joy and relief to go swimming in the rain, their bright cries perpetuating the deathless joke about how they were getting simply
230 drenched, and the children screaming with delight at the new sensation of bathing in the rain, and the joke about getting drenched linking the generations in a strong indestructible chain. And the comedian who waded in carrying an umbrella.

When the others went swimming my son said he was going in
235 too. He pulled his dripping trunks from the line where they had hung all through the shower, and wrung them out. Languidly, and with no thought of going in, I watched him, his hard little body,

skinny and bare, saw him wince slightly as he pulled up around his vitals the small, soggy, icy garment. As he buckled the swollen belt suddenly my groin felt the chill of death. 240

QUESTIONS

1. Like Mr. Wilson, Mr. White is not interested primarily in his own experience. He wants to make us understand a subtle but nearly universal experience, the way our feelings register the effect of time and thus, ultimately, the sense of mortality. Like Mr. Wilson, he starts with something which is apparently irrelevant but which turns out to be of considerable importance to the meaning of the selection; this is his description of the sea, of the *restlessness* of the tides, the *fearful* cold of the sea water, the *incessant* wind. In all these respects, the sea is in striking contrast to the lake, with its almost enchanted stillness. Make sure you understand this contrast and the way it foreshadows the conclusion of the selection.

2. Mr. White's statement about the sea wind "which blows across the afternoon and into the evening" (lines 11–12) is oddly phrased. It is so phrased because Mr. White is thinking of the wind as like time, which blows us incessantly through life; can you explain the feelings about time which suggest this comparison to Mr. White?

3. What is there about the lake which makes Mr. White describe it as "this holy spot" (lines 20–21)? Does he use this same idea in describing it later in the paragraph?

4. Mr. White is surprised to discover how much the lake is as he remembers it from his boyhood; still, it has changed in small ways which keep reminding him that he is not in his boyhood: the tarred road is there (lines 46–47), the girls at the farm have washed their hair (lines 115–116). Pick out other small things that keep reminding him, in spite of his general feeling, that time has been at work.

5. Mr. White is careful to tell us, before we get to the lake at all, how he remembers having sneaked out of the cottage early in the morning to canoe on the lake (lines 31–35). Why does he do so?

6. Mr. White first mentions directly the effect of this "going back" in lines 52–60. Notice that it is not a simple effect; it involves his identifying himself in one way with his small son and in another way with his father; why does it? Mr. White does not tell at this point—

perhaps he did not discover it himself until later in the experience—exactly why this illusion gave him "a creepy sensation" (line 60), but if we have read the whole selection, we should be able to say why and thus to show how precise the word "creepy" is here. Show how precise this adjective is by pointing to other passages where he repeats this idea and makes its meaning more specific.

7. In the paragraph beginning at line 61, Mr. White becomes convinced that "everything was as it always had been" (line 65) and he makes us share this conviction by telling us exactly how the experience of the past was happening again; what larger conclusion about life does this experience lead him to?

8. Why does Mr. White conclude the paragraph which begins at line 81 by saying, "There had been no years"? How does this conclusion explain his selection of the details in the paragraph and the way he describes them?

9. What is the relevance to Mr. White's theme of the general remarks about summertime with which he begins the paragraph that starts at line 118?

10. In the paragraph which begins at line 150, Mr. White tells us how the presence of outboard motors changes things, largely, he suggests, for the worse, and he ends the paragraph with an account of the great satisfaction there was with the old inboard motors in getting them to eat "out of your hand" (lines 167–170). Why does he say that you had to get really close to them "spiritually" (line 170) in order to do so? Why does he include in this paragraph a discussion of his son's great desire "to achieve singlehanded mastery over [their inboard motor], and authority" (line 164)? What is the point of his telling us exactly what such mastery consisted in (lines 164–167)?

11. In the preceding paragraph (beginning at line 134), Mr. White tells us about the excitement of arriving at the lake when he was a boy and about the things he remembers specifically that created that excitement (lines 136–144). The paragraph ends with some specific details about the way he and his son arrived at the lake (lines 146–149) which, he suggests, were not nearly so exciting as the events of arrival when he was a boy. Do you suppose his son found arriving "less exciting nowadays"? Do you think Mr. White meant us to think of what his son was feeling? Is there anything in the succeeding paragraph which suggests that he did mean us to think of his son's feelings?

12. Does Mr. White's handling of his son's attitude to the visit to

the lake in these two paragraphs (lines 134–184) help us to understand why he included his son's attitude in this essay and not just his own? What connection does the contrast between these two attitudes have with the central idea of the essay?

13. The thunderstorm which is described in the paragraph that begins at line 212 reminds Mr. White most strikingly of his own boyhood; he calls it a melodrama (line 213)—that is, something which looks tragic but which we know all along will turn out happily; the passing of the thunderstorm appears to him to bring a "return of light and hope and spirits," and in fact it does to many of the young campers around the lake (lines 226–233). But this appearance of being mere melodrama which the storm has for Mr. White is an illusion, and an illusion that is full of irony for him. How does the last paragraph make this clear to him and to us (lines 234–240)?

14. Explain why words like "deathless" (line 229) and "indestructible" (line 232) occur in Mr. White's description of the campers' reactions to the storm?

SUGGESTED TOPICS

1. Write a paragraph in which you explain as precisely as you can just how much Mr. White means and does not mean that "the years were a mirage and there had been no years" (lines 65–66).

2. In the paragraph which begins at line 118 and describes summertime, Mr. White remarks, "This was the American family at play . . ." (line 129). Write two paragraphs in which you compare these Americans at play with the Americans at play described by Mr. Wilson in "Miami."

3. All the details about a fresh-water lake which Mr. White gives in the paragraph that begins at line 81 will seem strictly accurate to anyone who has ever known such a lake. But they have another purpose than mere descriptive accuracy. Write a paragraph in which you explain that purpose and show how the details serve it, and another paragraph in which you explain why it is important that these details are strictly accurate.

33/ Farewell, My Lovely!*

LEE STROUT WHITE

I SEE BY THE NEW Sears Roebuck catalogue that it is still possible to buy an axle for a 1909 Model T Ford, but I am not deceived. The great days have faded, the end is in sight. Only one page in the current catalogue is devoted to parts and accesso-
5 ries for the Model T; yet everyone remembers the springtimes when the Ford gadget section was larger than men's clothing, almost as large as household furnishings. The last Model T was built in 1927, and the car is fading from what scholars call the American scene—which is an understatement, because to a few million who
10 grew up with it, the old Ford practically *was* the American scene.

It was the miracle God had wrought. And it was patently the sort of thing that could only happen once. Mechanically uncanny, it was like nothing that had ever come to the world before. Flourishing industries rose and fell with it. As a vehicle, it was hard-work-
15 ing, commonplace, heroic; and it often seemed to transmit those qualities to the persons who rode in it. My own generation identifies it with Youth, with its gaudy, irretrievable excitements; before it fades into the mist, I would like to pay it the tribute of a sigh that is not a sob, and set down random entries in a shape somewhat
20 less cumbersome than a Sears Roebuck catalogue.

The Model T was distinguished from all other makes of cars by the fact that its transmission was of a type known as planetary—

* Reprinted by permission, © 1936 The New Yorker Mazagine, Inc. Published in book form by G. P. Putnam under the title "Farewell to Model T."

which was half metaphysics, half sheer friction. Engineers accepted the word "planetary" in its epicycle sense, but I was always conscious that it also meant "wandering," "erratic." Because of the peculiar nature of this planetary element, there was always, in a Model T, a certain dull rapport between engine and wheels, and even when the car was in a state known as neutral, it trembled with a deep imperative and tended to inch forward. There was never a moment when the bands were not faintly egging the machine on. In this respect it was like a horse, rolling the bit on its tongue, and country people brought to it the same technique they used with draft animals.

Its most remarkable quality was its rate of acceleration. In its palmy days the Model T could take off faster than anything on the road. The reason was simple. To get under way, you simply hooked the third finger of the right hand around a lever on the steering column, pulled down hard, and shoved your left foot forcibly against the low-speed pedal. These were simple, positive motions; the car responded by lunging forward with a roar. After a few seconds of this turmoil, you took your toe off the pedal, eased up a mite on the throttle, and the car, possessed of only two forward speeds, catapulted directly into high with a series of ugly jerks and was off on its glorious errand. The abruptness of this departure was never equalled in other cars of the period. The human leg was (and still is) incapable of letting in a clutch with anything like the forthright abandon that used to send the Model T on its way. Letting in a clutch is a negative, hesitant motion, depending on a delicate nervous control; pushing down the Ford pedal was a simple, country motion—an expansive act, which came as natural as kicking an old door to make it budge.

The driver of the old Model T was a man enthroned. The car, with top up, stood seven feet high. The driver sat on top of the gas tank, brooding it with his body. When he wanted gasoline, he alighted along with everything else in the front seat; the seat was pulled off, the metal cap unscrewed, and a wooden stick thrust down to sound the liquid in the well. There were always a couple of these sounding sticks kicking around in the ratty sub-cushion

regions of a flivver. Refuelling was more of a social function then,
60 because the driver had to unbend, whether he wanted to or not.
Directly in front of the driver was the windshield—high, uncom-
promisingly erect. Nobody talked about air resistance, and the four
cylinders pushed the car through the atmosphere with a simple
disregard of physical law.

65   There was this about a Model T: the purchaser never regarded
his purchase as a complete, finished product. When you bought a
Ford, you figured you had a start—a vibrant, spirited framework
to which could be screwed an almost limitless assortment of decora-
tive and functional hardware. Driving away from the agency hug-
70 ging the new wheel between your knees, you were already full of
creative worry. A Ford was born naked as a baby, and a flourishing
industry grew up out of correcting its rare deficiencies and combat-
ting its fascinating diseases. Those were the great days of lily-
painting. I have been looking at some old Sears Roebuck cata-
75 logues, and they bring everything back so clear.

First you bought a Ruby Safety Reflector for the rear, so that
your posterior would glow in another car's brilliance. Then you
invested thirty-nine cents in some radiator Moto Wings, a popular
ornament which gave the Pegasus touch to the machine and did
80 something godlike to the owner. For nine cents you bought a fan-
belt guide to keep the belt from slipping off the pulley.

You bought a radiator compound to stop leaks. This was as
much a part of everybody's equipment as aspirin tablets are of a
medicine cabinet. You bought special oil to prevent chattering, a
85 clamp-on dash light, a patching outfit, a tool box which you bolted
to the running board, a sun visor, a steering-column brace to keep
the column rigid, and a set of emergency containers for gas, oil,
and water—three thin, disc-like cans which reposed in a case on the
running board during long, important journeys—red for gas, gray
90 for water, green for oil. It was only a beginning. After the car was
about a year old, steps were taken to check the alarming disintegration. (Model T was full of tumors, but they were benign.) A set
of anti-rattlers (98c) was a popular panacea. You hooked them on
to the gas and spark rods, to the brake pull rod, and to the steering-

rod connections. Hood silencers, of black rubber, were applied to 95 the fluttering hood. Shock-absorbers and snubbers gave "complete relaxation." Some people bought rubber pedal pads, to fit over the standard metal pedals. (I didn't like these, I remember.) Persons of a suspicious or pugnacious turn of mind bought a rear-view mirror; but most Model T owners weren't worried by what was com- 100 ing from behind because they would soon enough see it out in front. They rode in a state of cheerful catalepsy. Quite a large mutinous clique among Ford owners went over to a foot accelerator (you could buy one and screw it to the floor board), but there was a certain madness in these people, because the Model T, just as she 105 stood, had a choice of three foot pedals to push, and there were plenty of moments when both feet were occupied in the routine performance of duty and when the only way to speed up the engine was with the hand throttle.

Gadget bred gadget. Owners not only bought ready-made gadg- 110 ets, they invented gadgets to meet special needs. I myself drove my car directly from the agency to the blacksmith's, and had the smith affix two enormous iron brackets to the port running board to support an army trunk.

People who owned closed models builded along different lines: 115 they bought ball grip handles for opening doors, window antirattlers, and de-luxe flower vases of the cut-glass anti-splash type. People with delicate sensibilities garnished their car with a device called the Donna Lee Automobile Disseminator—a porous vase guaranteed, according to Sears, to fill the car with a "faint clean 120 odor of lavender." The gap between open cars and closed cars was not as great then as it is now: for $11.95, Sears Roebuck converted your touring car into a sedan and you went forth renewed. One agreeable quality of the old Fords was that they had no bumpers, and their fenders softened and wilted with the years and permitted 125 the driver to squeeze in and out of tight places.

Tires were 30 x 3½, cost about twelve dollars, and punctured readily. Everybody carried a Jiffy patching set, with a nutmeg grater to roughen the tube before the goo was spread on. Everybody was capable of putting on a patch, expected to have to, and did have to. 130

During my association with Model T's, self-starters were not a prevalent accessory. They were expensive and under suspicion. Your car came equipped with a serviceable crank, and the first thing you learned was how to Get Results. It was a special trick, and until you learned it (usually from another Ford owner, but sometimes by a period of appalling experimentation) you might as well have been winding up an awning. The trick was to leave the ignition switch off, proceed to the animal's head, pull the choke (which was a little wire protruding through the radiator), and give the crank two or three nonchalant upward lifts. Then, whistling as though thinking about something else, you would saunter back to the driver's cabin, turn the ignition on, return to the crank, and this time, catching it on the down stroke, give it a quick spin with plenty of That. If this procedure was followed, the engine almost always responded—first with a few scattered explosions, then with a tumultuous gunfire, which you checked by racing around to the driver's seat and retarding the throttle. Often, if the emergency brake hadn't been pulled all the way back, the car advanced on you the instant the first explosion occurred and you would hold it back by leaning your weight against it. I can still feel my old Ford nuzzling me at the curb, as though looking for an apple in my pocket.

In zero weather, ordinary cranking became an impossibility, except for giants. The oil thickened, and it became necessary to jack up the rear wheels, which, for some planetary reason, eased the throw.

The lore and legend that governed the Ford were boundless. Owners had their own theories about everything; they discussed mutual problems in that wise, infinitely resourceful way old women discuss rheumatism. Exact knowledge was pretty scarce, and often proved less effective than superstition. Dropping a camphor ball into the gas tank was a popular expedient; it seemed to have a tonic effect on both man and machine. There wasn't much to base exact knowledge on. The Ford driver flew blind. He didn't know the temperature of his engine, the speed of his car, the amount of his fuel, or the pressure of his oil (the old Ford lubricated itself by what was amiably described as the "splash system"). A speedometer cost money and was an extra, like a windshield-wiper. The dashboard of the early models was bare save for an ignition key; later models, grown effete, boasted an ammeter which pulsated alarmingly with the throbbing of the car. Under the dash was a box of coils, with vibrators which you adjusted, or thought you adjusted. Whatever the driver learned of his motor, he learned not through instruments but through sudden developments. I remember that the timer was one of the vital organs about which there was ample doctrine. When everything else had been checked, you "had a look" at the timer. It was an extravagantly odd little device, simple in construction, mysterious in function. It contained a roller, held by a spring, and there were four contact points on the inside of the case against which, many people believed, the roller rolled. I have had a timer apart on a sick Ford many times, but I never really knew what I was up to—I was just showing off before God. There were almost as many schools of thought as there were timers. Some people, when things went wrong, just clenched their teeth and gave the timer a smart crack with a wrench. Other people opened it up and blew on it. There was a school that held that the timer needed large amounts of oil; they fixed it by frequent baptism. And there was a school that was positive it was meant to run dry as a bone; these people were continually taking it off and wiping it. I remember once spitting into a timer; not in anger, but in a spirit of research. You see, the Model T driver moved in the realm of metaphysics. He believed his car could be hexed.

One reason the Ford anatomy was never reduced to an exact science was that, having "fixed" it, the owner couldn't honestly claim that the treatment had brought about the cure. There were too many authenticated cases of Fords fixing themselves—restored naturally to health after a short rest. Farmers soon discovered this, and it fitted nicely with their draft-horse philosophy: "Let 'er cool off and she'll snap into it again."

A Ford owner had Number One Bearing constantly in mind. This bearing, being at the front end of the motor, was the one that always burned out, because the oil didn't reach it when the car was climbing hills. (That's what I was always told, anyway.)

The oil used to recede and leave Number One dry as a clam flat;
you had to watch that bearing like a hawk. It was like a weak
205 heart—you could hear it start knocking, and that was when you
stopped and let her cool off. Try as you would to keep the oil supply right, in the end Number One always went out. "Number One
Bearing burned out on me and I had to have her replaced," you
would say, wisely; and your companions always had a lot to tell
210 about how to protect and pamper Number One to keep her alive.

Sprinkled not too liberally among the millions of amateur witch
doctors who drove Fords and applied their own abominable cures
were the heaven-set mechanics who could really make the car talk.
These professionals turned up in undreamed-of spots. One time,
215 on the banks of the Columbia River in Washington, I heard the
rear end go out of my Model T when I was trying to whip it up a
steep incline onto the deck of a ferry. Something snapped; the car
slid backward into the mud. It seemed to me like the end of the
trail. But the captain of the ferry, observing the withered remnant,
220 spoke up.

"What's got her?" he asked.

"I guess it's the rear end," I replied, listlessly. The captain leaned
over the rail and stared. Then I saw that there was a hunger in his
eyes that set him off from other men.
225 "Tell you what," he said, carelessly, trying to cover up his eager-
ness, "let's pull the son of a bitch up onto the boat, and I'll help
you fix her while we're going back and forth on the river."

We did just this. All that day I plied between the towns of
Pasco and Kennewick, while the skipper (who had once worked
230 in a Ford garage) directed the amazing work of resetting the bones
of my car.

Springtime in the heyday of the Model T was a delirious season.
Owning a car was still a major excitement, roads were still wonderful and bad. The Fords were obviously conceived in madness: any
235 car which was capable of going from forward into reverse without
any perceptible mechanical hiatus was bound to be a mighty challenging thing to the human imagination. Boys used to veer them
off the highway into a level pasture and run wild with them, as

though they were cutting up with a girl. Most everybody used the reverse pedal quite as much as the regular foot brake—it distributed 240 the wear over the bands and wore them all down evenly. That was the big trick, to wear all the bands down evenly, so that the final chattering would be total and the whole unit scream for renewal.

The days were golden, the nights were dim and strange. I still recall with trembling those loud, nocturnal crises when you drew 245 up to a signpost and raced the engine so the lights would be bright enough to read destinations by. I have never been really planetary since. I suppose it's time to say good-bye. Farewell, my lovely!

QUESTIONS

1. This selection is basically an account of the Model T Ford, but it uses the biographical method to give us the author's personal recollections of the Model T and thus to communicate to us the delight an owner felt in the eccentricities of the Model T. We can see that the Model T is the main subject if we notice the organization of the selection. It falls into six sections, an introduction, a section on the Model T's driving qualities, a section on extras, a section on starting, a section on caring for the Model T, and a conclusion. Where does each of these sections start. Why do they occur in the order in which they do?

2. In line 11 Mr. White is paraphrasing a Biblical statement, "What hath God wrought?" (Numbers, 23:23). Possibly, also, he is remembering that these were the first words ever sent by telegraph. In any event, this statement is partly an irony directed at those people who look on mechanical inventions as miracles. Explain why.

3. If the statement in line 11 is an irony, it is also partly serious and helps us to understand the feelings about the Model T which the author is trying to convey. In what sense, would you say, was the Model T a miracle and not merely a mechanical contrivance?

4. Why did the author always think of "planetary" as having the second sense he tells us about (lines 24–25)?

5. Why does he tell us, not only that the Model T in neutral "tended to inch forward," but also that "it trembled with a deep imperative" (lines 28–29)?

6. In lines 31–33 and lines 49–51, the author makes comparisons between handling a Model T and what he calls country motions or the handling of draft animals. Are these comparisons merely explanatory, or is he trying to convey something of his feelings about the Model T by them?

7. In the paragraph which begins at line 65, Mr. White speaks of the Model T's "vibrant, spirited framework" (line 67). These adjectives are metaphorical; where else in the paragraph does he use this metaphor? What does it suggest about the owner's feelings for the car?

8. In lines 73–74 Mr. White describes the days of the Model T as "the great days of lily-painting"; what does this remark mean? What does it have to do with the section of the selection which follows?

9. What does Mr. White mean by saying that the Moto Wings "did something godlike to the owner" (lines 78–80)?

10. What earlier metaphor leads Mr. White to speak of the Model T's having "tumors" that "were benign" and of "a popular panacea" (lines 92–93)?

11. Mr. White presumably puts "complete relaxation" (lines 96–97) in quotation marks because he is quoting directly from the Sears Roebuck catalogue; what other effect do these quotation marks have?

12. What does it mean to say that Model T owners "rode in a state of cheerful catalepsy" (line 102)?

13. Can you explain why the phrase "routine performance of duty" (lines 107–108) is comic understatement?

14. Why does Mr. White describe the much-dented fenders of the Model T as having "softened and wilted with the years" (line 125)?

15. What feelings on the part of the true lover of the Model T would have led him to be suspicious of the self-starter (lines 131–134)?

16. What feelings lead Mr. White, in his description of how a Model T was cranked, to refer to the car as an animal (line 138) and as "nuzzling" him (lines 150–151)?

17. What attitude on the part of the owner of the Model T is implied by Mr. White's describing him, when he is starting the car, as "nonchalant" (line 140), "whistling" (line 140) and sauntering (line 141)?

18. What does Mr. White mean by saying that "for some planetary reason" jacking the car up helped (lines 153–155)? Does this odd adjective occur elsewhere in the selection?

19. It is Mr. White's feeling that most of the elaborate lore on the subject of how to keep a Model T in operation was folklore; can you point to some of the places where he indicates this feeling to us? Does this feeling have something to do with his saying that when he took the timer apart he "was just showing off before God" (line 181) and that the Model T owner "believed his car could be hexed" (line 191)?

20. Why does Mr. White describe the skipper of the ferry as directing the work of "resetting the bones of my car" (lines 230–231)?

21. In the two paragraphs that begin at line 232, Mr. White tells us why he loved his Model T; why did he?

SUGGESTED TOPICS

1. Write a paragraph in which you analyze the feelings which would make a man prefer to live with a mad and troublesome car like the Model T rather than with a modern car which gives him no trouble at all and which was designed for the maximum ease of operation.

2. Write a paragraph in which you explain the attitude which led to the Model T owner's habit of adding endless gadgets to his car.

3. Write a paragraph in which you compare and contrast the description of how a Model T was started which Mr. White gives (lines 131–155) with the description of this process given by Frederick Lewis Allen (selection 18).

34/ Adventures of a Trout[*]

SALLY CARRIGHAR

T HE POND was all in motion, for the wind had risen. The wind had stirred the marsh for several days, with short lulls. The Trout sensed that it brought a change of season. He could even taste the proof of summer's end, as dust, seeds, crumbling
5 leaves and bark washed through the pond.

Bright-edged shadows of the waves were racing over the bottom silt. They swept across the underwater plants and seemed to shake them. The surface layer of the pond was blowing to the upper end of the backwash. There the water turned below, to sweep back
10 down along the bottom. Against the dam this flowing sheet rolled up. It pressed beneath the Trout's fins as a breeze will lift against the wings of a bird.

Whenever the wind would strain the top of the rigid dead tree, he could feel a pulling in the roots. Suddenly they began to writhe,
15 to tear. The Trout was out of the maze and back in the beaver house as if the water had parted for him.

The Osprey's tree, upturned by the wind, fell into the pond. Billows met rebounding billows, whirls and eddies struggled, surges rocked the Trout. Gradually the violence quieted. Through a
20 cloud of mud he dimly saw that the trunk of the tree was under the surface, propped up from the bottom on its boughs.

He settled himself to feel the current's long touch on his sides.

* Reprinted from *One Day at Teton Marsh* by Sally Carrighar. By permission of Alfred A. Knopf, Inc. Copyright 1946, 1947 by Sally Carrighar.

But what disturbing change was this: the water's stroking soon was regular, yet took a new course—not from his nose to tail but downward now. The water's pressure was becoming lighter and its color rosier. The top of the pond was falling.

Inherited memories warned him that the change was ominous. But he did not leave his shelter, for it seemed that a greater danger threatened him outside: the Otter had returned. Sometimes the Trout could hear him in the water, sometimes out along the narrowing shores. The Trout would not be caught through panic. He lay in his nook and watched the surface drop.

Only when it reached the nook itself did he nose outside. Feeling the Otter's surging near, he turned down to a refuge lower in the wall. The top of the pond descended on him there. The water, draining off the bank beside the house, was roily, so that he could not see where he would go. But he entered it and let its motion guide him.

The currents were not flowing in familiar paths. They all converged in a powerful new suction. Since the roots of the cottonwood tree had been interwoven with the dam, its fall had torn apart the beaver's masonry of mud and sticks. The whole marsh seemed to be swirling toward the gap and plunging through it.

The Trout turned back. He would escape to the brook. He sensed that he must leave the doomed pond and would seek the water's source, as the other fish had done. He could not reach it. While he, the one most wary, stayed in the house to escape the Otter, the pond had shrunk below the mouth of the brook. The only water now connecting them was a thin sheet crinkling over a pebble bar.

Gone, lost above the surface, were the undercut banks of roots, the grassy tunnels, brush, and other shoreline hideaways. The Trout returned to the lower end of the pond. He glided with his fins streamlined in the depressions in his sides, and with so slight a sculling that he might be trying to make smoothness hide him. As he approached the dam, he saw the Otter. Dodging up the botton toward the island, he slipped beneath the log, which drifted now with one end resting on the silt.

The Otter was walking on the pond floor, moving with a swing
60 from his shoulders to his high arched rump. He somersaulted to
the surface for a breath; then looped and tumbled through the
water. He straightened toward the hole in the dam. The fluent
column of his body merged with the strands of the current, and
he vanished.

65 The surface soon was shattered by a splash. The Otter was back.
He had climbed up over the dam, beside the gap. He dived in, dis-
appeared through the break, and again returned. A plunge, a join-
ing with the water's sweep, and a swift ride: he had found a game.

The Trout was holding down his top fin, tense with fear. He
70 spread it, and it struck the under side of the log. And yet his belly
touched the silt. The log was the pond's last refuge, but the water
soon would leave it.

Nothing in the Trout's experience could help him. He only
could give himself to the urge that so intensely pressed to have him
75 live. He waited until the Otter had dived and once more swung
out through the hold. Leaving the log with a jet of speed, the
Trout had reached the gap. A gushing force took hold of him. It
hurled him through the break. Too quick for thought he dodged
the wreckage of the dam. He leapt to pass the brink of the fall and
80 dropped in the foam beneath. The cascade lightened, slowed, and
he found himself in a shallow creek-bed, moving over cobblestones.

His high emotion quickened his choice of route: to the left,
through streamers of emerald algae; right, along a slit between the
stones; here a turn to miss a piece of driftwood, there to pass a
85 boulder. The air was seldom far above his topmost fin. Sometimes
he drew a breath of it, and it seared his gills with dryness. Avoiding one by one the unfamiliar hazards, he progressed.

His lateral lines were jarred by a new sound, a tremendous, heavy
pouring. He swam around a bend in the creek and slid across a bar.
90 And there a torrent plunged upon him, water more swift than any
he had known. He was in the river, the violent tumult of the
Snake.

It nearly overwhelmed him, but he found a milder flow along
the bank. A curve there held a pool as in a shell. The pool was

covered by a sweeper, a willow with its caught debris. The Trout 95
discovering the refuge, entered it, and spiraled down into the cool
green quiet.

Through the afternoon he stayed there, gaining back his poise
and fitting his spirit to the strange new shape of his life. Most of
the time he hung in the water, motionless, but now and then a 100
ripple ran through his fins, and he chopped his breaths as with
excitement. When the first gray wave of dusk washed over the pool,
he rose to the top.

He swam along the bank, where small ripples pattered into
crevices among the rocks. The motion of the water here was light 105
and peaceful like the pond's. Turning out, he met a crisper current, stimulating as the pond had never been. An even greater
challenge growled from the center of the river, from grinding rocks
that yielded to the push of water irresistibly strong. The Trout
began to slant his strokes into the torrent. With a leap he sprang 110
to the very heart of its taut pressure. Enormous weight bore down
upon him, but he gripped it, driving his way against it with exultant
power.

To fight! To fight the turbulent flow! To sharpen his nerves on
its chill; to cut quick arcs through the weaving water; to throw so 115
much force into his muscles' swing that they could drive him upstream, past the rocks beneath, with the whole flood pounding toward him; to fling himself out into the air and see the river under
him, a river wider than the pond, wide for his play—all this, the
heritage of a trout, he knew now for the first time. 120

He faced the flood and, sculling exactly at the current's pace,
remained above the same stone. Swirling past were many insects,
blown in the river. He stayed to take a cricket only, for exhilaration
sang in his nerves. He leapt—

But stopped, caught. Talons had stabbed into his flesh, were now 125
locked through it. They were holding him in the center of a splash.
A feathered throat was lowering before his eyes. Wings were sweeping down at the sides, enclosing him. The Osprey, forgotten in his
conquest of the river, had made its sunset dive.

His torn nerves stung the Trout to action. The claws were power- 130 ful that bound him, but his thrashing bent their grip. They almost rigidly resisted, but they did bend. They were a pressure, like the river's force—to fight!

His instinct focused on one urge, to get himself in deeper water. 135 Arching his body downward, he furiously tried to scull from side to side. The hawk's wings beat, attempting to lift his own weight and the Trout's. The wings and the driving paddle of the Trout's tail pulled against each other. So far the Trout had not been able to drag the bird down, but he held him under the surface of the 140 water.

The river was aiding the fish. For the Osprey was growing desperate for a breath. At first the spines on the pads of his feet had pierced the skin of the Trout. They pressed their hold no longer. And the Trout could feel the talons in his flesh release their clutch. 145 The hawk was trying to withdraw them, but their curving points were caught securely.

The bird and fish were swirling downstream. They jolted to a stop, snagged by the willow sweeper. The water's force was beating at them. It poured through the Osprey's feathers. The push of the 150 wings was weakening. They suddenly relaxed, awash in the flow. And the claws were limp.

The Trout had fought another pressure, his exhaustion. When the straining of the talons ceased, he too relaxed. For long enough to gather a little strength, he waited. Then he began an intermit- 155 tent thrashing. With bursts of effort he tried to jerk himself away. One by one the claws worked out, some slipping loose but more of them tearing through his sides. Finally a twist of his body sent him forward, free.

He turned down under the willow, lower and lower in the dark 160 pool. With his flesh so cut, his lateral lines no longer clearly caught the echo of his motions, thus to guide him. He was careful, therefore, not to swim against the bottom. His chin touched, and he sank upon a stone. The stone was smooth, and soft with slime-coat algae. Soon he had drifted over on his side. His eyes were dull and 165 his fins closed. His consciousness sank lower.

The Trout had been so stimulated by the river that he had

ignored his innate caution. But now he was listening again to instinct, not to the water's roar. As he lay and waited for his strength to seep back into him, no creature could have been more passive, none more acquiescent. 170

The water's cold had numbed the anguish in his severed nerves. It would draw his wounds together. Already it had put in winter sluggishness the parasites that possibly would enter his exposed flesh. And gradually, as he rested, the cold became a tonic to his temper. Cold was as sharpening to him as the warm sun is to in- 175 sects. By midnight he was swimming experimentally around the bottom. He circled higher. The Osprey was gone from the willow sweeper. The Trout moved out of the pool.

He found a backwash near the bank and held himself on the edge, where a smooth flow passed. Moonlight, falling on the sur- 180 face, showed that a drift of small debris was swirling by. Drowned insects should be in it. His eye discovered a bright bit up ahead. He swayed forward. His mouth opened, touched it, and it broke with a singing snap. More came floating toward him—little round stars. Some winked out. He let the others pass. 185

But here was what he liked, a mayfly. Earlier in the day the year's last swarm had left the river for their brief erotic life. Now their delicate spent bodies would be nourishment for the Trout. Many others came his way. After his hunger had been satisfied, he took one more, and shot it out of his mouth for the chance of catching 190 it again, of biting it in two and tossing out and snapping up the pieces.

Now he was not shaped like a smooth wedge, for the cover of one gill was hanging loose, and his sides were ragged. And so his balance in the turns of the water was not perfect. His fins were 195 spread, all needed to aid his sculling tail. Yet the fins were rippling with an easy motion, easy as a creature can be only when it feels that more of living is ahead.

The winter, when a trout is quiet, would be long enough for his wounds to heal, and for his nerves to sharpen. Soon the last migrat- 200 ing Osprey would be gone, but would come back. And otters might be hunting here. The Trout must learn the dangers of this flood,

and learn to be wary even while he was exhilarated by it. He would.
The wisdom of instinct, as of intelligence, can be disregarded, and
205 it also can be drawn upon.

By the time he would be ready to try his strength once more
against the river, the Snake would be a slapping, dodging, driving,
wild spring torrent.

QUESTIONS

1. This selection might be looked on as the autobiography of a
trout, and in fact the author makes brilliant use of the autobiographical
method to make us see what experience looks like to the trout. But
her main purpose is to explain to us the life of the trout, and to make
us understand the working of what she calls "the wisdom of instinct"
as distinguished from the wisdom of intelligence (lines 204–205). In
the first two paragraphs (lines 1–12) we see events from the point of
view of the trout, but what they mean to the trout must be given by
the author in terms we can understand, both because we cannot know
how a trout "knows" and because we could not understand that kind
of knowledge even if we could know it. Point out the places in these
first two paragraphs where the author puts us in the position of the
trout and shows us what things he must have been aware of.

2. In order to avoid what is sometimes called "The Pathetic Fal-
lacy," that is, the ascription of our feelings to things and creatures
actually incapable of such feelings, the author keeps to a minimum
the ascription of particular feelings to the trout; explain how she does
so, for example, in lines 15–16.

3. In the paragraph that begins at line 22 we discover that the level
of the water is falling; why does the author say, "The top of the pond
was falling" (line 26)?

4. How does the trout know that the otter is near (lines 27–35)?

5. What makes the trout decide to escape upstream, to the brook
(lines 35–45)?

6. Where in lines 35–44 does the author introduce information that
the trout could not have possessed in any form?

7. Why does the author say, "Gone, lost above the surface" (line
51) about the familiar landmarks of the pond? Why is "landmark"
an imprecise word in this question?

8. Why does the trout glide "with his fins streamlined in the depressions in his sides" in the paragraph that begins at line 51?

9. Why does the author spend two paragraphs on the otter before telling us that he is playing a game (lines 59–68)?

10. On what motive does the trout finally act when he escapes from the pond (lines 73–81)?

11. What form does the trout's knowledge of his dangers take as he escapes to the Snake River (lines 82–92)?

12. Why does the author double-space between lines 97 and 98?

13. Why does the trout seek the fast, heavy water of mid-stream (lines 107–124)? Point out the places where the author makes the exact character of the trout's impulse clear to us.

14. The author makes particularly skillful use of the trout's point of view in describing his battle with the osprey (lines 125–151); point out the places where this point of view determines what the author tells us.

15. What is the "moral" for the trout of his experience with the osprey?

16. What things help the trout to recover (lines 168–178)?

17. Why was the trout successful in escaping the dangers of the pond and almost fatally unsuccessful in escaping those of the river?

SUGGESTED TOPICS

1. Write a paragraph in which you explain and illustrate what the author gains by using the point of view of the trout in this selection.

2. Write a paragraph in which you show the precision with which the author has observed the relevant details of the events of her narration and what she gains from having done so.

3. Write two paragraphs in which you show the way this description of the actions of a trout illustrates Susanne K. Langer's idea that animals understand only what she calls "signs" (selection 2).

35 / Mason City*

ROBERT PENN WARREN

T O GET THERE you follow Highway 58, going northeast
out of the city, and it is a good highway and new. Or was
new, that day we went up it. You look up the highway and it is
straight for miles, coming at you, with the black line down the
5 center coming at and at you, black and slick and tarry-shining
against the white of the slab, and the heat dazzles up from the
white slab so that only the black line is clear, coming at you with
the whine of the tires, and if you don't quit staring at that line
and don't take a few deep breaths and slap yourself hard on the
10 back of the neck you'll hypnotize yourself and you'll come to just
at the moment when the right front wheel hooks over into the
black dirt shoulder off the slab, and you'll try to jerk her back on
but you can't because the slab is high like a curb, and maybe you'll
try to reach to turn off the ignition just as she starts the dive. But
15 you won't make it, of course. Then a nigger chopping cotton a mile
away, he'll look up and see the little column of black smoke standing up above the vitriolic, arsenical green of the cotton rows, and
up against the violent, metallic, throbbing blue of the sky, and
he'll say, "Lawd God, hit's a-nudder one done done hit!" And
20 the next nigger down the next row, he'll say, "Lawd God," and the
first nigger will giggle, and the hoe will lift again and the blade will
flash in the sun like a heliograph. Then a few days later the boys
from the Highway Department will mark the spot with a little

* From *All the King's Men* by Robert Penn Warren. Copyright 1946 by
Harcourt, Brace and Company, Inc., and reprinted with their permission.

metal square on a metal rod stuck in the black dirt off the shoulder, the metal square painted white and on it in black a skull and cross- 25 bones. Later on love vine will climb up it, out of the weeds.

But if you wake up in time and don't hook your wheel off the slab, you'll go whipping on into the dazzle and now and then a car will come at you steady out of the dazzle and will pass you with a snatching sound as though God-Almighty had ripped a tin roof 30 loose with his bare hands. Way off ahead of you, at the horizon where the cotton fields are blurred into the light, the slab will glitter and gleam like water, as though the road were flooded. You'll go whipping toward it, but it will always be ahead of you, that bright, flooded place, like a mirage. You'll go past the little white 35 metal squares set on metal rods, with the skull and crossbones on them to mark the spot. For this is the country where the age of the internal combustion engine has come into its own. Where every boy is Barney Oldfield, and the girls wear organdy and batiste and eyelet embroidery and no panties on account of the 40 climate and have smooth little faces to break your heart and when the wind of the car's speed lifts up their hair at the temples you see the sweet little beads of perspiration nestling there, and they sit low in the seat with their little spines crooked and their bent knees high toward the dashboard and not too close together for the cool, 45 if you could call it that, from the hood ventilator. Where the smell of gasoline and burning brake bands and red eye is sweeter than myrrh. Where the eight-cylinder jobs come roaring round the curves in the red hills and scatter the gravel like spray, and when they ever get down in the flat country and hit the new slab, God 50 have mercy on the mariner.

On up Number 58, and the country breaks. The flat country and the big cotton fields are gone now, and the grove of live oaks way off yonder where the big house is, and the whitewashed shacks, all just alike, set in a row by the cotton fields with the cotton grow- 55 ing up to the doorstep, where the pickaninny sits like a black Billiken and sucks its thumb and watches you go by. That's all left behind now. It is red hills now, not high, with blackberry bushes along the fence rows, and blackjack clumps in the bottoms

60 and now and then a place where the second-growth pines stand
close together if they haven't burned over for sheep grass, and if
they have burned over, there are the black stubs. The cotton
patches cling to the hillsides, and the gullies cut across the cotton
patches. The corn blades hang stiff and are streaked with yellow.

65   There were pine forests here a long time ago but they are gone.
The bastards got in here and set up the mills and laid the narrow-
gauge tracks and knocked together the company commissaries and
paid a dollar a day and folks swarmed out of the brush for the
dollar and folks came from God knows where, riding in wagons
70 with a chest of drawers and a bedstead canted together in the
wagon bed, and five kids huddled down together and the old
woman hunched on the wagon seat with a poke bonnet on her
head and snuff on her gums and a young one hanging on her tit.
The saws sang soprano and the clerk in the commissary passed out
75 the blackstrap molasses and the sowbelly and wrote in his big
book, and the Yankee dollar and Confederate dumbness col-
laborated to heal the wounds of four years of fratricidal strife, and
all was merry as a marriage bell. Till, all of a sudden, there weren't
any more pine trees. They stripped the mills. The narrow-gauge
80 tracks got covered with grass. Folks tore down the commissaries for
kindling wood. There wasn't any more dollar a day. The big boys
were gone, with diamond rings on their fingers and broadcloth on
their backs. But a good many of the folks stayed right on, and
watched the gullies eat deeper into the red clay. And a good hand-
85 ful of those folks and their heirs and assigns stayed in Mason City,
four thousand of them, more or less.

You come in on Number 58, and pass the cotton gin and the
power station and the fringe of nigger shacks and bump across the
railroad track and down a street where there are a lot of little
90 houses painted white one time, with the sad valentine lace of
gingerbread work around the eaves of the veranda, and tin roofs,
and where the leaves on the trees on the yard hang straight down
in the heat, and above the mannerly whisper of your eighty-horse-
power valve-in-head (or whatever it is) drifting at forty, you hear
95 the July flies grinding away in the verdure.

QUESTIONS

1. This first-hand description of a trip up Highway 58 to Mason City is primarily concerned to make us feel all that an intelligent and aware person ought to feel about such a trip; that is why it is written in the second person ("you"), which includes both the author and the reader. That is why, too, it attempts to make us feel everything that is suggested by the trip, from the immediate sensation of driving fast on a good, new highway to the way history, going back to the Civil War, has contributed to making the scene we are observing. Finally, it wishes to leave us with a general feeling about life as a whole which the author thinks is illustrated by this trip, an amused but sardonic feeling about the way haste and passion, greed and stupidity, get men into trouble. In the opening passage, where the author is describing one of the common effects of driving fast on a good highway (lines 1–10) he repeats over and over, in only slightly changed phrases, that the black line down the center of the road comes at you; what is the point of this repetition?

2. Why does the author conclude this description by saying, "But you won't make it, *of course.*" (lines 14–15)?

3. What effect does the reaction of the negroes (lines 15–22) have on our feelings about the death of "you" which has just been imagined by the author?

4. The little metal square put up by "the boys from the Highway Department" is of course meant to warn future drivers by reminding them that a fatal accident took place at this point on the highway (lines 22–26). But it also serves as a kind of memorial to "you." What does the author feel about it as a memorial? Why does he conclude by remarking that "later on love vine will climb up it, out of the weeds" (line 26)?

5. Why does the author compare the sound of a passing car to the sound of God-Almighty ripping "a tin roof loose with his bare hands" (lines 29–31)? What does it add to the effect of this comparison that he uses in it the exaggerated colloquial language of the tall tale ("God-Almighty," "with his bare hands")?

6. Why does the author describe us as always moving toward a "bright, flooded place, like a mirage" which we never reach, always passing "the little white metal squares . . . with the skull and cross-bones on them" (lines 31–37)?

7. The next section of this paragraph (lines 37–51) seeks to remind us of the feelings which are closely associated for us with automobiles; can you say what these feelings are? Why does the author say, "every boy is Barney Oldfield" (line 39)? Why does he combine "the smell of gasoline and burning brake bands and red eye" (lines 46–47), and why does he say they are "sweeter than myrrh"? Why does he say, "God have mercy on the mariner" (lines 50–51)?

8. What kind of country is the area described in lines 58–64? How is our impression of its character intensified by what the author says in lines 52–57)?

9. The paragraph that begins at line 65 explains to us how Mason City came into existence; this explanation requires the author to go all the way back to the Civil War and allows him the particularly sardonic reference to that conflict that he makes in lines 76–77; how does what he has said up to this point in the paragraph fit this generalization?

10. In what sense was all "merry as a marriage bell" (line 78)?

11. Why does the author refer to the descendents of the mill workers as "their heirs and assigns" (line 85)?

12. What, beyond the appearance of the houses, does the author suggest when he says these houses were "painted white one time" (line 90)?

13. What is "sad" about the "valentine lace of gingerbread work" on these houses (lines 90–91)?

14. What point is the author driving home by telling us that we can hear the "flies grinding away in the verdure" above "the mannerly whisper" of the car (lines 93–95)? Is this point emphasized by "mannerly" and "grinding"?

SUGGESTED TOPICS

1. Write three paragraphs in which you describe the attitude toward life of the speaker in this selection.

2. In line 70 the author says the chest of drawers and the bedstead were "canted" together. Most of the work of making us see the contents of the wagon clearly is done by that verb. Pick out two or three other places where the author makes a single word or a phrase do this amount of work and explain how it works.

3. Nearly every paragraph in this selection could be divided into two paragraphs. Take one paragraph, show where you would divide it, and explain why.

GEOFFREY SCOTT

PAUL F. GEMMILL

AND

RALPH H. BLODGETT

FRANCIS BACON

JAMES THURBER

THORSTEIN VEBLEN

ROBERT L. HEILBRONER

GEORGE ORWELL

vi. Definition

36 / The Architecture of Humanism*

GEOFFREY SCOTT

THE ARCHITECTURE of humanism rose in Greece; and of the Greeks it has been said that they first made man "at home in the world." Their thought was anthropocentric: so also was their architecture. Protagoras, who first made humanity the centre of a metaphysic, and "the measure of all things"; the poets who, in the labours of Heracles and Theseus and the strife of the gods with centaurs, celebrated the conquest by human reason of a corner in the darkened world; Socrates, who drew down speculation from the flattery of the stars to the services of the conscience; the dramatists, who found tragedy a savage rite and left it a mirror of life, not as it is but as our mind demands: these were the first humanists. Among these men, and to satisfy this same proclivity, was created an architecture whose several elements were drawn indeed from primitive necessities, but so ordered and so chosen that its constructive need and coarse utility were made to match the delight of the body and mock the image of the mind. Matter—the very antithesis of spirit—matter with its mere weight and mass and balance; space, the mere void we recognize as nothing, became, for them, the spirit's language. Within the world of concrete forms indifferent to man, they constructed a world as man desires it, responsive to his instinct and his stature.

* From *The Architecture of Humanism* by Geoffrey Scott. Reprinted by permission of Charles Scribner's Sons.

But humanism has its practical aspect as well as its ideal; and the values which the Greek defined and founded, the Roman fixed impregnably upon the earth. Roman architecture, less fastidious than the Greek, and less restricted, preserved the principles of mass, space, line and coherence for rougher uses, wider and more general. It ensured their survival, their independence of the time and place whence they had sprung. In architecture as in thought it is to Rome, not Greece, that humanism owes its deep and racial hold upon the West.

The architecture which thus rose with humanism was with humanism eclipsed and with humanism restored. To pass from Roman architecture or that of the Renaissance to the fantastic and bewildering energy of Gothic, is to leave humanism for magic, the study of the congruous for the cult of the strange. It is to find that the logic of inhuman science has displaced the logic of the human form. It is to discover resplendent beauty of detail in glass and bronze and ivory and gold; it is to lose architecture in sculpture. Here is structure, certainly—daring, intricate, ingenious; but seldom humanized structure. Here is poetry, curious craftsmanship, exquisite invention. But the supreme, the distinctive quality of architecture—that pure identity between the inner and the outer world—is unattempted. The lines of this amazed construction are at one moment congruous with our movement, at the next they contradict it with a cramped and angular confusion. Mass is too often lost in multiplicity. Space and coherence come, if at all, unsought and unregarded; and when they come it is most often because the ritual of the Church, preserving something of the pagan order it inherits, imposed a harmony upon the plan. Divorced from this ritual, Gothic, as its domestic building and its streets suffice to prove, admits its deep indifference to ordered form. It is entangled, like the medieval mind itself, in a web of idle thoughts of which man as he is has ceased to be the centre.

When, in the Renaissance, that centre was recovered, and humanism became once more a conscious principle of thought, Roman design in architecture came with it as of right. But there was now a difference in its intent. Humanism has two enemies—chaos

and inhuman order. In antiquity humanism strove principally
against the primitive confusion of the world: its emphasis was
laid on order: it clung to discipline and rule. Hence Greek archi-   60
tecture is the strictest of all styles of building, and Rome, in whatever outposts of Spain and Britain her legions were remotely quar-
tered, there set a tiny Forum, and preserved without concession
the imperial order of its plan. But in the thought of the Renaissance humanism was pitted, not against chaos, but against the in-   65
human rigour of a dead scholastic scheme, whose fault was not
lack of logic, but excess of logic with a lack of relevance to man.
Thus the emphasis of Renaissance humanism, in all its forms, was
less on order than on liberty. And, in architecture, while it rebelled
against the mere constructive logic of the Gothic style, while it   70
returned with passion to the aesthetic logic of antiquity, it makes
that logic serve the keen variety of life. It is no longer content to
rest for ever in the restraint of classic equipoise and calm. It has
learned the speech of architecture from Greece and Rome, but the
Renaissance itself will choose what things that speech will say.   75
Every value, every avenue of promise, it will explore, enjoy, express. Hence the insatiate curiosity, the haste, the short duration
of its styles; hence the conversion of classic forms to the gay uses
of baroque and rococo invention; hence the pliancy and swift re-
coveries of taste. But not the less does the Renaissance employ   80
the language of Humanism; and hence its unsevered ties with classic
architecture, its reliance on the "Orders," its perpetual study of the
past. Still, as in antiquity, it speaks by mass, space, line, coherence;
as in antiquity, it still builds through these a congruous setting to
our life. It makes them echo to the body's music—its force and   85
movement and repose. And the mind that is responsive to that
harmony, it leads enchantingly among the measures of a dance in
stone.

COMMENTARY

THIS SELECTION attempts to define a kind of architecture, what
the author calls "The Architecture of Humanism." This is clearly not

a kind of architecture that was limited to one period or style; it constitutes a larger class than the ones we are used to, such as "Greek" or "Baroque." Thus the author is faced with a particularly difficult problem in definition. He is not faced with the at least comparatively simple problem of defining to our satisfaction a class of objects with which, as a class, we are already to some extent familiar; he has to make us understand the characteristics which define what is for us a new class and, at the same time, to show us why the objects we are used to seeing in separate classes belong together in this new class. In addition, though he is perhaps not logically obligated to do so, Scott seeks to make us agree that this new class he is setting up is important.

Mostly as a convenience, he takes up the objects which he feels belong together in this class in chronological order: his readers, he knows, will be used to thinking of them in that order. But his point is to show us that, with some minor exceptions, the chronological distinctions between Greek and Roman architecture, between Roman and Renaissance, are unimportant; that, in the ways that really count, these architectures are all alike. The chronological framework has another advantage for him: it allows him to draw our attention quickly and easily to the characteristics by which the various periods of architecture have usually been defined and then to show us that these characteristics are only superficial. In each section of his essay, he takes up a familiar period of architecture and shows us how its characteristics do—or, in the case of Gothic architecture, do not—satisfy the requirements of what he calls "humanism." Notice how carefully he has paragraphed his essay to make this arrangement clear. The first paragraph discusses Greek architecture (and the word "Greece" appears in the first sentence); the second paragraph discusses Roman architecture (and again the subject is mentioned in the first sentence). The third paragraph discusses Gothic architecture, which the author looks on as an unfortunate interruption of the tradition that he is concerned with. He therefore begins this paragraph with a sentence telling us that humanism was eclipsed in the centuries between two periods of humanism, the period of Roman architecture and the period of Renaissance architecture. Only then does he mention the subject of the paragraph—Gothic architecture. The fourth paragraph deals with the Renaissance, which it mentions immediately, and the last paragraph, by generalizing its observations on the Renaissance, returns to an abstract idea, the definition of "the architecture of humanism," with which Scott began in the first paragraph. Thus the plan of Scott's definition, like a well-constructed building, reflects its meaning in its design.

The great advantage of this design for the purposes of definition is that it allows Scott gradually to accumulate around the bare statement about humanism a whole series of superficially different but fundamentally similar illustrations; he thus makes us feel that we have a thorough and particularized knowledge of what "the architecture of humanism" really is, not simply as an abstract idea, but as an idea realized in actual architectural forms.

Arranging his definition chronologically has yet another advantage for Scott. The most serious drawback to definition is that it has no inherent form, or way of arranging what it wants to say. There is no clear reason for putting one point before or after another in a definition. Therefore, an essay which is constructed like a definition may easily decline into a disorderly jumble of ideas which are hard for us to follow because we never quite know why we are moving from one idea to another in the order we are. At its most jumbled, such an essay will look like a pile of notes on a subject thrown together at random. The chronological arrangement of his definition protects Scott from all these dangers, and at the same time permits him to make the best possible use of his greatest talent as a writer, his almost old-fashioned gift for arranging ideas, within sentences and within paragraphs, in a clear and precise way.

Notice, for example, how, starting with the Greeks, as chronology suggests he should, he makes clear to us at once exactly *why* "the architecture of humanism rose in Greece" (line 1). This "why" requires him to discuss the nature of Greek thought and to show us how it was "anthropocentric" (line 3). Notice how skillfully he keeps us aware that, though he is going to write several sentences about the character of Greek thought, his main interest is in Greek architecture: the Greeks "first made man 'at home in the world.' Their thought was anthropocentric: *so also was their architecture*" (lines 3–4). This constitutes a very exact outline of the paragraph which follows; we are first given eight lines about the philosophers, poets, and dramatists of Greece which suggest to us the way Greek thought sought to make man "at home in the world" (lines 4–12). Notice that these lines are all worked into a single sentence by a series of nearly parallel clauses that lead up to the colon, in line 11, which introduces the point Scott has been driving at throughout the sentence: "these [men] were the first humanists," another way of stating the idea with which the paragraph began, that Greek thinkers sought to make men "at home in the world." We now have at least the beginnings of a definition of "humanism."

The second half of this first paragraph consists of exactly the same number of lines—eight—about Greek architecture (remember Scott's topic sentence, "Their thought was anthropocentric: so also was their architecture"). Scott makes sure we realize that he is shifting to the second half of his topic at this point: "Among these men, and to satisfy this same proclivity, was created an architecture. . . ." (lines 12–13). In the following eight lines he tells us what there was about Greek architecture that made it humanist. First, however, he makes a concession to people who stress the idea that architecture is not an art but only a way of satisfying a practical necessity, that there is really no such thing as architecture, there is only building. Greek architecture, he says, did indeed draw its several elements from primitive necessities (lines 13–14), but what it did with these elements was done to satisfy needs in men beyond those of primitive necessity; these elements drawn from primitive necessity in the first instance were "made to match the delight of the body and mock the image of the mind" (lines 15–16). We thus arrive at a general statement of the way architecture can display the values of "humanism." So important is this point to Scott's argument that twice more before he comes to the end of the paragraph he restates and elaborates it (lines 14–21).

This first paragraph illustrates very clearly the sharpness and precision of Scott's thought, despite its difficulty and novelty, and the exactness with which the structure of his sentences and paragraphs follows the movement of his thought. Nothing is more important to exposition than such precision of thought and such exactness of structure and, to achieve them in your own writing, you would do well to study carefully the way Scott achieves them. Neither, as you will discover, is easy, even with the simplest subject matter. What is more important, you cannot achieve exactness of structure unless your thought is clear and precise. You can write parallel sentences, perhaps, and carefully introduce transitions; such things *can* be done merely mechanically. But unless your ideas have first been clearly distinguished in your mind, brought into parallel, and arranged in the right order, this merely mechanical exactness of the sentences will be like the false, two-story fronts on the stores in the cow-towns of the old west, which fooled no one and only seemed pretentious. On the other hand, when you have gotten your thoughts clear and have reasoned out exactly the relations among them and the order in which you wish to take them, then it is necessary to make the sentences you put them in reflect this order as exactly as possible; there is no more unjustified defense of a piece of writing than the one frequently heard from inexperienced writers, that "What I meant to say was. . . ."

After the first paragraph, Scott's thought moves chronologically, first to the Romans, who, he tells us, made the humanist principles established by the Greeks a permanent part of the heritage of Western civilization by using them, not simply for the work of great and rare occasions, but for the public buildings in which the everyday life of Roman society was conducted. Then, with the decline of Rome, there came a break in the tradition of humanism and consequently a break in the continuity of "the architecture of humanism." Notice how, at the opening of the third paragraph, Scott clearly indicates this hiatus (lines 31–34): "[The architecture of humanism] rose with humanism was with humanism eclipsed and with humanism restored. To pass from Roman architecture or that of the Renaissance to . . . Gothic. . . ." These opening sentences make clear to us not only the topic of this paragraph, but the way Scott wishes us to look at it, and they foreshadow the movement of thought throughout the rest of the selection, since he will, in the final paragraph, "pass to" the architecture of the Renaissance and show us that, as "humanism [was] restored" in that period, so also was "the architecture of humanism." In this paragraph Scott does full justice to Gothic architecture's achievements; he does not run it down. At the same time, as he is pointing out the brilliance of Gothic architecture, he manages to remind us at each step that it reflects, not the ideals of humanism, but another set of ideals which he clearly feels are inferior. Thus, even while he is talking about the period in which architecture was not humanist, he is adding to our understanding of "the architecture of humanism" by using the device of comparison and contrast. The world out of which Gothic architecture grew and whose ideals it reflected, he tells us, substituted magic, the cult of the strange, for humanism, the study of the congruous (line 35); notice how the parallelism of the phrases helps to make the parallel and contrast of the ideas in this line clear to us. In this way, each observation about

Gothic architecture in what follows adds to our understanding of "the architecture of humanism." Unlike Gothic, "the architecture of humanism" does not substitute sculpture for architecture (line 38); it does not dehumanize structure (lines 39–40). It does seek "that pure identity between the inner and the outer world" (line 42); it does achieve mass, space, and coherence (lines 45–46); it is concerned with "ordered form" (line 51). And it does all these things because the humanist mind, unlike the medieval mind, is not entangled "in a web of idle thoughts of which man as he is has ceased to be the centre" (lines 52–53).

But with the decline of the Middle Ages and the coming of the Renaissance, "that centre" (that is, man; notice how the repetition of this term carries our thought over from the previous paragraph) was recovered. Nonetheless, the architecture of the Renaissance, while basically humanist, differed strikingly in its surface characteristics from the architecture of Greece and of Rome. Scott's task in this paragraph is to make us see how this difference in surface characteristics came about and why it is not a basic difference but rather an expression of the fundamental humanist attitude which is fitted to Renaissance times. He does so by arguing that, whereas Greek and Roman civilizations were confronted by something like chaos and therefore needed the maximum rigidity of thought, Renaissance civilization was confronted by the elaborate and—as it seems to him—inhuman rigor of medieval scholastic thought and therefore needed the maximum of freedom. Thus, whereas Greek and Roman thought expressed itself architecturally with strictness, Renaissance thought expressed itself—though always in the classical and humanist idiom—with great flexibility and variety.

Nonetheless, despite these adjustments in the Renaissance to changed circumstances and the consequent differences in the superficial appearances of its architecture, the Renaissance remained essentially humanist, and therefore Scott can sum up his argument and return to the general definition of "the architecture of humanism," which he established in the opening paragraph about Greek architecture, simply by summing up the essential characteristics of Renaissance architecture. Notice the careful and orderly way in which he repeats in this last paragraph (in line 83) the architectural ideas about mass, space, and coherence which he had used to describe Greek architecture in the first paragraph (lines 16–19) and had denied to

Gothic architecture in the third paragraph (lines 45–47). Notice that he is equally careful to reassert the ideas about the body and the mind (in lines 85–88) which he believes a civilization must hold in order to produce a real "architecture of humanism" and which he has previously pointed out to us as strikingly characteristic of Greek civilization (lines 1–12) and strikingly absent from medieval thought (lines 34–35 and 51–53). In this way Scott rounds off and balances the structure of this selection, not simply in a general way, but with a precision and an exactness of detail of which a good humanist architect might well be proud.

37 / Communism*

PAUL F. GEMMILL AND
RALPH H. BLODGETT

K ARL MARX held that economic matters are dominant
in determining the course of history and that the form
of government, family system, moral standards, and literature of a
society are but reflections or by-products of economic activities and
5 institutions. An important feature of capitalism, according to
Marx, is the continuous class struggle. The two opposing classes
are called by different names at different times in history, he said,
but the struggle goes on all the time. The class struggle at present
is supposed to be between the capitalist (or owning) class and the
10 proletariat (or working) class.

Prominent among Marx's theories were those relating to value
and what he termed "surplus value." He held that all commodities,
regardless of differences in size, shape, composition, and usefulness,
contain a certain common element; that is, the labor used in pro-
15 ducing them. Capital, though useful in production, he regarded
merely as past labor congealed in a more or less permanent form.
The values of commodities in terms of each other depend upon
the amount of socially necessary labor contained in them. For example, a commodity that takes twice as much socially necessary

labor to produce as another commodity has twice as much ex- 20
change value.

From this theory of value, Marx derived his explanation of the
method by which workers are exploited by capitalists. Under capitalism, the workers cannot work for themselves because they are unable to acquire the land and capital needed in production. Conse- 25
quently, they must work for the capitalists who own these material
means of production. As a condition of employment, the workers
must turn their products over to the capitalists who are free to sell
them for whatever they will bring, which will be an amount propor-
tionate to the labor contained in the products. On the other hand, 30
the wages which the capitalists pay to the workers need only be
high enough to maintain the laborers and their families, and to
permit them to raise enough children to take their places. The difference between the value created by the workers in production
and the wages paid to them is called "surplus value," and goes to 35
the capitalists as an unearned increment. The workers cannot refuse to make this bad bargain, because they are dependent upon
the capitalists for a chance to work and because in a capitalistic system there is always a reserve of unused laborers waiting to take the
places of those already employed. In this exploitation of the workers 40
and appropriation of surplus value by the capitalists lies the cause
of the class struggle.

According to Marx, the thirst of the capitalists for gain is so
great that they seize every possible opportunity to increase the
amount of the surplus value. This leads to increasing misery and 45
suffering among the workers and to the formation of an ever larger
labor reserve. Moreover, it brings about an increasing concentration of capital in the hands of a few individuals; for the large enter-
prisers are more efficient than the small ones, and force the latter
out of business, taking over their land and capital. As this process 50
goes on, society will become more and more the victim of commercial crises or depressions until finally will come that last crisis
in which the proletariat will rise up, dethrone the capitalists, and
operate the material means of production in their own interests.
Eventually will come a classless order in which all workers will 55

share the income of society and the state will dwindle away—for Marx regarded the bourgeois state as an instrument for protecting the owning class in its favored position.

Marx wrote three large volumes to elucidate and elaborate his
60 theories, and many books of criticism of his theories have appeared since his time. However, we shall be able here merely to suggest why his theories have been very largely discredited. First of all, the idea that all of man's activities can be explained in terms of his economic activities and institutions is based upon an overemphasis
65 of the economic aspects of life. History must certainly take economic matters into account, but there are many human actions which cannot be explained wholly on economic grounds. As for the class struggle, it is obvious that there are differences between capital and labor and that their relations might be loosely termed a strug-
70 gle. However, this struggle is not the only, or necessarily the most important, feature of the capitalistic system. Marx, thinking of the proletariat as an ideal theoretical class, attributed to the workers a unity of purpose and action which they do not possess. Workers have varied interests, many of which are not economic in character.
75 Moreover, there is little reason to suppose that workers always act in accordance with their economic interests, to the exclusion of interests of other kinds. It must also be remembered that there are economic differences between different classes of labor, and these differences *in degree* may sometimes be quite as important as the
80 difference *in kind* that exists between capitalists and laborers.

The Marxian theory of value has also been sharply and successfully attacked. According to Marx, the only element common to things which have exchange value is the labor contained in them. This contention led him to say that articles of wealth which have
85 not been produced by human labor have *use value*, but not *exchange value*. However, as we know, natural resources which are in no sense the product of human labor have exchange value just as truly as have the economic goods produced by human labor. Marx never demonstrated that the value of a commodity depends upon
90 the amount of labor contained in it. He merely attempted to show

that there could be no other element common to different commodities—and this is by no means the same thing. Marx also overlooked the element of utility in connection with exchange value. His analysis of value was incomplete in that it approached the question of value entirely from the side of supply. For it should be clear that utility is an element common to all goods which have exchange value, and an element which plays an important role in the actual pricing of commodities in our economic system.

The theory of surplus value, also, has fared badly since Marx's time. In explaining surplus value, Marx divided capital into two parts. He said that constant capital (which we would today call fixed capital) consists of such things as machinery and buildings, and is not a source of gain to the capitalist, since this capital merely reproduces itself into the value of the things produced. He regarded variable capital, used to pay wages, as the source of the surplus value and the gain of the capitalists. But if, as Marx thought, all gain to the capitalists comes from variable capital and not from constant capital, it is difficult to understand why capitalists should introduce machinery into their industries to make use of increasing amounts of fixed capital. For the greater the quantity of fixed capital goods used, the less would be the gains in the form of further surplus value. The rate of gain to capitalists would be highest in industries using much labor and little fixed capital, and lowest in industries using little labor and much capital; and yet Marx's prediction of revolution was based upon the growth of a great army of unemployed labor, which supposedly was to result from an increasing use of labor-saving machinery.

In describing the return received by the capitalists as a surplus value filched from the laborers, Marx overlooked the element of time and the important function of waiting performed by those who save and thus make possible the formation of capital. He also largely disregarded the important administrative and managerial functions which are often performed by capitalists. Finally, he failed to explain why the capitalists, under competition—since they were making a large gain from each worker used—did not bid against one another in the attempt to hire more of these profitable laborers until they reached the point at which the contribution of the marginal worker to production equaled, and only just equaled, the wages which had to be paid to get his services.

130   It would seem that Marx was not an especially good prophet, if we may judge by subsequent events. The population has not become divided into two distinct classes, bourgeoisie and proletariat. Instead, a large middle class has continued to exist, and there are surveys which show that most individuals, whether relatively well-
135 to-do or poor, consider themselves members of the middle class. Under the development of the corporation and industrial combinations, there has been a considerable concentration of capital, but the concentration of *control* over capital has been more pronounced than that concentration of *ownership* which was so prominent in
140 the Marxian analysis.

The lot of the workers has not been one of increasing degradation, misery, and squalor, in an absolute sense, since Marx's time. It is true, of course, that for some years following the Industrial Revolution the trend in the condition of the working class seemed
145 to be in that direction; but labor organization and governmental intervention in the form of labor legislation and social insurance— measures in which Marx had no faith—have helped to reverse the trend. However, it is possible to argue that workers have become relatively worse off, and that the disparity between rich and poor has
150 increased since Marx's time. For some years we have had a reserve of idle labor and this reserve has been large in times of severe depression, but it has hardly reached the proportions predicted by Marx.

Business depressions have probably increased in severity, in the
155 absolute sense, as our economic system has become more extensive and more complex, but it is not clear that they have become relatively more severe. Finally, the time when all material means of production will be owned by a few, and the militant masses of the population (the proletariat) will rise up in their might and destroy
160 these few capitalists, does not indeed appear to be imminent.

QUESTIONS

1. This selection has a double purpose, to define for us the main characteristics of Marx's theory and to define for us the respects in which that theory appears to be faulty. It therefore falls into two parts which, as we shall see, are very carefully related to one another. Where do the authors move from their definition of Marx's theory to their definition of its faults?

2. The central proposition of Marx's theory was that of the class struggle: his analysis of the history of capitalism was largely devoted to showing how capitalism produced and inevitably intensified the class struggle, and his prediction of the future was based on the way he thought this struggle would end. Therefore the authors of this selection begin (lines 1–10) by defining what Marx meant by the class struggle in a capitalist society. When do they get back to this idea of the class struggle?

3. The authors begin their explanation of Marx's theory of how capitalism leads to class struggle by defining Marx's "labor theory of value," though they do not give us that name (lines 11–21). Explain this theory of value.

4. The authors mention "surplus value" in line 12, but note that they say they are going to talk about "theories . . . relating to value and what he termed 'surplus value' " (lines 11–12). It was logically necessary for them to use this elaborate phrase; why?

5. In lines 33–36 the authors finally reach the point where they can tell us what "surplus value" is; outline the steps by which they reach this definition.

6. In the paragraph that begins at line 43, the authors show us the line of reasoning by which Marx demonstrated, to his own satisfaction, that the existence of surplus value would lead to a crisis in which "the proletariat will rise up" and destroy capitalism. Outline the steps in Marx's argument.

7. Beginning at line 59 the authors take up a series of Marx's theories and criticize them. What determines the order in which they take up these theories?

8. To Marx's theory of the class struggle the authors offer four specific objections. What are they?

9. To "the Marxian theory of value" (line 81) the authors offer four objections; what are they?

10. Why do the authors divide their criticism of Marx's theory of surplus value into two paragraphs (lines 99–129)? Altogether they offer five objections to the theory of surplus value; what are they?

11. The paragraph that begins at line 130 starts, "It would seem that Marx was not an especially good prophet . . ." (line 130); this phrase indicates that we have reached an important dividing point in the authors' criticism of Marx; what aspect of Marxism do they criticize in the rest of the selection? How does it differ from the aspect they were criticizing in lines 59–129?

12. With what paragraph in the explanation of Marx's theory (lines 1–58) does the last section of criticism (lines 130–160) correspond?

13. Why do the authors divide their criticism of Marx as a prophet (lines 130–160) into three paragraphs?

SUGGESTED TOPICS

1. To each of the paragraphs at the beginning of this selection, where the authors are explaining Marx's theory, there is an answer in the last part, where they are criticizing it; write four brief paragraphs in which you indicate the answers to each of the four theories given in the first part of the selection, and show where the authors give these answers.

2. Take one of the Marxian theories which the authors explain and write a paragraph in which you explain this theory in your own words.

3. The paragraph that begins at line 81 states a number of objections to Marx's theory of value. Take one of these objections and write a paragraph in which you make it clear why the objection is valid.

38 / Of Marriage and Single Life

FRANCIS BACON

H E that hath wife and children hath given hostages to
fortune, for they are impediments to great enterprises,
either of virtue or mischief. Certainly the best works, and of greatest merit for the public, have proceeded from the unmarried or
childless men; which both in affection and means have married 5
and endowed the public. Yet it were great reason that those that
have children should have greatest care of future times; unto which
they know they must transmit their dearest pledges. Some there
are, who though they lead a single life, yet their thoughts do end
with themselves, and account future times impertinences. Nay, 10
there are some other that account wife and children but as bills of
charges. Nay more, there are some foolish rich covetous men, that
take a pride in having no children, because they may be thought
so much the richer. For perhaps they have heard some talk, *Such
an one is a great rich man,* and another except to it, *Yea, but he* 15
hath a great charge of children; as if it were an abatement to his
riches. But the most ordinary cause of a single life is liberty, especially in certain self-pleasing and humorous minds, which are so
sensible of every restraint, as they will go near to think their girdles
and garters to be bonds and shackles. Unmarried men are best 20
friends, best masters, best servants; but not always best subjects;
for they are light to run away; and almost all fugitives are of that
condition. A single life doth well with churchmen; for charity will
hardly water the ground where it must first fill a pool. It is indif-

25 ferent for judges and magistrates; for if they be facile and corrupt,
you shall have a servant five times worse than a wife. For soldiers,
I find the generals commonly in their hortatives put men in mind
of their wives and children; and I think the despising of marriage
amongst the Turks maketh the vulgar soldier more base. Certainly
30 wife and children are a kind of discipline of humanity; and single
men, though they may be many times more charitable, because
their means are less exhaust, yet, on the other side, they are more
cruel and hardhearted (good to make severe inquisitors,) because
their tenderness is not so oft called upon. Grave natures, led by
35 custom, and therefore constant, are commonly loving husbands; as
was said of Ulysses, *vetulam suam praetulit immortalitati:* [he pre-
ferred his old wife to immortality]. Chaste women are often proud
and froward, as presuming upon the merit of their chastity. It is
one of the best bonds both of chastity and obedience in the wife,
40 if she think her husband wise; which she will never do if she find
him jealous. Wives are young men's mistresses; companions for
middle age; and old men's nurses. So as a man may have a quarrel
to marry when he will. But yet he was reputed one of the wise men,
that made answer to the question, when a man should marry?—A
45 *young man not yet, an elder man not at all.*[1] It is often seen that
bad husbands have very good wives; whether it be that it raiseth
the price of their husband's kindness when it comes; or that the
wives take a pride in their patience. But this never fails, if the bad
husbands were of their own choosing, against their friends' con-
50 sent; for then they will be sure to make good their own folly.

QUESTIONS

1. When this essay was written, in 1612, the modern habit of indi-
cating the structure of the discourse by paragraphing was not customary; but because Bacon's essay is all one paragraph, we ought not
to conclude that its thought has no structure; it has, and that structure
is clear and systematic enough to allow us to indicate the points at

---

[1] Thales was the wise man who made this remark.

which a modern writer would have paragraphed this essay. Do not be misled in looking for this structure by the fact that Bacon shows in this essay two of the common convictions of his time; first, that the way to measure the value of an institution is above all to determine its advantages and disadvantages for society as a whole; second, that men are more important than women. For these reasons he starts with a general statement about the effectiveness of married and single men in "great enterprises" which have "merit for the public" (lines 2–4). At what point do you think he completes this statement and begins another subject which might lead a modern writer to start a new paragraph?

2. Having asserted that experience shows single men are most likely to perform acts of great service to the public, Bacon goes on to point out that nonetheless, in the majority of cases, the reasons men have for remaining single are selfish reasons. He gives four such reasons, adding an extra sentence of explanation for the third one and reaching a climax with the fourth one. What are these four reasons, and which sentence is devoted to each?

3. Bacon then turns to another subject, the various activities for which single and married men are best fitted. At what point does he start on this subject?

4. Bacon deals with the subject of the activities for which married and unmarried men are best fitted in what might be described as an A–B–A order; why does he use this order?

5. The last section of Bacon's essay is devoted to the subject of married life itself. Where does he start on this subject?

6. Bacon discusses the characteristics of wives and husbands from the point of view of the man rather than from some neutral point; indicate some of the things in his discussion which show that he is doing so.

7. Why is it logical for Bacon, with the particular assumption he makes about life, to leave his discussion of marriage to the end of his essay?

8. Much of the effectiveness of Bacon's essay depends on its succinct and epigrammatic style. This is no style for a beginner to venture on, since it requires the kind of ideas which only much thought will produce and a control over words which not even long experience will always provide. Bacon is particularly effective in his use of brief, homely, and often ironic metaphors, such as the one in lines 23–24.

We must be sure we follow these metaphors, and that means we must be sure we understand the words and know the things used in the comparison; since Bacon's essay was written over three hundred years ago, we shall have to look up some words in order to do so. For instance, in the metaphor Bacon uses in lines 23–24, he uses the word "charity" in a sense that was very common in his day but which exists for us today only in the Bible's use of this word. (The Bible we read was translated into English during Bacon's lifetime and was first published just a year before this essay.) Explain the meaning of "charity" in this sentence. What is "the ground" the churchman's charity ought to water? What is "the pool" it would have to fill were he not single?

9. What does it mean to say that a man with a wife and children "hath given hostages to fortune" (lines 1–2)?

10. What is the meaning of "impertinences" in line 10? of "bills of charges" in lines 11–12?

11. You will discover that you must go all the way down to the fifth sense of "liberty" in *Webster's New Collegiate Dictionary* before you find the meaning the word has in line 17; it is important to do so, because this is a meaning we usually associate with the word "license" rather than with the word "liberty." What does the word "humorous" mean in line 18?

12. Do you know enough about an Elizabethan gentleman's dress to explain what his girdle and garters were and why they make a good metaphor here (lines 19–20)?

13. What is the meaning of "hortatives" (line 27)? of "vulgar" (line 29)?

14. What does Bacon mean by saying that some women *presume* "upon the merit of their chastity" (lines 37–38)?

15. There is a very rich observation of life behind the neatly paralleled phrase in lines 41–42; explain each of these phrases. Be careful not to give the word "mistress" the wrong meaning.

16. How does the dictionary define the meaning of the word "quarrel" in line 42?

SUGGESTED TOPICS

1. Write a paragraph in which you summarize the main point of each of the four parts of Bacon's essay and arrange these points, with proper transitions, in the same order Bacon does.

2. Take one of Bacon's epigrammatic remarks (for example, lines 1–3, 23–24, 41–42) and write a paragraph in which you make clear the view of human nature which it depends on.

3. Take the activities Bacon lists in lines 20–29 and show why Bacon prefers for each the kind of man he does.

39 / Ladies' and Gentlemen's Guide to Modern English Usage*

JAMES THURBER

I—*Which*

THE relative pronoun "which" can cause more trouble than any other word, if recklessly used. Foolhardy persons sometimes get lost in which-clauses and are never heard of again. My distinguished contemporary, Fowler, cites several tragic cases,
5 of which the following is one: "It was rumoured that Beaconsfield intended opening the Conference with a speech in French, his pronunciation of which language leaving everything to be desired . . ." That's as much as Mr. Fowler quotes because, at his age, he was afraid to go any farther. The young man who originally
10 got into that sentence was never found. His fate, however, was not as terrible as that of another adventurer who became involved in a remarkable which-mire. Fowler has followed his devious course as far as he safely could on foot: "Surely what applies to games should also apply to racing, the leaders of which being the very people from
15 whom an example might well be looked for . . ." Not even Henry James could have successfully emerged from a sentence with "which," "whom," and "being" in it. The safest way to avoid such things is to follow in the path of the American author, Ernest Hemingway. In his youth he was trapped in a which-clause one time
20 and barely escaped with his mind. He was going along on solid

* Reprinted by permission of the author. Originally published in *The New Yorker*, May 4, June 22, and August 17, 1929. Copyright 1929 by James Thurber.

ground until he got into this: "It was the one thing of which, being very much afraid—for whom has not been warned to fear such things—he . . ." Being a young and powerfully built man, Hemingway was able to fight his way back to where he had started, and begin again. This time he skirted the treacherous morass in this way: "He was afraid of one thing. This was the one thing. He had been warned to fear such things. Everybody has been warned to fear such things." Today Hemingway is alive and well, and many happy writers are following along the trail he blazed.

What most people don't realize is that one "which" leads to another. Trying to cross a paragraph by leaping from "which" to "which" is like Eliza crossing the ice. The danger is in missing a "which" and falling in. A case in point is this: "He went up to a pew which was in the gallery, which brought him under a colored window which he loved and always quieted his spirit." The writer, worn out, missed the last "which"— the one that should come just before "always" in that sentence. But supposing he had got it in! We would have: "He went up to a pew which was in the gallery, which brought him under a colored window which he loved and which always quieted his spirit." Your inveterate whicher in this way gives the effect of tweeting like a bird or walking with a crutch, and is not welcome in the best company.

It is well to remember that one "which" leads to two and that two "whiches" multiply like rabbits. You should never start out with the idea that you can get by with one "which." Suddenly they are all around you. Take a sentence like this: "It imposes a problem which we either solve, or perish." On a hot night, or after a hard day's work, a man often lets himself get by with a monstrosity like that, but suppose he dictates that sentence bright and early in the morning. It comes to him typed out by his stenographer and he instantly senses that something is the matter with it. He tries to reconstruct the sentence, still clinging to the "which," and gets something like this: "It imposes a problem which we either solve, or which, failing to solve, we must perish on account of." He goes to the water-cooler, gets a drink, sharpens his pencil, and grimly tries again. "It imposes a problem which we either solve or which

we don't solve and . . ." He begins once more: "It imposes a problem which we either solve, or which we do not solve, and from
which . . ." The more times he does it the more "whiches" he
60 gets. The way out is simple: "We must either solve this problem,
or perish." Never monkey with "which." Nothing except getting
tangled up in a typewriter ribbon is worse.

II—The Perfect Infinitive

It is easy enough to say that a person should live in such a way
as to avoid the perfect infinitive after the past conditional, but it
65 is another matter to do it. The observance of the commonest
amenities of life constantly leads us into that usage. Let us take
a typical case. A gentleman and his wife, calling on friends, find
them not at home. The gentleman decides to leave a note of regret
couched in a few well-chosen words, and the first thing he knows
70 he is involved in this: "We would have liked to have found you
in." Reading it over, the gentleman is assailed by the suspicion
that he has too many "haves," and that the whole business has
somehow been put too far into the past. His first reaction is to
remedy this by dating the note: "9 p.m. Wednesday, Jan. 21,
75 1931." This at once seems too formal, and with a sigh he starts
in again on the sentence itself. That is where he makes a fatal
mistake. The simplest way out, as always, is to seek some other
method of expressing the thought. In this case the gentleman
should simply dash off, "Called. You were out. Sorry," and go
80 home to bed. What he does, however, is to lapse into a profound
study of this particular grammatical situation, than which there is
no more hazardous mental occupation. His wife should, above all
things, not choose this time to nag at him, or hurry him. His condition now calls for the utmost kindness and consideration.
85   First the victim will change the sentence to: "We would have
liked to find you in." Now as a matter of fact, this is correct (bar-
ring the use of "would" instead of "should"), but, alas, the gentleman does not realize it. Few people ever do realize it. This is because the present infinitive, "to find," seems to imply success. They
90 therefore fall back on the perfect infinitive, "to have found," be-

cause it implies that the thing hoped for did not come to pass. They have fallen back on it so often that, after the ordinary past tenses, its use has come to be counted as idiomatic, even though it is incorrect. After past conditionals, however—such as our gentleman caller has got into—the use of the perfect infinitive is not even idiomatic. It is just dangerous.

The gentleman, with two variants on his hands, takes to mumbling them to himself, first one and then the other—"We would have liked to have found you in," "We would have liked to find you in." After he does this several times, both expressions begin to sound meaningless. They don't make any sense at all, let alone make precise sense. His mental feeling is analogous to the terror that strikes into children's minds when they get to repeating some common word, like "saucer," over and over again, until it sounds idiotic and legendary. At this point it would be infinitely better not to leave any note at all, but the gentleman's education and his strength of mind have been challenged. He takes an envelope out of his pocket and grimly makes a list of all the possible combinations, thus getting: "We would have liked to have found," "We would have liked to find," "We would like to have found," and "We would like to find." A dull pain takes him back of the ears. This is the danger sign, and his wife should have the presence of mind to summon assistance, for he is now out of hand and uncontrollable. What she does, however, is to say, "Here, let me write it." He instantly snarls, "I'm no child" or "Get away" or some such thing, and his difficulties are added to by the quarrel which follows. At length he has the bright inspiration of going into the hope clauses and turns out: "We had hoped to have been able to have found." If he has married the right kind of woman, she will hastily scratch a brief word on a calling card, shove it under the door, and drag her husband away. Otherwise he will sink rapidly into a serious mental state, from which it may take him weeks to emerge.

There is a simple rule about past conditionals which will prevent a lapse into that deep contemplation which is so often fatal. After "would have liked," "would have hoped," "would have feared,"

etc., use the present infinitive. The implication of non-fulfillment is inherent in the governing verb itself, that is, in the "would have liked," etc. You don't have to shade the infinitive to get a nice note
130 of frustration. Let it alone. Dr. Fowler himself says: "Sometimes a writer, dimly aware that 'would have liked to have done' is wrong, is yet so fascinated by the perfect infinitive that he clings to that at all costs." That's what it is—a fascination—like a cobra's for a bird. Avoid the perfect infinitive after the past conditional
135 as you would a cobra.

III—The Subjunctive Mood

The importance of correct grammar in the home can not be overestimated. Two young people should make sure that each is rhetorically sound before they get married, because grammatical precision, particularly in mood, is just as important as anything
140 else. Rhetoric and sex, in fact, are so closely related that when one becomes confused they both become confused. Take the subjunctive. Fowler, in his book on modern English usage, says the subjunctive is dying, but adds that there are still a few truly living uses, which he groups under "Alives, Revivals, Survivals, and Ar-
145 rivals." Curiously enough, he leaves out Departures, which it seems to me are just as important as Arrivals. Let us examine the all too common domestic situation where the husband arrives just after another gentleman has departed—or just after he thinks another gentleman has departed (Suppositional Departures lead to just as
150 much bitterness, and even more subjunctives, than Actual Departures).

The wife, in either case, is almost sure to go into the subjunctive —very likely before any accusation is made. Among the most common subjunctives which she will be inclined to use are those of in-
155 dignation and hauteur, such as "Be that as it may," "Far be it from me," etc. For the moment, she is safe enough in the subjunctive, because her husband has probably gone into it, too, using "Would God I were," "If there be justice," and so on. Wives select the subjunctive usually because it is the best mood in which
160 to spar for time, husbands because it lends itself most easily to

ranting and posturing. As long as they both stay in it they are safe. Misunderstandings are almost certain to arise, however, when the husband goes into the indicative, as he is pretty sure to do. He usually does this preparatory to dismissing his suspicions, a step toward which every husband is impelled by his natural ego- 165 tism. First he will begin with a plain past-tense indicative if-clause —just to show that he knows who the man is—prior to dismissing him.

"If George Spangrell was here," the husband will begin, lighting a cigarette, "I . . ." 170

"Well, what would you do if he *were?*" demands the wife.

The confusion, which begins at this point, is pretty intricate. The husband has gone into the indicative, but his wife has stayed in the subjunctive and, furthermore, she thinks that he is still there, too. Thus she thinks he intended to say: "If George 175 Spangrell was here [that is, now] I would tell him what I think of him, the low scoundrel." There is no excuse for a wife prematurely imputing such a suspicion or such a rhetorical monstrosity to her husband. What he probably intended to say was merely something like this: "If George Spangrell was here, I wouldn't 180 like it, but of course I know he wasn't, dear." However, misunderstandings now begin to pile up. The husband is instantly made suspicious by her "What would you do if he *were?*" He considers her "were" tantamount to "is." (This quick-tempered construction, of course, makes the "would" in his wife's sentence ridiculous, 185 for, had she meant "is" instead of "were," she would have substituted "will" for "would.") The situation is much too involved now, however, for the husband to make an effort to parse anything. He instantly abandons all grammatical analysis, and begins to look about, peering into the wardrobe, swishing under beds with 190 a cane or umbrella.

His wife now has the advantage of him, not only in mood, but in posture. A woman must naturally view with disdain and contempt any man who is down on all fours unless he has taken that position for the purpose of playing horse with some children—an 195 extenuation which we need not discuss here. To meet her on even

terms, the husband should walk, not crawl, from wardrobe to chaise-longue, using the mandatory subjunctive in a firm voice, as follows: "If anyone be in (or under) there, let him come out!"
200 ["Come out" is better here than "emerge" because stronger, but a husband should not fall into the colloquial "Come on out of that!" He may, however, if he so wishes, address the gentleman, whether he be present or not, as "Spangrell" but never "Mr. Spangrell" (Hypocritical Dignification) and certainly never as "George"—the use
205 of the given name being in extreme bad taste where no endearment is intended.]

The wife of course will resent all these goings-on, and the quarrel that results will probably last late into the night.

There are several ways to prevent a situation like this. In the
210 first place, when a husband says "was" a wife should instantly respond with "wasn't." Most husbands will take a "wasn't" at its face value, because it preserves their egotism and self-respect. On the other hand, "if . . . were" is always dangerous. Husbands have come to know that a wife's "if . . . were" usually means that
215 what she is presenting as purely hypothetical is, in reality, a matter of fact. Thus, if a wife begins, one evening after an excellent dinner, "Dear, what would you do, if I were the sort of woman who had, etc.," her husband knows full well that it is going to turn out that she is the sort of woman who has. Husbands are suspicious of
220 all subjunctives. Wives should avoid them. Once a woman has "if . . . were'd" a Mr. Spangrell, her husband is, nine times out of ten, going to swish under the chaise-longue. Even if he finds no one, the situation becomes extremely awkward, and there is of course always the plaguey hundredth chance that he may discover
225 a strange cane or pair of gloves.

The best of all ways out is for the husband to go instantly into the future indicative and say, with great dignity, "I shall go down to the drugstore." Ordinarily, his wife would reply, "Oh, no you won't," but with all the doubt and suspicion in the air, she will be
230 inclined to humor him and let him have his way. She is certain to, if Spangrell is in the clothes hamper.

QUESTIONS

1. This selection actually consists of three, brief essays of the same kind which are connected with one another by their common general subject, grammar, and their common method. In each one Mr. Thurber takes up a familiar and—for most people—baffling grammatical problem, and in each he treats the subject by inventing a human situation in which the confusion over the grammatical problem motivates the action (the first essay varies this scheme slightly, as we shall see). In this way he is able to define the grammatical situation and at the same time make us see that it is not just a theoretical problem but a problem in our daily lives—and just incidentally, he is also able to amuse us. The first essay, on "Which," does not present a story, but it does something similar. Notice, for example, that the first paragraph (lines 1–29) sets up a comparison between the anonymous writers of the terrible sentences it quotes and adventurers or explorers who are always in danger. For instance, *"Foolhardy persons sometimes get lost in which-clauses and are never heard of again"* (lines 2–3). Read through this paragraph carefully and point out the other places where Mr. Thurber uses this comparison.

2. Why does Mr. Thurber refer to Fowler (the author of the most famous of all grammar handbooks, *Modern English Usage*) as *"My distinguished contemporary"* (line 4)?

3. In the sentence Mr. Thurber imagines Hemingway struggling with (lines 20–23), there is a glaring grammatical blunder. Can you point it out and explain why it is a blunder? Why do you think Mr. Thurber introduced it?

4. Mr. Thurber has devoted the first paragraph to the way writers can get lost in "which-clauses"; to what does he devote the next two paragraphs (lines 30–62)?

5. Why does Mr. Thurber say that your inveterate whicher "is not welcome in the best company" (lines 40–42)?

6. In the third paragraph (lines 43–62), Mr. Thurber invents a little situation in which he imagines the fatal sentences being written. What is that situation? At what points does Mr. Thurber indicate it to us? Why is the last sentence of this paragraph (lines 61–62) an ideal conclusion for it?

7. What kind of writer is Mr. Thurber parodying in the first sentence of the second essay (lines 63–65)?

8. In describing the man who wishes to leave a note for his friends, Mr. Thurber says that he "decides to leave a note of regret couched *in a few well-chosen words*" (lines 68–69). Why does he use this phrasing?

9. What is Mr. Thurber suggesting about the man's effort to solve the grammatical problem when he says the man should dash off a rough note "and go home to bed" (lines 78–80)?

10. In the last sentence of this paragraph (lines 83–84) Mr. Thurber begins an idea which runs through the whole narrative of this essay. What is it? Where else does he refer to it?

11. What creates the grammatical problem Mr. Thurber is dealing with in this essay. What is the right solution of it and why do people fall into the wrong solution?

12. When Mr. Thurber sets up the situation of the third essay in lines 136–141 it sounds as if he were merely trying to make a joke. But the story he tells, which is by no means implausible, supports the opening assertions. Do you see the advantage he gains by beginning with an assertion that we are likely not to take seriously?

13. What is there about the subjunctive that makes it quite true that "Suppositional Departures lead to . . . even more subjunctives than Actual Departures" (lines 149–151)? What makes Mr. Thurber capitalize these terms? Does he use this trick elsewhere?

14. On what grammatical fine points is Mr. Thurber depending in lines 175–177 and 183–187?

15. For all Mr. Thurber's fooling, jokes like his depend very much on the shrewdness and insight with which he portrays his characters; point out some examples of shrewdness and insight in the paragraph that begins at line 209.

SUGGESTED TOPICS

1. Write a paragraph in which you explain why the sentence Mr. Thurber is working over in the second essay is correctly written, "We should have liked to find you in," and a second paragraph in which you explain why the alternative versions he gives are wrong.

2. Write a paragraph in which you explain why a series of which-clauses of the kind Mr. Thurber is discussing in the first essay gets writers into trouble.

3. Write a paragraph in which you explain the meanings—correct and incorrect but plausible—of the sentences in lines 169–181 which led to the misunderstanding between the husband and wife.

40 / The Economic Theory of Woman's Dress*

THORSTEIN VEBLEN

I N HUMAN APPAREL the element of dress is readily distinguishable from that of clothing. The two functions—of dress
and of clothing the person—are to a great extent subserved by the
same material goods, although the extent to which the same ma-
5 terial serves both purposes will appear very much slighter on second
thought than it does at first glance. A differentiation of materials
has long been going on, by virtue of which many things that are
worn for the one purpose no linger serve, and are no longer expected to serve, the other. The differentiation is by no means com-
10 plete. Much of human apparel is worn both for physical comfort
and for dress; still more of it is worn ostensibly for both purposes.
But the differentiation is already very considerable and is visibly
progressing.

But, however united in the same object, however the two pur-
15 poses may be served by the same material goods, the purpose of
physical comfort and that of a reputable appearance are not to be
confounded by the meanest understanding. The elements of clothing and of dress are distinct; not only that, but they even verge on
incompatibility; the purpose of either is frequently best subserved
20 by special means which are adapted to perform only a single line

* From *Essays in Our Changing Order* by Thorstein Veblen. Reprinted by
permission of The Viking Press, Inc.

of duty. It is often true, here as elsewhere, that the most efficient tool is the most highly specialized tool.

Reputability [of appearance] is in the last analysis, and especially in the long run, pretty fairly coincident with the pecuniary strength of the social unit in question. Woman, primarily, originally because she was herself a pecuniary possession, has become in a peculiar way the exponent of the pecuniary strength of her social group; and with the progress of specialization of functions in the social organism this duty tends to devolve more and more entirely upon the woman. The best, most advanced, most highly developed societies of our time have reached the point in their evolution where it has (ideally) become the great, peculiar, and almost sole function of woman in the social system to put in evidence her economic unit's ability to pay. That is to say, woman's place (according to the ideal scheme of our social system) has come to be that of a means of conspicuously unproductive expenditure.

The admissible evidence of the woman's expensiveness has considerable range in respect of form and method, but in substance it is always the same. It may take the form of manners, breeding, and accomplishments that are, *prima facie*, impossible to acquire or maintain without such leisure as bespeaks a considerable and relatively long-continued possession of wealth. It may also express itself in a peculiar manner of life, on the same grounds and with much the same purpose. But the method in vogue always and everywhere, alone or in conjunction with other methods, is that of dress. "Dress," therefore, from the economic point of view, comes pretty near being synonymous with "display of wasteful expenditure."

The extra portion of butter, or other unguent, with which the wives of the magnates of the African interior anoint their persons, beyond what comfort requires, is a form of this kind of expenditure lying on the border between primitive personal embellishment and incipient dress. So also the brass-wire bracelets, anklets, etc., at times aggregating some thirty pounds in weight, worn by the same class of persons, as well as, to a less extent, by the male population of the same countries. So also the pelt of the arctic

fur seal, which the women of civilized countries prefer to fabrics that are preferable to it in all respects but that of expense. So also the ostrich plumes and the many curious effigies of plants and
60 animals that are dealt in by milliners. The list is inexhaustible, for there is scarcely an article of apparel of male or female, civilized or uncivilized, that does not partake largely of this element, and very many may be said, in point of economic principle, to consist of virtually nothing else.

65   The first principle of dress, therefore, is conspicuous expensiveness. As a corollary under this principle, but of such magnificent scope and consequence as to claim rank as a second fundamental principle, there is the evidence of expenditure afforded by a constant supersession of one wasteful garment or trinket by a new one.
70 This principle inculcates the desirability, amounting to a necessity wherever circumstances allow, of wearing nothing that is out of date. In the most advanced communities of our time, and so far as concerns the highest manifestations of dress—e. g., in ball dress and the apparel worn on similar ceremonial occasions, when the canons
75 of dress rule unhampered by extraneous considerations—this principle expresses itself in the maxim that no outer garment may be worn more than once.

This requirement of novelty is the underlying principle of the whole of the difficult and interesting domain of fashion. Fashion
80 does not demand continual flux and change simply because that way of doing things is foolish; flux and change and novelty are demanded by the central principle of all dress—conspicuous waste.

But apart from the exhibition of pecuniary strength afforded by an aggressive wasteful expenditure, the same purpose may also
85 be served by conspicuous abstention from useful effort. The woman is, by virtue of the specialization of social functions, the exponent of the economic unit's pecuniary strength, and it consequently also devolves on her to exhibit the unit's capacity to endure this passive form of pecuniary damage. She can do this by putting in evidence
90 the fact (often a fiction) that she leads a useless life. Dress is her chief means of doing so. The ideal of dress, on this head, is to demonstrate to all observers, and to compel observation of the

fact, that the wearer is manifestly incapable of doing anything that is of any use. The modern civilized woman's dress attempts this demonstration of habitual idleness, and succeeds measurably.   95

Herein lies the secret of the persistence, in modern dress, of the skirt and of all the cumbrous and otherwise meaningless drapery which the skirt typifies. The skirt persists because it is cumbrous. It hampers the movement of the wearer, and disables her, in great measure, for any useful occupation. So it serves as an advertise- 100 ment (often disingenuous) that the wearer is backed by sufficient means to be able to afford the idleness, or impaired efficiency, which the skirt implies. The like is true of the high heel, and in less degree of several other features of modern dress.

The cardinal principles of the theory of woman's dress, then, 105 are these three:

1. Expensiveness: Considered with respect to its effectiveness as clothing, apparel must be uneconomical. It must afford evidence of the ability of the wearer's economic group to pay for things that are in themselves of no use to anyone concerned—to pay without 110 getting an equivalent in comfort or gain. From this principle there is no exception.

2. Novelty: Woman's apparel must afford *prima facie* evidence of having been worn but for a relatively short time, as well as, with respect to many articles, evidence of inability to withstand any ap- 115 preciable amount of wear. Exceptions from this rule are such things as are of sufficient permanence to become heirlooms, and of such surpassing expensiveness as normally to be possessed only by persons of superior (pecuniary) rank. The possession of an heirloom is to be commended because it argues the practice of waste 120 through more than one generation.

3. Ineptitude: It must afford *prima facie* evidence of incapacitating the wearer for any gainful occupation; and it should also make it apparent that she is permanently unfit for any useful effort, even after the restraint of the apparel is removed. From this rule 125 there is no exception.

There are, further, minor principles that may or may not be present, some of which are derivatives of the great central requisite

of conspicuous waste; others are of alien origin, but all are none
130 the less subject to the controlling presence of the three cardinal
principles enumerated above. These three are essential and constitute the substantial norm of woman's dress, and no exigency can
permanently set them aside so long as the chance of rivalry between persons in respect of wealth remains. Given the possibility
135 of a difference in wealth, and the sway of this norm of dress is inevitable. Some spasm of sense, or sentiment, or what not, may
from time to time create a temporary and local diversion in
woman's apparel; but the great norm of "conspicuous waste" cannot be set aside or appreciably qualified so long as this its economic
140 ground remains.

QUESTIONS

1. Veblen's title tells us that he is giving us a definition of women's
dress from the economic point of view and—he might have added—
an almost anthropological one. About this explanation Veblen is, it
is clear, on the whole quite serious, but he is aware that it emphasizes
in a very striking way certain of the absurdities of women's dress and
his language shows that he is fully aware of these absurdities. The
same thing is true of the way his economic explanation suggests that
in matters of dress, and indeed in all others, the real motives of society
have little or no connection with common sense. Like Freud and a
good many other modern thinkers, Veblen not only does not think
this fact weakens his theory, but, on the contrary, thinks that only
an explanation which runs counter to common sense is likely to be
true. Near the end of this selection (lines 105–126) Veblen sums up
the three characteristics of women's dress which constitute his definition of it. Which parts of his essay deal with each of the characteristics
he lists here?

2. Veblen begins by making an introductory distinction between
what he calls "dress" and what he calls "clothing." Define succinctly
what he means by each of these terms (lines 1–13).

3. What does Veblen mean by saying, "still more of [human ap-
parel] is worn ostensibly for both purposes" (line 11)? Does this assertion parallel one he has made earlier in the paragraph?

4. What purpose is served by the second paragraph (lines 14–22)?

5. With the third paragraph Veblen comes to the heart of his thesis, that women's dress puts "in evidence her economic unit's ability to pay" (lines 33–34). Notice the careful steps by which he has moved from his definition of dress to this point. There are four intervening logical steps; what are they?

6. When Veblen speaks of the "best" (line 30) and the "ideal scheme of our social system" (line 35) he is using these terms to describe what must logically be so if one judges from the actual practice of the society, but these words have an ironic effect because we usually derive their meaning from something else. Explain how they gain this ironic effect.

7. In the paragraph that begins at line 37, Veblen lists a number of minor ways in which women may display expensiveness (lines 37–44); how do manners and breeding display expensiveness?

8. Why do you suppose Veblen began his proof that "dress" is, from the economic point of view, practically synonymous with "display of wasteful expenditure" with the practices of African savages (lines 49–56)? What leads him to refer to these women as "the wives of the magnates of the African interior" (line 50)?

9. What does Veblen suggest about civilized women by referring to the decorations on their hats as "curious effigies of plants and animals" (lines 59–60)?

10. With the paragraph that begins at line 65, Veblen shifts to what he calls "a corollary" under the first principle, which he has just discussed. What is this corollary?

11. What are the "extraneous considerations" by which the canons of dress rule unhampered on "ceremonial occasions" (lines 73–75)? What is the effect of Veblen's calling these entertainments "ceremonial occasions"?

12. In lines 79–82 Veblen not only does not seem to think that a thing is unlikely to happen if it is foolish; he seems, on the contrary, to think we may suppose this a good reason for believing it will happen, and that he must disabuse us of this expectation. Reconstruct the underlying course of reasoning here.

13. Veblen has now arrived at the third characteristic of women's dress which is important to his economic definition of the subject. What is it? What is Veblen's economic explanation of it?

14. In lines 119–121 Veblen says that "the possession of an heir-

loom is to be commended. . . ." Does he mean that he thinks such possession a good thing? What does lead him to use this verb?

15. At the end of this selection, Veblen asserts an idea about the nature of human affairs that is fundamental to the whole argument of this selection (lines 136–140); what is it?

SUGGESTED TOPICS

1. Write a paragraph in which you explain the expression, "the most efficient tool is the most highly specialized tool" (lines 21–22), and illustrate it from Veblen's essay.

2. Write a paragraph in which you discuss the economic conditions which must exist in a society if Veblen's argument about dress is to hold good (Veblen makes these conditions explicit at one or another point in the selection).

3. Write a paragraph in which you define the characteristics of women's dress that Veblen is concerned with.

41 / The Savage World of Thorstein Veblen*

ROBERT L. HEILBRONER

THORSTEIN VEBLEN had the quality of isolation to the nth degree. He walked through life as if he had descended from another world, and the goings on which appeared so natural to the eyes of his contemporaries appeared to him as piquant, exotic, and curious as the rituals of a savage community to the eye 5 of an anthropologist. Other economists—and this includes both Adam Smith and Karl Marx—were not only in their society but they were *of* it; sometimes full of admiration for the world about them and sometimes filled with despair and rage at what they saw. Not Thorstein Veblen. In the bustling, boosting, gregarious com- 10 munity in which he lived, he stood apart: uninvolved, unentangled, remote, aloof, disinterested, a stranger.

Because he was a stranger, he was a nonconformist, but not a radical. The world to Veblen was uncomfortable and forbidding; he adapted to it as a missionary might to a land of primitives, re- 15 fusing to go native, but preserving his integrity at the cost of frightful solitude. Many admired, even loved him, but he had no friends: there was no man he called by his first name, and no woman he could wholly love.

As might be expected, he was a mass of eccentricities. He re- 20 fused to have a telephone, kept his books stacked along the wall in

* From *The Worldly Philosophers* by Robert L. Heilbroner. Reprinted by permission of Simon and Shuster, Inc.

311

their original packing cases, and saw no sense in daily making up the beds; they were thrown back in the morning and pulled up again at night. Lazy, he allowed the dishes to accumulate until the
25 cupboard was bare and then washed the whole messy heap by turning the hose on them. Taciturn, he would sit for hours in silence when all his visitors were eager to hear his pronouncements. A flouter of convention, he gave all his students the same grade, regardless of their work, but when one student needed a higher mark
30 to qualify for a scholarship, Veblen gladly changed a C into an A. And perhaps strangest of all, this sardonic and unprepossessing man had that indefinable quality of being attractive to women. He was always engaged in one liaison or another, and not always of his own doing. "What are you to do if the woman moves in on
35 you?" he once inquired of a friend.

A bewildering and complex personality, locked within itself and with only one avenue for expression: he wrote in razorlike English in a style much like himself, involuted and laden with esoteric scientific terminology, a kind of surgical style that left the world
40 raw and exposed but perfectly bloodless, so fine-edged was his blade. He wrote of philanthropy and called it "essays in pragmatic romance"; of religion and characterized it as "the fabrication of vendible imponderables in the nth dimension." He wrote of the main ecclesiastical organizations as "chainstores" and of the in-
45 dividual church as a "retail outlet"—cruel but telling phrases. He described a walking stick as "an advertisement that the bearer's hands are employed otherwise than in useful effort" and he noted also that it was a weapon: "The handling of so tangible and primitive a means of offense is very comforting to anyone who is gifted
50 with even a moderate share of ferocity." *Gifted* with ferocity! what a savage and yet curiously dry phrase.

But what had this to do with economics? Nothing, in the conventional sense of the word. Economics for Veblen had no relation to the neat but unreal game of the Victorians in which the ways
55 of the world were justified by the differential calculus, and it bore little kinship with the efforts of earlier economists to explain how things worked themselves out. Veblen wanted to know something

else: why things were as they were in the first place. Hence his inquiry began not with the economic play, but with the players; not with the plot, but with the whole set of customs and mores which resulted in that particular kind of a play called "the business system." In a word, he delved into the nature of economic man and his economic rites and rituals, and in this almost anthropological approach it was as important for him to notice that gentlemen carried walking sticks and went to church as that landlords received something which society called rent. He was seeking to penetrate to the true nature of the society in which he lived, and in that search through a maze of deceptions and conventions, he would have to take hints and evidences wherever they revealed themselves: in dress, manners, speech or polite usage. Like the psychoanalyst he often fastened on the smallest trivium when he believed it to be the projecting handle of some important but buried reality, and again like the psychoanalyst he sought for meanings which were often strange and even repugnant to common sense.

His examination of society is merciless. But its biting quality comes not so much from a wish to disparage as from the peculiar coldness with which our fondest notions are appraised. It is as if nothing were familiar to Veblen, nothing too commonplace to merit his attention, and therefore nothing beyond judgment. Only a singularly detached mind, after all, would see in a walking stick both a disguised advertisement of leisure and a barbaric weapon.

And there is a final conclusion to be drawn. The notion of man as a civilized barbarian does more than explain the presence of a leisure class and the acceptance of display as the norm of expenditure. It gives a clue to the nature of social cohesion itself. For the earlier economists were not too successful in explaining what bound society together in the face of the powerful divergent interests of its component classes. If Marx's view was right, for example, and the proletariat was irreconcilably and diametrically opposed to the capitalist, what prevented the revolution from breaking out at once? Veblen provides an answer. The lower classes are not at swords' points with the upper; they are bound up with them

by the intangible but steely bonds of common attitudes. The work-
95 ers do not seek to displace their managers; they seek to *emulate*
them. They themselves acquiesce in the general judgment that the
work they do is somehow less "dignified" than the work of their
masters, and their goal is not to rid themselves of a superior class
but to climb up to it. In the theory of the leisure class lies the
100 kernel of a theory of social stability.

Most of all, the man gave so much to economics—a new pair of
eyes with which to see the world. After Veblen's savage description
of the mores of daily life, the Classical picture of society as a well-
mannered tea party became increasingly difficult to maintain. His
105 scorn of the old school was bitingly expressed when he once wrote:
"A gang of Aleutian Islanders, slushing about in the wrack and
surf with rakes and magical incantations for the capture of shell-
fish, are held to be engaged on a feat of hedonistic equilibration in
rent, wages, and interest," and just as he ridiculed the Classical at-
110 tempt to resolve the primitive human struggle by fitting it into a
fleshless and bloodless framework, so he highlighted the emptiness
of trying to understand the actions of modern man in terms which
derived from an incomplete and outmoded set of preconceptions.
Man, said Veblen, is not to be comprehended in terms of sophisti-
115 cated "economic laws" in which his innate ferocity and creativity
are both smothered under a cloak of rationalization. He is better
dealt with in the less flattering but more fundamental vocabulary
of the anthropologist or the psychologist: a creature of strong and
irrational drives, credulous, untutored, ritualistic. Leave aside the
120 preconceptions of another age, he asks of the economists, and find
out why man actually behaves as he does.

QUESTIONS

1. The purpose of this selection is to describe Thorstein Veblen,
but Veblen has two aspects, namely, what he was as a man, in his
daily life, and what he was in his writing, especially in what he wrote
as an economist. Therefore this description of Veblen falls into two

parts, a description of his personality and a description of his work. Where does Mr. Heilbroner move from the first to the second part?

2. If Mr. Heilbroner's descriptions of Veblen's personality and of his work are true, they will show the same thing; Mr. Heilbroner emphasizes the similarities between Veblen's personality and his work in order to convince us that they do show the same thing. The main point that these descriptions have in common is indicated by Mr. Heilbroner's title. This title really has two meanings; in what two ways was the world, for Veblen—as both his life and his writing show—"savage"?

3. The key word in the summing-up sentence of the first paragraph is "disinterested" (line 12), a word often used incorrectly. Mr. Heilbroner uses it correctly; make sure you know what he means by it. How does Veblen's disinterestedness distinguish him from Adam Smith and Karl Marx as they are described in lines 6–9? Why does Heilbroner choose these two economists for comparison?

4. Outline the sequence of ideas by which Mr. Heilbroner gets from his discussion of Veblen's view of the world to his discussion of Veblen's personality?

5. In the third paragraph (beginning at line 20) Mr. Heilbroner gives a list of Veblen's personal characteristics and an illustration of each; explain how he uses parallelism to make his purpose clear to us.

6. What opinion must Veblen have held if he was glad to change a student's grade from a C to an A in order to get the student a scholarship (lines 29–30)?

7. What is there about Veblen's thought as it is illustrated by the examples in lines 41–51 that leads Mr. Heilbroner to use the comparison he does in lines 37–41?

8. Perhaps you can see at a glance what attitude toward organized religion led Veblen to compare it to a system of chain stores (lines 43–45), but it is necessary to think carefully about a phrase like "the fabrication of vendible imponderables in the nth dimension" (lines 42–43) in order to see how precisely every word is used in the phrase and how exactly it cuts out the meaning Veblen is looking for. Make sure you understand the exact meaning of this phrase. What way of looking at men leads Veblen to say that handling a means of offense like a cane "is very comforting to anyone who is gifted with . . . ferocity" (lines 48–50)? Has Mr. Heilbroner already discussed this way of looking at men?

9. Put in a sentence the purpose of Veblen's economic studies as that purpose is described by Mr. Heilbroner in lines 53–75.

10. How does Veblen's preoccupation with looking at men as he does in the quotation at the end of the fourth paragraph (lines 48–50) lead logically to what Mr. Heilbroner tells us about Veblen's conception of economics (lines 53–75)?

11. In the paragraph that starts at line 76, Mr. Heilbroner sums up for us what Veblen's work shows about him; does this correspond with what Veblen's personality shows? What previous passage must you refer to in order to make sure?

12. Describe in a sentence what Veblen was able to explain more satisfactorily than Marx was (lines 83–100).

13. The quotation in lines 106–109 contrasts Veblen's way of seeing society with that of the Classical economists; explain how Veblen's conception of these two ways of seeing society determines the comparisons he uses for each in this quotation?

14. The closing sentences of this selection (lines 109–121) consist of two explanatory paraphrases of the quotation in lines 106–109. Which parts of this passage go with the first half of the quotation and which parts go with the second half?

SUGGESTED TOPICS

1. Write two paragraphs in which you show how Veblen's essay on "The Economic Theory of Woman's Dress," pages 304–308, supports Mr. Heilbroner's account of Veblen's purpose and method in lines 52–75.

2. Write a paragraph in which you explain, as fully and precisely as you can, one of the quotations from Veblen in this selection.

3. Write two paragraphs in which you define what Mr. Heilbroner calls Veblen's "almost anthropological approach" to society (lines 63–64) and give an illustration of that approach which you relate to your definition.

42 / Reflections on Gandhi*

GEORGE ORWELL

O F LATE YEARS it has been the fashion to talk about
Gandhi as though he were not only sympathetic to the
Western Left-wing movement, but were integrally part of it. Anarchists and pacifists, in particular, have claimed him for their own,
noticing only that he was opposed to centralism and State violence 5
and ignoring the other-worldly, anti-humanist tendency of his doc-
trines. But one should, I think, realize that Gandhi's teachings
cannot be squared with the belief that Man is the measure of all
things and that our job is to make life worth living on this earth,
which is the only earth we have. They make sense only on the 10
assumption that God exists and that the world of solid objects is
an illusion to be escaped from. It is worth considering the disciplines which Gandhi imposed on himself and which—though he
might not insist on every one of his followers observing every detail—he considered indispensable if one wanted to serve either 15
God or humanity. First of all, no meat-eating, and if possible no
animal food in any form. (Gandhi himself, for the sake of his
health, had to compromise on milk, but seems to have felt this to
be a backsliding.) No alcohol or tobacco, and no spices or condi-
ments even of a vegetable kind, since food should be taken not for 20
its own sake but solely in order to preserve one's strength. Sec-

---

ondly, if possible, no sexual intercourse. If sexual intercourse must happen, then it should be for the sole purpose of begetting children and presumably at long intervals. Gandhi himself, in his mid-
25 dle thirties, took the vow of *brahmacharya*, which means not only complete chastity but the elimination of sexual desire. This condition, it seems, is difficult to attain without a special diet and frequent fasting. One of the dangers of milk-drinking is that it is apt to arouse sexual desire. And finally—this is the cardinal point—for
30 the seeker after goodness there must be no close friendships and no exclusive loves whatever.

Close friendships, Gandhi says, are dangerous, because "friends react on one another" and through loyalty to a friend one can be led into wrong-doing. This is unquestionably true. Moreover, if
35 one is to love God, or to love humanity as a whole, one cannot give one's preference to any individual person. This again is true, and it marks the point at which the humanistic and the religious attitude cease to be reconcilable. To an ordinary human being, love means nothing if it does not mean loving some people more than
40 others. The autobiography leaves it uncertain whether Gandhi behaved in an inconsiderate way to his wife and children, but at any rate it makes clear that on three occasions he was willing to let his wife or a child die rather than administer the animal food prescribed by the doctor. It is true that the threatened death never
45 actually occurred, and also that Gandhi—with, one gathers, a good deal of moral pressure in the opposite direction—always gave the patient the choice of staying alive at the price of committing a sin: still, if the decision had been solely his own, he would have forbidden the animal food whatever the risks might be. There must,
50 he says, be some limit to what we will do in order to remain alive, and the limit is well on this side of chicken broth. This attitude is perhaps a noble one, but, in the sense which—I think—most people would give to the word, it is inhuman. The essence of being human is that one does not seek perfection, that one *is* sometimes
55 willing to commit sins for the sake of loyalty, that one does not push asceticism to the point where it makes friendly intercourse

impossible, and that one is prepared in the end to be defeated and broken up by life, which is the inevitable price of fastening one's love upon other human individuals. No doubt alcohol, tobacco, and so forth, are things that a saint must avoid, but sainthood is a thing that human beings must avoid. There is an obvious retort to this, but one should be wary about making it. In this yogi-ridden age, it is too readily assumed that "non-attachment" is not only better than a full acceptance of earthly life, but that the ordinary man only rejects it because it is too difficult: in other words, that the average human being is a failed saint. It is doubtful whether this is true. Many people genuinely do not wish to be saints, and it is probable that some who achieve or aspire to sainthood have never felt much temptation to be human beings. If one could follow it to its psychological roots, one would, I believe, find that the main motive for "non-attachment" is a desire to escape from the pain of living, and above all from love, which, sexual or non-sexual, is hard work. But it is not necessary here to argue whether the other-worldly or the humanistic ideal is "higher." The point is that they are incompatible. One must choose between God and Man, and all "radicals" and "progressives," from the mildest Liberal to the most extreme Anarchist, have in effect chosen Man.

However, Gandhi's pacificism can be separated to some extent from his other teachings. Its motive was religious, but he claimed also for it that it was a definite technique, a method, capable of producing desired political results. Gandhi's attitude was not that of most Western pacifists. *Satyagraha*, first evolved in South Africa, was a sort of non-violent warfare, a way of defeating the enemy without hurting him and without feeling or arousing hatred. It entailed such things as civil disobedience, strikes, lying down in front of railway trains, enduring police charges without running away and without hitting back, and the like. Gandhi objected to "passive resistance" as a translation of *Satyagraha*: in Gujarati, it seems, the word means "firmness in the truth." In his early days Gandhi served as a stretcher-bearer on the British side in the Boer War, and he was prepared to do the same again in the

war of 1914–18. Even after he had completely abjured violence he
was honest enough to see that in war it is usually necessary to take
sides. He did not—indeed, since his whole political life centered
95 round a struggle for national independence, he could not—take
the sterile and dishonest line of pretending that in every war both
sides are exactly the same and it makes no difference who wins.
Nor did he, like most Western pacifists, specialize in avoiding awkward questions. In relation to the late war, one question that every
100 pacifist had a clear obligation to answer was: "What about the
Jews? Are you prepared to see them exterminated? If not, how do
you propose to save them without resorting to war?" I must say
I have never heard, from any Western pacifist, an honest answer to
this question, though I have heard plenty of evasions, usually of
105 the "you're another" type. But it so happens that Gandhi was
asked a somewhat similar question in 1938 and that his answer
is on record in Mr. Louis Fischer's *Gandhi and Stalin*. According
to Mr. Fischer, Gandhi's view was that the German Jews ought to
commit collective suicide, which "would have aroused the world
110 and the people of Germany to Hitler's violence." After the war he
justified himself: the Jews had been killed anyway, and might as
well have died significantly. One has the impression that this attitude staggered even so warm an admirer as Mr. Fischer, but
Gandhi was merely being honest. If you are not prepared to take
115 life, you must often be prepared for lives to be lost in some other
way. When, in 1942, he urged non-violent resistance against a
Japanese invasion, he was ready to admit that it might cost several
million deaths.

One may feel, as I do, a sort of aesthetic distaste for Gandhi, one
120 may reject the claims for sainthood made on his behalf (he never
made any such claim himself, by the way), one may also reject
sainthood as an ideal and therefore feel that Gandhi's basic aims
were anti-human and reactionary: but regarded simply as a politician, and compared with the other leading political figures of our
125 time, how clean a smell he has managed to leave behind!

QUESTIONS

1. The structure of Orwell's description of Gandhi appears at first glance easy and casual, so strong is the suggestion of Orwell's style that he is just thinking out loud. This easy informality is a very desirable effect; it gives what Orwell has to say all the interest of some one talking to us personally. But actual thinking out loud usually produces only muddle and confusion, and the structure of this selection is, we see when we inspect it closely, clear and orderly. Orwell is at pains, at the very beginning, to list the characteristics of Gandhi and his thought which will, he believes, define what Gandhi actually was and will distinguish this actual Gandhi from the imaginary one that the "Western Left-wing movement" thought of as one of its members. These characteristics are given us in lines 4–5; they are that Gandhi "was opposed to centralism and State violence" (i.e., that he opposed a highly organized and tyrannical government and was a kind of pacifist), that Gandhi was "other-worldly" (i.e., that he believed the purpose of man's existence was to be found in the next world, not in this one), and that he was, therefore, "anti-humanist" (i.e., that he was prepared to ignore the things that "make life worth living on this earth," line 9). The remainder of this selection follows the pattern suggested by this list, though Orwell does not take up these topics in the exact order in which he gives them in lines 4–5. Indicate which part of the selection is used to elaborate each of these characteristics

2. The point that Gandhi was "other-worldly" and the point that he was "anti-humanist" are logically connected; where does Orwell make this connection clear?

3. In lines 12–13, Orwell says that "it is worth considering the disciplines which Gandhi imposed on himself." How does our considering these disciplines support what Orwell has made (lines 7–12) the topic of this paragraph?

4. What is Orwell's purpose in ending the first paragraph with the sentence in lines 29–31?

5. Orwell thinks both the opinions he ascribes to Gandhi at the beginning of the second paragraph are true (lines 32–36); but he does

not agree with them; why not? Does his explanation of his reasons have a connection with the main ideas of this selection as they were stated at the beginning (lines 1–10)?

6. In lines 53–65 Orwell explains what he thinks the essence of being human is; what has this explanation got to do with his discussion of Gandhi?

7. Why *must* human beings avoid sainthood (lines 60–61)?

8. Orwell evidently thinks that being "human" is as difficult as being "saintly" (lines 59–77); why does he think so?

9. What is Orwell referring to when he speaks of the "temptation to be human beings" (line 69)?

10. Orwell's discussion of whether or not most people are failed saints (line 66) is slightly off the main line of his discussion of Gandhi; in what way? At what point does he get back on the main line of his discussion?

11. In the third paragraph, beginning at line 78, Orwell takes up the final characteristic of Gandhi's teaching which he listed at the beginning, his pacificism. Why does he take this characteristic up last?

12. What leads Orwell to begin by distinguishing Gandhi's *Satyagraha* from Western pacifism (lines 79–82)?

13. After briefly describing *Satyagraha* in lines 82–89, Orwell uses the rest of this paragraph to make two points about Gandhi's pacifism which Orwell thinks show Gandhi superior to Western pacifists; what are these two points?

14. Orwell thinks that Fischer, a Westerner, was staggered by Gandhi's policy for German Jews (lines 107–114); what was there about Gandhi's fundamental position which made this policy less outrageous in his own eyes than it appears to Westerners?

15. Orwell uses his final paragraph (lines 119–125) partly to sum up what he has been saying in the body of the selection; how does this summary make it clear that Orwell has followed a consistent plan from the beginning to the end of the selection?

16. Throughout this selection Orwell has praised Gandhi for his honesty, for his willingness to face facts and consequences which are unpleasant; is there anything in this last paragraph (lines 119–125) which suggests to you that Orwell had the same kind of honesty?

SUGGESTED TOPICS

1. The attitude that Orwell is taking in this selection is a very good illustration of the humanism which Professor Panofsky defines in selection 7. Write a paragraph in which you show that it is.

2. On several occasions Orwell gives us examples of how Gandhi acted (for instances, lines 16–22, 40–49, 89–94). Take one of these examples and show how it fits logically with Gandhi's basic attitude.

3. Write a paragraph in which you summarize Orwell's argument in support of the proposition that the other-worldly ideal and the humanistic ideal are incompatible (lines 73–74).